2005
Moon Sign
Book

Interior Illustrations:
Kerigwen, 135, 150, 172, 192, 211, 212, 255
Interior clip art: Dover Publications.
Illustration on page 136, 271: Getty Images
Chart wheels were produced by the Kepler program by permission of
Cosmic Patterns Software, Inc. (www.AstroSoftware.com)

Copyright 2004 Llewellyn Worldwide.
All rights reserved. Printed in the U.S.A.
Editor/Designer: Sharon Leah
Cover Design & Art: Kevin R. Brown
Special thanks to Aina Allen
for astrological proofreading.
ISBN 0-7387-0136-X

LLEWELLYN WORLDWIDE
P.O. Box 64383 Dept. 0136-X
St. Paul, MN 55164-0383 U.S.A.

2005

JANUARY

S	M	T	W	T	F	S
						1
2	◐	4	5	6	7	8
9	●	11	12	13	14	15
16	◑	18	19	20	21	22
23	24	○	26	27	28	29
30	31					

FEBRUARY

S	M	T	W	T	F	S
		1	◐	3	4	5
6	7	●	9	10	11	12
13	14	◑	16	17	18	19
20	21	22	○	24	25	26
27	28					

MARCH

S	M	T	W	T	F	S
		1	2	◐	4	5
6	7	8	9	●	11	12
13	14	15	16	◑	18	19
20	21	22	23	24	○	26
27	28	29	30	31		

APRIL

S	M	T	W	T	F	S
					◐	2
3	4	5	6	7	●	9
10	11	12	13	14	15	◑
17	18	19	20	21	22	23
○	25	26	27	28	29	30

MAY

S	M	T	W	T	F	S
◐	2	3	4	5	6	7
●	9	10	11	12	13	14
15	◑	17	18	19	20	21
22	○	24	25	26	27	28
29	◐	31				

JUNE

S	M	T	W	T	F	S
			1	2	3	4
5	●	7	8	9	10	11
12	13	◑	15	16	17	18
19	20	21	○	23	24	25
26	27	◑	29			

JULY

S	M	T	W	T	F	S
					1	2
4	5	●	7	8	9	
10	11	12	13	◑	15	16
17	18	19	20	○	22	23
24	25	26	◐	28	29	30
31						

AUGUST

S	M	T	W	T	F	S
	1	◐	3	4	5	6
7	●	9	10	11	12	13
14	15	◑	17	18	19	20
21	22	○	24	25	26	27
28	29	30	31			

SEPTEMBER

S	M	T	W	T	F	S
				1	2	●
4	5	6	7	8	9	10
◑	12	13	14	15	16	○
18	19	20	21	22	23	24
◐	26	27	28	29	30	31

OCTOBER

S	M	T	W	T	F	S
						1
2	●	4	5	6	7	8
9	◑	10	12	13	14	15
16	○	18	19	20	21	22
23	◐	25	26	27	28	29
30	31					

NOVEMBER

S	M	T	W	T	F	S
		●	2	3	4	5
6	7	◑	9	10	11	12
13	14	○	16	17	18	19
20	21	22	◐	24	25	26
27	28	29	30			

DECEMBER

S	M	T	W	T	F	S
				●	2	3
4	5	6	7	◑	9	10
11	12	13	14	○	16	17
18	19	20	21	22	◐	24
25	26	27	28	29	●	31

Table of Contents

Advertise (Internet) • Advertise (Print) • Automobiles • Animals • Animals (Breed) • Animals (Declaw) • Animals (Neuter or spay) • Animals (Sell or buy) • Animals (Train) • Animals (Train dogs to hunt) • Baking Cakes • Beauty Treaments (Massage, etc.) • Borrow (Money or goods) • Brewing • Build (Start foundation) • Business (Start new) • Buy Goods • Canning • Clothing • Collections • Concrete • Construction (Begin new) • Consultants (Work with) • Contracts (Bid on) • Copyrights/Patents • Coronations and Installations • Cultivate • Cut Timber • Decorating or Home Repairs • Demolition • Dental and Dentists • Dressmaking • Egg-Setting • Electronic (Repair) • Electronics (Buying) • Electricity and Gas (Install) • Entertain Friends • Eyes and Eyeglasses • Fence Posts • Fertilize and Compost • Find Hidden Treasure • Find Lost Articles • Fishing • Friendship • Grafting or Budding • Habit (Breaking) • Haircuts • Harvest Crops • Health • Home Furnishings (Buy new) • Home (Buy new) •

Home (Make repairs) • Home (Sell) • Job (Start new) •
Legal Matters • Loan (Ask for) • Machinery, Appliances,
or Tools (Buy) • Make a Will • Marriage • Medical
Treatment for the Head • Medical Treatment for the
Eyes • Medical Treatment for the Nose • Mining •
Mow Lawn • Move to New Home • Negotiate • Occupa-
tional Training • Paint • Party (Host or attend) • Pawn •
Pick Mushrooms • Plant • Promotion (Ask for) • Prune
• Reconcile People • Roof a Building • Romance •
Sauerkraut • Select a Child's Sex • Sell or Canvas • Sign
Papers • Spray and Weed • Staff (Fire) • Staff (Hire) •
Stocks (Buy) • Surgical Procedures • Travel (Air) • Travel
(Automobile) • Visit • Wean Children • Weight (Reduce)
• Wine and Drink Other Than Beer • Write

If you are among the rapidly increasing numbers who believe that the universe is operated upon a well-defined plan wherein each individual has a chance to advance and achieve success according to his or her degree of understanding and effort put forth toward that objective . . . this BIG little book may truly be for you a guide to victory.

Llewellyn George

To Readers

Llewellyn's *Moon Sign Book* celebrates its 100th anniversary with this 2005 edition. As in years past, you'll find your favorites: entertaining and informative articles, economic and weather forecasts, Moon void-of-course tables, retrograde tables, the Moon Tables and Lunar Aspectarian, the Favorable and Unfavorable Days tables; and the best dates for hunting and fishing, setting eggs, planting, and for doing other garden-related activities. Last year, we gathered all the various elected activities into one section and listed them alphabetically for your convenience.

This year, you'll find an expanded list of activities to help you with your important decisions.

If this is the first time you've used the *Moon Sign Book*, you may be wondering how and why it is different from other almanacs. Well, read on.

Why This Almanac Is Different from Some Almanacs

Readers have asked why the *Moon Sign Book* says that the Moon is in Taurus when some almanacs indicate that the Moon is Aries? It's because there are two different zodiac systems in use today: the tropical and the sidereal zodiac. The *Moon Sign Book* is based on the tropical zodiac.

The tropical zodiac takes 0 degrees of Aries to be the Spring Equinox in the Northern Hemisphere. This is the time and date when the Sun is directly overhead at noon along the equator, usually about March 20–21. The rest of the signs are positioned at 30 degree intervals from this point.

The sidereal zodiac, which is based on the location of fixed stars, uses the positions of the fixed stars to determine the starting point of 0 degrees of Aries. In the sidereal system, 0 degrees of Aries always begins at the same point. This does create a problem though, because the positions of the fixed stars, as seen from Earth, have changed since the constellations were named. The term "precession of the equinoxes" is used to describe the change.

Precession of the equinoxes describes an astronomical phenomenon brought about by the Earth's wobble as it rotates and orbits the Sun. The Earth's axis is inclined toward the Sun at an angle of about 23½ degrees, which creates our seasonal weather changes. Although the change is slight, because one complete circle of the Earth's axis takes 25,800 years to complete, we can actually see that the positions of the fixed stars seem to shift. The result is that each year, in the tropical system, the Spring Equinox occurs at a slightly different time.

Does Precession Matter?

There is an accumulative difference of about 23 degrees between the Spring Equinox (0 degrees Aries in the tropical zodiac and 0 degrees Aries in the sidereal zodiac) so that 0 degrees Aries at Spring Equinox in the tropical zodiac actually occurs at about 7 degrees Pisces in the sidereal zodiac system. You can readily see that those who use the other almanacs may be planting seeds (in the garden and in their individual lives) based on the belief that it is occurring in a fruitful sign, such as Taurus, when in fact it would be occurring in Gemini, one of the most barren signs of the zodiac. So, if you wish to plant and plan activities by the Moon, it is important to follow the *Moon Sign Book*. Before we go on, there are important things to understand about the Moon, her cycles, and their correlation with everyday living. We'll start by looking at some basic astrological principles.

How Important Is the Moon?

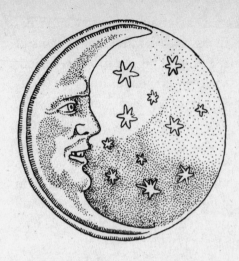

Before we move on, there are other important things to understand about the Moon, her cycles, and their correlation with everyday living. We'll start by looking at some basic astrological principles.

Everyone has seen the Moon wax (increase) and wane (decrease) over a period of approximately twenty-nine days. This succession from New Moon to New Moon is called the lunation cycle. The cycle is divided into parts, called quarters or phases. The astrological system of naming the lunar phases does not always correspond to systems used in other almanacs and calendars. (See explanation on page 7.) It is therefore important to follow only Llewellyn's *Moon Sign Book* or our *Astrological Calendar* for timing events defined in this book.

The Moon is the most important planet in any election. Time and experience have proven that anything started when the Moon is weak by sign and aspect is unlikely to prosper.

What Makes the Moon Weak or Strong?

When astrologers talk about the Moon's strength, they are not referring to physical strength, nor to emotional strength or weakness. The Moon's strength is an assessment of its energy in other signs—its attitude—when compared to how the Moon is expressed in Cancer, the sign it rules and where it enjoys its purest form of expression. The Moon is said to be strong in Cancer because her symbolism is closely associated with Cancer's traits of mothering, nurturing, feeling, and intuiting. On the other hand, the Moon's expression in Capricorn is thought to be weak because the qualities of goal setting, detachment, and achieving, which are common to Capricorn, are not in sync with the Moon's natural mode of expression.

When the Moon is not in its home sign of Cancer or the sign of its exaltation, Taurus, its strength is judged according to its position in the chart. If it is in the first, fourth, seventh, or tenth house, it will have more impact on the outcome of the election than it would have if located in the third, sixth, ninth, or twelfth house.

The Moon is considered weak when she is void-of-course (near the end of a sign and not aspecting other planets). Experience has proven that activities begun during a void-of-course Moon often have a different ending than what was expected.

In electional astrology, the worst zodiacal position of the Moon is the 30 degrees referred to as the "Via Combusta" (15 degrees Libra to 15 degrees Scorpio). This is especially unfavorable for buying, selling, travelling, and marrying.

The Moon can also be debilitated if it is in difficult aspect to Saturn, Mars, Uranus, Neptune, or Pluto.

Moon Phases

The Moon's phase is important to the success of your election, too. Some elections will have better success if the Moon is in its waxing (increasing) phase, and other elections will benefit from having the Moon in its waning (decreasing) phase.

The first twelve hours after the exact moment of the New Moon are considered unfavorable for many things. The next seventy-two hours (until the time of the first quarter) are considered favorable. The twelve hours beginning with the exact time of the first quarter are unfortunate. This pattern continues throughout the Moon's cycle.

The Moon Tables (pages 74–96) or Llewellyn's *Astrological Calendar* can show you what sign the Moon is in, when it changes Quarter phase; and the tables on pages 101–06 show when it goes void-of-course.

First Quarter

The first quarter begins at the New Moon, when the Sun and Moon are conjoined (the Sun and Moon are in the same degree of the same zodiac sign). The New Moon phase is a time for new beginnings that favor growth and to draw things to you. During this phase, the lunar and solar forces work together, pulling things in the same direction. Toward the end of the first quarter is the best time to finalize plans. In nature, it is the time when things germinate and begin to emerge.

Second Quarter

The second quarter begins when the Sun and Moon are ninety degrees apart (about seven days into the lunation cycle), and it ends with the Full Moon. This half Moon rises about noontime and sets near midnight, and it can be seen in the western sky during the first half of the night. It represents growth, development, and the expression of things that already exist.

If your plans are taking shape, concentrate on completing or adding to projects at this time. It should be noted that every thing has its own timeline. Events occurring now may be the result of something initiated in a different lunation cycle, year, or even a different "season" of life.

Third Quarter

The third quarter quarter begins at the Full Moon (about fourteen days into the lunation cycle), when the Sun and Moon are opposite, which allows the Sun's full light to shine on the Moon. Early in this phase, the Moon can be seen rising in the east at sunset, and then rising a little later each evening. The Full Moon stands for illumination, completion, unrest, and using what we worked to create. Toward the end of the third quarter is a time of maturity, fruition, and fulfillment.

Fourth Quarter

The fourth quarter begins about day twenty-one of the lunation cycle, or halfway between the Full Moon and next New Moon. The Sun and Moon are again at ninety degrees apart, or in square aspect. A waning Moon rises at midnight and it can be seen in the east during the last half of the night, reaching the overhead position at about the time the Sun is rising. The fourth quarter is a time of disintegration, drawing back for reorganization, reflecting on what has past, and ridding yourself of what has become unnecessary in order to make room for what is new to come in.

Moon Aspects

The aspects the Moon will make during the times you are considering are also important. A trine or sextile, sometimes a conjunction, are considered favorable aspects. A trine or sextile between the Sun and Moon is an excellent foundation for success. Whether or not a conjunction is considered favorable depends upon the planet the Moon is making a conjunction to. If it's joining the Sun, Venus, Mercury, Jupiter, or even Saturn, the aspect is favorable. If the Moon joins Pluto or Mars, however, that would not be considered favorable. There may be exceptions, but it would depend on what you are electing to do. For example, a trine to Pluto might hasten the end of a relationship you want to be free of.

It is important to avoid times when the Moon makes an aspect to or is conjoining any retrograde planet, unless, of course, you want the thing started to end in failure.

After the Moon has completed an aspect to a planet, that planetary energy has passed. For example, if the Moon squares Saturn at 10:00 am, you can disregard Saturn's influence on your activity if it will occur after that time. You should always look ahead at aspects the Moon will make on the day in question, though, because if the Moon opposes Mars at 11:30 pm on that day, you can expect events that stretch into the evening to be affected by the Moon-Mars aspect. A testy conversation might lead to an argument, or more.

Moon Signs

Much agricultural work is ruled by earth signs—Virgo, Capricorn, and Taurus; and the air signs—Gemini, Aquarius, and Libra—rule flying and intellectual pursuits.

Each planet has one or two signs in which its characteristics are enhanced or "dignified," and the planet is said to "rule" that sign. The Sun rules Leo and the Moon rules Cancer, for example. The ruling planet for each sign is listed below. These should not be considered complete lists. We recommend that you purchase a book of planetary rulerships for more complete information.

Aries Moon

The energy of an Aries Moon is masculine, dry, barren, and fiery. Aries provides great start-up energy, but things started at this time may be the result of impulsive action that lacks research or necessary support. Aries lacks staying power.

Use this assertive, outgoing Moon sign to initiate change, but have a plan in place for someone to pick up the reins when you're impatient to move on to the next thing. Work that requires skillful, but not necessarily patient, use of tools—hammering, cutting down trees, etc.—is appropriate in Aries. Expect things to occur rapidly but to also quickly pass. If you are prone to injury or accidents, exercise caution and good judgment in Aries-related activities.

RULER: Mars

IMPULSE: Action

RULES: Head and face

PLANTS: Aloe, buttercup, and star thistle

LOCATIONS: Large cities, corner houses, east, east corner rooms, east walls, and entryways

MOST COMPATIBLE WITH: Gemini, Leo, Sagittarius, and Aquarius

Taurus Moon

A Taurus Moon's energy is feminine, semi-fruitful, and earthy. The Moon is exalted—very strong—in Taurus. Taurus is known as the farmer's sign because of its associations with farmland and precipitation that is typically of the day-long "soaker" type. Taurus energy is good to incorporate into your plans when patience, practicality, and perseverance are needed. Be aware, though, that you may also experience stubbornness in this sign.

Things started in Taurus tend to be long lasting and to increase in value. This can be very supportive energy in a marriage election. On the downside, the fixed energy of this sign resists change or the letting go of even the most difficult situations. A divorce following a marriage that occurred during a Taurus Moon may be difficult and costly to end. Things begun now tend to become habitual and hard to alter. If you want to make changes in something you start, it would be better to wait for Gemini. This is a good time to get a loan, but expect the people in charge of money to be cautious and slow to make decisions.

RULER: Venus

IMPULSE: Stability

RULES: Neck, throat, and voice

PLANTS: Columbine, daisy, cow-slip, goldenrod, and violet

LOCATIONS: Quiet places, center rooms, middle of the block, fields, landscaped areas near a building, safes, storerooms, and southeast

MOST COMPATIBLE WITH: Cancer, Virgo, Capricorn, and Pisces

Gemini Moon

A Gemini Moon's energy is masculine, dry, barren, and airy. People are more changeable than usual and may prefer to follow intellectual pursuits and play mental games rather than apply themselves to practical concerns.

This sign is not favored for agricultural matters, but it is an excellent time to prepare for activities, to run errands, and write letters. Plan to use a Gemini Moon to exchange ideas, meet people, go on vacations that include walking or biking, or be in situations that require versatility and quick thinking on your feet.

> RULER: Mercury
>
> IMPULSE: Versatility
>
> SIGN RULES: Shoulders, hands, arms, lungs, and nervous system
>
> PLANTS: Ferns, lily of the valley, vervain, yarrow, and woodbine
>
> LOCATIONS: High places, grain elevators, roads of all kinds, subways, schools, and upper rooms
>
> MOST COMPATIBLE WITH: Aries, Leo, Aquarius, and Libra

Cancer Moon

A Cancer Moon's energy is feminine, fruitful, moist, and very strong. Use this sign when you want to grow things—flowers, fruits, vegetables, commodities, stocks, or collections—for example. This sensitive sign stimulates rapport between people. Considered the most fertile of the signs, it is often associated with mothering. You can use this moontime to build personal friendships that support mutual growth.

Cancer is associated with emotions and feelings. Prominent Cancer energy promotes growth, but it can also turn people pouty and prone to withdrawing into their shells.

> RULER: The Moon
>
> IMPULSE: Tenacity

Rules: Chest area, breasts, and stomach

Plants: Iris, lotus, white rose, white lily, night-blooming and water plants

Locations: Near water, gardens, shady places, ditches, kitchens, eating areas, grocery stores, warehouses, cellars, north, and north walls

Most compatible with: Virgo, Scorpio, Pisces, Taurus, and Leo

Leo Moon

A Leo Moon's energy is masculine, hot, dry, fiery, and barren. Use it whenever you need to put on a show, make a presentation, or entertain colleagues or guests. This is a proud yet playful energy that exudes self-confidence and is often associated with romance.

This is an excellent time for fund-raisers and ceremonies, or to be straight forward, frank, and honest about something. It is advisable not to put yourself in a position of needing public approval or where you might have to cope with underhandedness, as trouble in these areas can bring out the worst Leo traits. There is a tendency in this sign to become arrogant or self-centered.

Ruler: The Sun

Impulse: I am

Rules: Heart, upper back

Plants: Daffodil, dill, poppy, eye-bright, fennel, red rose, mistletoe, marigolds, sunflower, and saffron

Locations: Outdoors, mountains, ballrooms, castles, dance halls, forests, stadiums, and sunrooms

Most compatible with: Aries, Gemini, Libra, and Sagittarius

Virgo Moon

A Virgo Moon is feminine, dry, barren, earthy energy. It is favorable for anything that needs painstaking attention—especially those things where exactness rather than innovation is preferred.

Use this sign for activities when you must analyze information, or when you must determine the value of something. Virgo is the sign of bargain hunting. It's friendly toward agricultural matters with an emphasis on animals and harvesting vegetables. It is an excellent time to care for animals, especially training them and veterinary work.

This sign is most beneficial when decisions have already been made and now need to be carried out. The inclination here is to see details rather than the bigger picture.

There is a tendency in this sign to overdo. Precautions should be taken to avoid becoming too dull from all work and no play. Build a little relaxation and pleasure into your routine from the beginning.

RULER: Mercury

IMPULSE: Discriminating

RULES: Abdomen and intestines

PLANTS: Azalea, lavender, skullcap, woodbine, and grains

LOCATIONS: Rural areas, closets, dairies, gardens, lands that are level and productive, meadows, pantries, sick rooms, rooms that are kept locked, and southwest

MOST COMPATIBLE WITH: Cancer, Scorpio, Capricorn, and Taurus

Libra Moon

The Moon's energy is masculine, semi-fruitful, and airy in Libra. This energy will benefit any attempt to bring beauty to a place of thing. Libra is considered good energy for starting things of an intellectual nature. Libra is the sign of partnership and unions, making it an excellent time to form partnerships of any kind, to make agreements, and to negotiate. Even though this sign is good for initiating things, working with a partner who will provide incentive and encouragement is crucial. A Libra Moon accentuates teamwork (particularly teams of two) and artistic work (especially work that involves color). Make use of this sign when you are decorating your home or shopping for better quality clothing.

RULER: Venus

IMPULSE: Balance

RULES: Lower back, kidneys, and buttocks

PLANTS: Lemon-thyme, strawberries, flowers

LOCATIONS: Beauty salons, bedrooms, boutiques, corner building facing west, west corner room, west wall of room, garrets, and upper airy rooms

MOST COMPATIBLE WITH: Aquarius, Sagittarius, Gemini, and Leo

Scorpio Moon

The energy of a Scorpio Moon is feminine, fruitful, cold, and moist. It is useful when intensity (that sometimes borders on obsession) is needed. Scorpio is considered a very psychic sign. Use this Moon sign when you must back up something you strongly believe in, such as union or employer relations. There is strong group loyalty here, but a Scorpio Moon is also a good time to end connections thoroughly. This is also a good time to conduct research.

The desire nature is so strong here that there is a tendency to manipulate situations to get what one wants, or to not see one's responsibility in an act.

RULER: Pluto, Mars (traditional)

IMPULSE: Transformation

RULES: Reproductive organs, genitals, groin, and pelvis

PLANTS: Honeysuckle, heather, thistle, wormwood, and poisonous plants

LOCATIONS: Near stagnant water, cemeteries, morgues and mortuaries, drugstores, bathrooms, rubbish dumps, northeast, and northeast walls

MOST COMPATIBLE WITH: Cancer, Virgo, Capricorn, and Pisces

Sagittarius Moon

The Moon's energy is dry, barren, and fiery in Sagittarius, encouraging flights of imagination and confidence in the flow of life. Sagittarius is the most philosophical sign. Candor and honesty are enhanced when the Moon is here. This is an excellent time to "get things off your chest," to deal with institutions of higher learning, publishing companies, and the law. It's also a good time for sport and adventure.

Sagittarians are the crusaders of this world, and this is a good time to tackle things that need improvement. Don't try to be the diplomat while influenced by this energy, though. Opinions can run strong and the tendency to proselytize is increased.

RULER: Jupiter

IMPULSE: Expansion

RULES: Thighs and hips

PLANTS: Mallow, feverfew, holly, and carnation

LOCATIONS: High and airy places, army barracks, banks, churches, foreign countries, universities, racetracks, upper rooms, and ships

MOST COMPATIBLE WITH: Libra, Aries, Leo, and Aquarius

Capricorn Moon

In Capricorn the Moon's energy is feminine, semi-fruitful, and earthy. Because Cancer and Capricorn are polar opposites, the Moon's energy is thought to be debilitated here. This energy encourages the need for structure, discipline, and organization. This is a good time to set goals and plan for the future, tend to family business, and to take care of details requiring patience or a businesslike manner. Institutional activities are favored. This sign should be avoided if you're seeking favors as those in authority can be insensitive under this influence.

RULER: Saturn

IMPULSE: Ambitious

RULES: Bones, skin, and knees

PLANTS: Moss, amaranth, plantain, black poppies, and hemlock

LOCATIONS: Abandoned places, old churches, tombs, ore mines, places hard to reach, pyramids, south, south rooms, south wall of room, vaults, and vaulted passages

MOST COMPATIBLE WITH: Taurus, Virgo, and Pisces

Aquarius Moon

An Aquarius Moon's energy is masculine, barren, dry, and airy. Activities that are unique, individualistic, concerned with humanitarian issues, society as a whole, and making improvements are favored under this Moon. It is this quality of making improvements that has caused this sign to be associated with inventors and new inventions.

An Aquarius Moon promotes the gathering of social groups for friendly exchanges. People tend to react and speak from an intellectual rather than emotional viewpoint when the Moon is in this sign.

RULER: Uranus, Saturn

IMPULSE: Reformer

RULES: Calves and ankles

PLANTS: Frankincense

LOCATIONS: High places where there is activity, movie theaters, airplanes, airplane hangers, and lecture halls

MOST COMPATIBLE WITH: Aries, Libra, Sagittarius, and Gemini

Pisces Moon

A Pisces Moon is feminine, fruitful, cool, and moist. This is an excellent time to retreat, meditate, sleep, pray, or make that dreamed-of escape into a fantasy vacation. However, things are not always what they seem to be with the Moon in Pisces. Personal boundaries tend to be fuzzy, and you may not be seeing things clearly. People tend to be idealistic under this sign, which can prevent them from seeing reality.

There is a live and let live philosophy attached to this sign, which in the idealistic world may work well enough, but chaos is frequently the result. That's why this sign is also associated with alcohol and drug abuse, drug trafficking, and counterfeiting. On the lighter side, many musicians and artists are ruled by Pisces. It's only when they move too far away from reality that the dark side of substance abuse, suicide, or crime takes away life.

RULER: Jupiter and Neptune

IMPULSE: Empathetic

RULES: Feet

PLANTS: Water lily, water ferns, and mosses that grow in water

LOCATIONS: Ponds, oceans, convents, gasoline stations, hospitals, institutions, rooms with low ceilings, southeast, southeast wall, and submarines

MOST COMPATIBLE WITH: Taurus, Capricorn, Cancer, and Scorpio

More About Zodiac Signs

Element (Triplicity)

Each of the zodiac signs is classified as belonging to the element of fire, earth, air, or water. These are the four basic elements. Aries, Sagittarius, and Leo are fire signs. Fire signs are action oriented, outgoing, energetic, and spontaneous. Taurus, Capricorn, and Virgo are earth signs. The earth signs are stable, conservative, practical, and oriented to the physical and material realm. Gemini, Aquarius, and Libra are air signs. Air signs are sociable, critical, and tend to represent intellectual responses rather than feelings. Cancer, Scorpio, and Pisces are water signs. The water signs are emotional, receptive, intuitive, and can be very sensitive.

Quality (Quadruplicity)

Each zodiac sign is further classified as being cardinal, mutable, or fixed. There are four signs in each quadruplicity, one sign from each element.

The cardinal signs of Aries, Cancer, Libra, and Capricorn represent beginnings. They initiate new action. The cardinal signs initiate each new season in the cycle of the year.

Fixed signs want to maintain the status quo through stubbornness and persistence. Taurus, Leo, Scorpio, and Aquarius represent that between time. For example, Leo is the month when summer really is summer.

Mutable signs adapt to change and tolerate situations. Pisces, Gemini, Virgo, and Sagittarius represent the last month of each season, when things are changing in preparation for the next season.

Nature and Fertility

In addition to a sign's element and quality, each sign is further classified as either fruitful, semi-fruitful, or barren. This classification is the most important for readers who use the gardening information in the *Moon Sign Book* because the timing of most events depends on the fertility of the sign occupied by the Moon. The water signs of Cancer, Scorpio, and Pisces are the most fruitful. The semi-fruitful signs are the earth signs Taurus and Capricorn, and the air sign Libra. The barren signs correspond to the fire signs Aries, Leo, and Sagittarius; the air signs Gemini and Aquarius; and the earth sign Virgo.

Planetary Rulerships

Each sign and planet rules many things, including specific parts of the body. The lists that begin on the following page are not meant to be complete, but they will give you some idea about what activities are ruled over by each planet. We recommend that you refer to a book of planetary and sign rulerships if you are going to use electional astrology. There are several books on the planet rulerships available, including Rex E. Bills' *The Rulership Book* and Dr. Lee Lehman's *The Book of Rulerships*. Maria K. Simms' book *A Time for Magick* is another excellent resource if you want help with timing elections.

The Moon

The Moon rules over things that are constantly changing: the tides, emotions and feelings, and fluctuating character. She also rules the public in general. Other things ruled by the Moon include:

Babies
Bakers and bakeries
Bars, bartenders
Baths
Breasts
Cafes
Childbirth
Cleaning
Collectors and collections
Dairys
Domestic life
Ferries
Fish
Fortunetellers
Furniture
Germination
Homes
Houseboats
Kitchens
Land
Landscape gardeners
Lamps
Mariners
Midwives
Monday
Nurses
Oceans
Pantries
Procreation
Public opinion
Reproduction
Water pipes
Water-related occupations
Women in general

Mercury

Driving and other forms of travel are Mercury ruled, as are most forms of communication. So, for example, hard aspects to Mercury or Mercury retrograde may result in lost letters, snarled traffic, delayed mail delivery, and faulty office equipment. Other things ruled by Mercury include:

Advertising
Agents
Amnesia
Animals, small and domestic
Animals, training
Audits
Bookcases
Books and bookstores
Briefcases
Communications
Commuting
Conferences

Contracts
Coughs
Editors
Early education
Employees
Eyeglasses
Fennel
Hay fever
Humor and humorists
Insomnia
Interviews
Invoices
Manuscripts
Neighbors
Research
Telephones
Socializing
Traffic
Vehicles
Veterinarians
Wednesday
Writing
Written agreements

Venus

Parties and social events planned when Venus is receiving good aspects from other planets are more apt to be fun and successful. When she is receiving less favorable aspects, parties are likely to be boring or poorly attended.

Other things ruled by Venus include:

Apparel, women's
Art
Art dealers and museums
Artists
Ballrooms
Banks, banking, bankers
Bank notes
Brokers
Brides, bridegrooms
Brotherhoods
Carpets
Cashiers
Chimes
Costumes
Customers
Dressmakers
Friday
Furnishings
Hairdressers
Handicrafts
Gardens, gardeners
Hotels
Interest, interest rates
Jewelry
Maids, servant
Opera, opera singers
Paperhangers
Popularity
Profits
Romance
Shops, shopping

Social gatherings
Vacations
Wallets
Wine

Sun

You will make a more favorable impression when meetings or interviews are scheduled at times the Sun makes a favorable aspect to your natal Ascendant. If the Sun is afflicted by hard aspects to Saturn or Mars, however, business dealings should be avoided. Things ruled by the Sun include:

Authorities
Ballrooms
Bragging
Casinos
Chief executives
Commanders
Confidence
Coronations
Empires
Favors
Foremen
Games, professional
Gambling, gamblers
Grants
Government
Government service
Honors

Leadership
Managers
Moneylenders
Parks, park keepers
Playgrounds
Politicians
Principals
Recreation
Resorts
Self-expression
Showboats
Solariums
Speculation, speculators
Stock brokering
Stock market
Sunday
Theaters

Mars

Avoid or postpone potential confrontations when Mars is squaring a sensitive point in your birth chart as power struggles will likely be the outcome. However, when Mars is transiting your Ascendant, it will often bring a strong sense of self-confidence to you. Mars rules over:

Accidents
Ambition
Ammunition
Arenas

Armed forces
Atheletes
Barbers
Battles
Blacksmiths
Blemishes
Carpenters
Chimneys
Crime, criminals
Dentists, dentistry
Enemies
Fire
Firefighters, fire departments
Furnaces
Guards
Leadership
Piercing
Prizefighters
Sports, competitive
Surgery, surgeons
Tattoos
Tools, sharp
Wreckers
Wrenches
Wrestlers

Jupiter

When you make important life changes, Jupiter is the most important planet to consider. Favorable Jupiter aspects are beneficial if you are starting an education program or publish-ing. Jupiter can bring about excesses such as agreeing to too much, or overspending. Other things Jupiter rules include:

Accumulation
Advertising, long-range
Animals, large
Appraisals, appraisers
Assessors
Attorneys
Banquets
Benefactors
Bondsmen
Capitalism, capitalists
Celebrations
Clergy
Commerce, general
Costumes
Courts of law
Exports
Financial gain
Indorsements
Inheritances
Journeys, long
Law, legal affairs
Plaintiffs
Profits
Publishing
Reimbursement
Shops and shopkeepers
Sports enthusiasts
Taxation
Vows

Saturn

You are apt to succeed at projects that require a long-term commitment if Saturn is making good aspects to your birth chart when the work begins. If Saturn is squaring your Midheaven or Sun, failure is more likely to be the outcome. Some things Saturn rules are:

Abandoned places
Aging people
Archeology
Architects
Bankruptcy
Basements
Barriers
Blood clots
Bones
Builders, buildings in general
Buyers
Cement
Clothing, work
Constrictions
Contraction
Day laborers
Decomposition
Earthy occupations
Embargoes
Employment
Engineers
Farms, farmhands

Foreclosures
Grudges
Government buildings
Harshness
Hoarding
Knees
Landowners
Ore
Reunions
Refrigeration
Rejection
Reservoirs
Saturday
Self-control
Solitude
Subways
Tenements
Watches, watchmakers

Uranus

This energy tends to create unstable conditions. Your ability to adjust to change will determine if the energy is felt positively or negatively. Uranus' ability to time events is impressive. Squares from this planet to your natal planets can bring disruption in your life. Other things Uranus rules include:

Aeronautics
Agitators
Aloofness

Airplanes, airports
Astrologers
Boycotts
Cartoons, cartoonists
Colleagues
Computers
Convulsion
Discrepancies
Electricians
Electricity
Elevators
Explorers
Flying
Free trade
Garages, repair
Gasoline stations
Hearing aids
Helicopters
Highways
Immigration
Inventions
Inversions
Magic and magicians
Mechanisms
Miracles
Music (electronic)
Passports
Radio
Repair people
Research, researchers
Revolution
Science, scientists
Telephones
Television
Transformation
Violations

Neptune

Neptune transits are subtle. Changes that occur under Neptune's influence are so gradual they often go undetected until some time has passed. Neptune rules:

Actors, actresses
Addicts
Admirals
Alcohol, alcoholism
Aquariums
Artists
Baptism
Barges
Bartenders
Baths, bathing
Bayous, bays, beaches
Boats
Butterflies
Camouflage
Charity
Chemicals
Cigarettes
Confessions
Con artists
Drains
Dreams
Espionage

Fog
Liars
Magicians
Missionaries
Obsession
Prisoners
Secrets
Ships
Wasting diseases

Pluto

Pluto transits are profound and have lasting affects. You may experience big changes in life direction when this transit is interacting with your natal birth chart. Pluto rules:

Abduction
Ambulances
Autopsies
Betrayal
Coffins
Coroners
Death
Decay
Destruction
Detectives
Disasters
Espionage
Funerals
Gangs, gang leaders
Garbage
Legacies
Lewdness
Massacres
Pestilence
Petroleum
Plutonium
Poisons
Pornography
Puzzles
Rape
Satire
Septic systems
Snakes
Vandals
Viruses
Wars

Zodiac Signs and Their Corresponding Body Parts

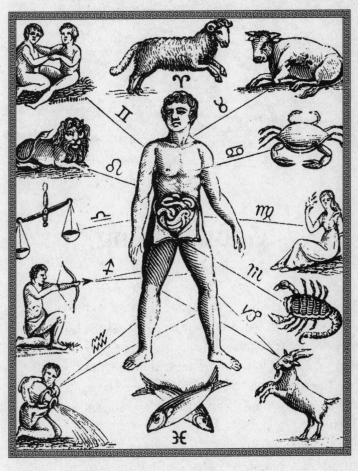

♈	= Aries	♎	= Libra
♉	= Taurus	♏	= Scorpio
♊	= Gemini	♐	= Sagittarius
♋	= Cancer	♑	= Capricorn
♌	= Leo	♒	= Aquarius
♍	= Virgo	♓	= Pisces

Good Timing

by Sharon Leah

Electional astrology is the art of "electing" times to begin any undertaking. Say, for example, you start a business. That business will experience ups and downs, as well as reach its potential, according to the promise held in the universe at the time the business was started—its birth time. The horoscope (birth chart) set for the time that a business was started would indicate its path.

So, you might ask yourself the question: If the horoscope for a business start can show success or failure, why not begin at a time that is more favorable to the venture? Well, you can.

While no time is "perfect," there are better times and better days to undertake specific activities. There are thousands of examples that prove electional astrology is not only practical, but that it can make a difference in our lives. The benefit of considering the Moon's sign and phase when planting was proven to me during two consecutive summers.

Two years running I was away at an astrology conference at the end of May, during the time when Zone 4 gardens should be planted. Upon returning home the first year, I transplanted tomatoes into the garden and planted corn and green bean seeds, even though the *Astrological Calendar* indicated that it was the wrong Moon sign and phase to plant in.

To say the crops were bad that year would not be an understatement. The corn stalks were weak and the ears of corn that did set on were small and filled with deformed kernels. Rabbits ate the beans so I don't know what would have happened to them, and I don't think we got twelve good tomatoes from six plants. The best thing I can say for the effort we put into the garden that year is that weeds didn't completely take over the space.

Before leaving for the conference the second year, I glanced at the calendar and saw that I would miss the "best" planting time again, and there wouldn't be another good opportunity to plant until the third week in June. Even though it would be very late in the planting season, I decided to wait. What a difference it made! The tomato vines were vigorous, and the yield was phenomenal. The tomatoes were big, beautiful, and very tasty. (I didn't plant any beans for the bunnies that year.)

If you could schedule meetings so that attendees would be awake, attentive, and cooperative, wouldn't you do it? And wouldn't most of us prefer to enjoy the clothing we buy for a longer time than only the day we bought them? I hate it when I buy on a whim, only to realize days later that I'll never wear the item again.

There are rules for electing times to begin various activities. You'll find detailed instructions about how to make elections beginning on page 41.

Personalizing Elections

The election rules in this almanac are based upon the planetary positions at the time for which the election is made. They do not depend on any type of birth chart. However, a birth chart based upon the time, date, and birthplace of an event has advantages.

Why is a birth chart important if you can make elections without one? Because no election is effective for every person. For example, you may leave home to begin a trip at the same time as a friend, but each of you will have a different experience according to whether or not your birth chart favors the trip.

Not all elections require a birth chart, but the timing of very important events—business starts, marriages, etc.—would benefit from the additional accuracy a birth chart provides. To order a birth chart for yourself or a planned event, visit our web site at www.llewellyn.com.

Some Things to Consider

You've probably experienced good timing in your life. Maybe you were at the right place at the right time to meet a friend whom you hadn't seen in years. Frequently, when something like that happens, it is the result of following an intuitive impulse—that "gut instinct."

While no time is "perfect," there are definitely better times and better days to undertake specific activities. Electional astrology is a tool that can help you to align with energies, present and future, that are available due to planetary placements.

Significators

Decide upon the important "significators" (planets, signs, and houses ruling the matter) for which the election is being made. The Moon is the most important significator in any election, so the Moon should always be "fortified" (strong by sign, and making favorable aspects to other planets). The Moon's aspects to other planets are more important than the sign the Moon is in, however.

The other important significators are the Ascendant and Midheaven with their rulers, the house ruling the election matter, and the ruler of the sign on that house cusp. Finally, any planet or sign that has a general rulership over the matter in question should be taken into consideration.

A list of significators (rulerships) begins on page 24.

Nature and Fertility

Determine the general nature of the sign that is appropriate for your election. For example, much agricultural work is ruled by the earth signs of Virgo, Capricorn, and Taurus; while the air signs—Gemini, Aquarius, and Libra—rule intellectual pursuits.

One Final Comment

Use common sense. If you must do something, like plant your garden or take an airplane trip on a day that doesn't have the best aspects, proceed anyway, but try to minimize problems. For example, leave early for the airport to avoid being left behind due to delays in the security lanes. When you have no other choice, do the best that you can under the circumstances at the time.

Planetary Hours

Choosing the "best" time to have an event—meeting, marriage, trips, buying a home—begin is one of the great benefits you gain from using electional astrology. You've read that planets have rulership over specific days and things. Planets have rulership over specific times during each day, too.

The astrological day begins at the exact moment of local sunrise in your area, and the night begins at local sunset. The first planetary hour of the day depends on what day of the week it is. Sunday and the first planetary hour of Sunday are ruled by the Sun, the second hour is ruled by the Moon, the third hour by Mars, and so on, until the eighth hour after sunrise, which is again ruled by the Sun.

Monday and the first hour after sunrise on Monday are ruled by the Moon. The second hour is ruled by Mars, the third by Mercury, and so on. Tuesday and the first hour after sunrise on Tuesday are ruled by Mars. Wednesday and the first hour after sunrise on Wednesday are ruled by Mercury. Thursday and the first hour after sunrise on Thursday are ruled by Jupiter. Friday and the first hour after sunrise on Friday are ruled by Venus. Saturday and the first hour after sunrise on Saturday are ruled by Saturn.

The length of a planetary hour varies, depending on the time of the year, because days are longer in summer than they are in winter (in the Northern Hemisphere). So to find the length of a planetary hour, you must first know the length of time between sunrise and sunset in hours and minutes. You divide that time by twelve, which gives you the length of a planetary hour on a specific date. It is easier to work with the time if you convert hours to sixty-minute segments. Divide the total time by twelve. Do the same to find the length of a night time planetary hour.

The Advantage of Using Planetary Hours

It is easier and less time consuming to figure out an hour table than it is to learn how to set up an election chart. There are books available, including Maria K. Simms *A Time for Magick* (Llewellyn, 2001), that have the hour tables already figured out for you. You will also find more complete information on planetary hours in the book.

Your may also find information about planetary hours on various Web sites. An Internet search at the time of this writing turned up several resources. It would be best if you conducted your own search, though, because Internet addresses change frequently and without warning.

If you elect to begin an activity that involves writing, for example, you could start the letter or project on a Wednesday (Mercury rules writing and communications), or during a Mercury hour. But if you wanted to begin a courtship or some other activity that involves a woman, choosing to begin on a Friday (Venus rules courtship, women, and matters relating to women) or during a Venus hour would be to your advantage.

Houses in the Horoscope

You'll find this information more useful if you have a horoscope (birth chart) for yourself or the event in question. If you do not have access to a horoscope, please do not attempt to apply these additional qualifications to your elections.

Each house in the horoscope represents an area of life, and the planets found in a house will have direct bearing on the outcome of your elections. For example, if Saturn is in the first house, you might expect something to hinder the election. Things may go slower than expected, there might be restrictions or obstacles you didn't expect, and so on. The planets and their aspects to other planets in other houses also influence the election.

The House Ruling the Election Is Important

The ruling house is the house that relates strongly to your event. If your personal interests are important, you would look to the first house for information. If your concern is about career or reputation, the tenth house would be the ruling house. Following is general list of the houses and what they rule.

- The first house relates to you and your personal interests in an election; the business or organization in question; the home team in sports; the head.

- The second house relates to budgets, finances, earnings, and spending power; personal possessions or resources; person(s) who handles financial matters; the ears and throat.

- The third house relates to local travel by taxi, bus, bike, automobile, walking, and running; extended family, siblings, and neighbors; communications; shoulders, arms, lungs, and nervous system.

- The fourth house relates to buildings, property, and real estate investments; family, the father; endings; breast, stomach, and digestive organs.

- The fifth house relates to children; recreation and entertaining activities; developing resources and products for speculation; gambling; creative work; the heart and upper part of the back.

- The sixth house relates to daily routine, habits, and schedules; employees and labor unions; small animals; personal well-being and illness; the solar plexus and bowels.

- The seventh house relates to partnerships, mergers, agreements, your opponent, and competitive relationships; the public; kidneys, ovaries, and lower back.

- The eighth house relates to loans, debts, joint finances, profits and losses from death or inheritance, sharing, borrowed money, and investments; divorce; sexuality; the muscular system, bladder, and sex organs.

- The ninth house relates to publishing, advertising, and legal matters; foreign travel; higher education; liver and thighs.

- The tenth house relates to career, management, status, reputation, one's public image; the government; mothers; the knees.

- The eleventh house relates to groups of friends, organizations, and group activities; condition of employer; wishes and expectations; the ankles.

- The twelfth house relates to secret activities, plots, and intelligence gathering; confinement, hospitals, institutions; large animals; occult matters; the feet.

Choose the Best Time
for Your Activities

When rules for elections refer to "favorable" and "unfavorable" aspects to your Sun or other planets, please refer to the Favorable and Unfavorable Day Tables and Lunar Aspectarian for more information. You'll find instructions and the tables beginning on page 67.

The material in this section came from several sources including: *The New A to Z Horoscope Maker and Delineator* by Llewellyn George (Llewellyn, 1999), *Moon Sign Book* (Llewellyn, 1945), and *Electional Astrology* (Slingshot Publishing, 2000) by Vivian Robson. Robson's book was originally published in 1937.

Advertise (Internet)

The Moon should be conjunct, sextile, or trine Mercury or Uranus; and in the sign of Gemini, Capricorn, or Aquarius.

Advertise (Print)

Write ads on a day favorable to your Sun. The Moon should be conjunct, sextile, or trine Mercury or Venus. Avoid hard aspects to Mars and Saturn. Ad campaigns produce the best results when the Moon is well aspected in Gemini (to enhance communication) or Capricorn (to build business).

Automobiles

When buying an automobile, select a time when the Moon is conjunct, sextile, or trine to Mercury, Saturn, or Uranus; and in the sign Gemini or Capricorn.

Animals

Take home new pets when the day is favorable to your Sun, or when the Moon is trine, sextile, or conjunct Mercury, Venus, or Jupiter, or in the sign of Virgo or Pisces. However, avoid days when the Moon is either square or opposing the Sun, Mars, Saturn, Uranus, Neptune, or Pluto. When selecting a pet, have the Moon well aspected by the planet that rules the animal. Cats are ruled by the Sun, dogs by Mercury, birds by Venus, horses by Jupiter, and fish by Neptune. Buy large animals when the Moon is in Sagittarius or Pisces, and making favorable aspects to Jupiter or Mercury. Buy animals smaller than sheep when the Moon is in Virgo with favorable aspects to Mercury or Venus.

Animals (Breed)

Animals are easiest to handle when the Moon is in Taurus, Cancer, Libra, or Pisces, but try to avoid the Full Moon. To encourage healthy births, animals should be mated so births occur when the Moon is increasing in Taurus, Cancer, Pisces, or Libra. Those born during a semi-fruitful sign (Taurus and Capricorn) will produce leaner meat. Libra yields beautiful animals for showing and racing.

Animals (Declaw)

Declaw cats in the dark of the Moon. Avoid the week before and after the Full Moon and the sign of Pisces.

Animals (Neuter or spay)

Have livestock and pets neutered or spayed when the Moon is in Sagittarius, Capricorn, or Pisces; after it has passed through Scorpio, the sign that rules reproductive organs. Avoid the week before and after the Full Moon.

Animals (Sell or buy)

In either buying or selling, it is important to keep the Moon and Mercury free from conjunction or any aspect to Mars. Aspects to Mars will create discord and increase the likelihood of wrangling over price and quality. The Moon should be passing from the first quarter to full and sextile or trine Venus or Jupiter. When buying racehorses, let the Moon be in air sign. The Moon should be in air signs when you buy birds. If the birds are to be pets, let the Moon be in good aspect to Venus.

Animals (Train)

Train pets when the Moon is in Virgo or when the Moon trines Mercury.

Animals (Train dogs to hunt)

Let the Moon be in Aries in conjunction with Mars, which makes them courageous and quick to learn. But let Jupiter also be in aspect to preserve them from danger in hunting.

Baking Cakes

Your cakes will be have a lighter texture if you see that the Moon is in Gemini, Libra, or Aquarius, and in good aspect to Venus or

Mercury. If you are decorating the cake or confectionary are being made, place the Moon in Libra.

Beauty Treatment (Massage, etc.)

See that the Moon is in Taurus, Cancer, Leo, Libra, or Aquarius, and in favorable aspect to Venus. In the case of plastic surgery, aspects to Mars should be avoided, and the Moon should not be in the sign ruling the part to be operated on.

Borrow (Money or goods)

See that the Moon is not placed between 15 degrees Libra and 15 degrees Scorpio. Let the Moon be waning and in Leo, Scorpio (16 to 30 degrees), Sagittarius, or Pisces. Venus should be in good aspect to the Moon, and the Moon should not be square, opposing, or conjunct either Saturn or Mars.

Brewing

Start brewing during the third or fourth quarter, when the Moon is in Cancer, Scorpio, or Pisces.

Build (Start foundation)

Turning the first sod for the foundation marks the beginning of the building. For best results, excavate the site when the Moon is in the first quarter of a fixed sign and making favorable aspects to Saturn.

Business (Start new)

When starting a business, have the Moon be in Taurus, Virgo, or Capricorn, and waxing. The Moon should be sextile or trine Jupiter or Saturn, but avoid oppositions or squares. The planet ruling the business should be well aspected, too.

Buy Goods

Buy during the third quarter, when the Moon is in Taurus for quality, or in a mutable sign (Gemini, Sagittarius, Virgo, or Pisces) for savings. Good aspects to Venus or the Sun are desirable. If you are buying for yourself, it is good if the day is favorable for your Sun sign. You may also apply rules for buying specific items.

Canning

Can fruits and vegetables when the Moon is in either the third or fourth quarter, and in the water sign Cancer or Pisces. Preserves and jellies use the same quarters and the signs Cancer, Pisces, or Taurus.

Clothing

Buy clothing on a day that is favorable for your Sun sign, and when Venus or Mercury is well aspected. Avoid aspects to Mars and Saturn. Buy your clothing when the Moon is in Taurus if you want to remain satisfied. Do not buy clothing or jewelry when the Moon is in Scorpio or Aries. See that the Moon is sextile or trine the Sun during the first or second quarters.

Collections

Try to make collections on days when your Sun is well aspected. Avoid days when the Moon is opposing or square Mars or Saturn. If possible, the Moon should be in a cardinal sign (Aries, Cancer, Libra, or Capricorn). It is more difficult to collect when the Moon is in Taurus or Scorpio.

Concrete

Pour concrete when the Moon is in the third quarter of the fixed sign Taurus, Leo, or Aquarius.

Construction (Begin new)

The Moon should be sextile or trine Jupiter. According to Hermes, no building should be begun when the Moon is in Scorpio or Pisces. The best time to begin building is when the Moon is in Aquarius.

Consultants (Work with)

The Moon should be conjunct, sextile, or trine Mercury or Jupiter.

Contracts (Bid on)

The Moon should be in Gemini or Capricorn, and either the Moon or Mercury should be conjunct, sextile, or trine Jupiter.

Copyrights/Patents

The Moon should be conjunct, trine, or sextile Mercury or Jupiter.

Coronations and Installations

Let the Moon be in Leo and in favorable aspect to Venus, Jupiter, or Mercury. The Moon should be applying to these planets.

Cultivate

Cultivate when the Moon is in a barren sign and waning, ideally the fourth quarter in Aries, Gemini, Leo, Virgo, or Aquarius. The third quarter in the sign of Sagittarius will also work.

Cut Timber

Timber cut during the waning Moon does not become worm-eaten, it will season well, and not warp, decay, or snap during burning. Cut when the Moon is in Taurus, Gemini, Virgo, or Capricorn—especially in August. Avoid the water signs. Look for favorable aspects to Mars.

Decorating or Home Repairs

Have the Moon waxing, and in the sign of Libra, Gemini, or Aquarius. Avoid squares or oppositions to either Mars or Saturn. Venus in good aspect to Mars or Saturn is beneficial.

Demolition

Let the waning Moon be in Leo, Sagittarius, or Aries.

Dental and Dentists

Visit the dentist when the Moon is in Virgo, or pick a day marked favorable for your Sun sign. Mars should be marked sextile, conjunct, or trine; and avoid squares or oppositions to Saturn, Uranus, or Jupiter.

Teeth are best removed when the Moon is in Gemini, Virgo, Sagittarius, or Pisces, and during the first or second quarter. Avoid the Full Moon! The day should be favorable for your lunar cycle, and Mars and Saturn should be marked conjunct, trine, or sextile. Fillings should be done in the third or fourth quarters in the sign of Taurus, Leo, Scorpio, or Pisces. The same applies for dentures.

Dressmaking

William Lilly wrote in 1676: "Make no new clothes, or first put them on when the Moon is in Scorpio or afflicted by Mars, for they will be apt to be torn and quickly worn out." Design, repair, and sew clothes in the first and second quarters of Taurus, Leo, or Libra on a day marked favorable for your Sun sign. Venus, Jupiter, and Mercury should be favorably aspected, but avoid hard aspects to Mars or Saturn.

Egg-setting

Eggs should be set so chicks will hatch during fruitful signs. To set eggs, subtract the number of days given for incubation or gestation from the fruitful dates. Chickens incubate in twenty-one days, turkeys and geese in twenty-eight days.

A freshly laid egg loses quality rapidly if it is not handled properly. Use plenty of clean litter in the nests to reduce the number of dirty or cracked eggs. Gather eggs daily in mild weather and at least two times daily in hot or cold weather. The eggs should be placed in a cooler immediately after gathering and stored at 50 to 55°F. Do not store eggs with foods or products that give off pungent odors since eggs may absorb the odors.

Eggs saved for hatching purposes should not be washed. Only clean and slightly soiled eggs should be saved for hatching. Dirty eggs should not be incubated. Eggs should be stored in a cool place with the large ends up. It is not advisable to store the eggs longer than one week before setting them in an incubator.

Electronic (Repair)

The Moon should be sextile or trine Mars or Uranus in a fixed sign (Taurus, Leo, Scorpio, Aquarius).

Electronics (Buying)

Choose a day when the Moon is in an air sign (Gemini, Libra, Aquarius) and well aspected by Mercury and/or Uranus when buying electronics.

Electricity and Gas (Install)

The Moon should be in a fire sign, and there should be no squares, oppositions, or conjunctions with Uranus (ruler of electricity), Neptune (ruler of gas), Saturn, or Mars. Hard aspects to Mars can cause fires.

Entertain Friends

Let the Moon be in Leo or Libra and making good aspects to Venus. Avoid squares or oppositions to either Mars or Saturn to by the Moon or Venus.

Eyes and Eyeglasses

Have your eyes tested and glasses fitted on a day marked favorable for your Sun sign, and on a day that falls during your favorable lunar cycle. Mars should not be in aspect with the Moon. The same applies for any treatment of the eyes, which should also be started during the Moon's first or second quarter.

Fence Posts

Set posts when the Moon is in the third or fourth quarter of the fixed sign Taurus or Leo.

Fertilize and Compost

Fertilize when the Moon is in a fruitful sign (Cancer, Scorpio, Pisces). Organic fertilizers are best when the Moon is waning. Use chemical fertilizers when the Moon is waxing. Start compost when the Moon is in the fourth quarter in a water sign.

Find Hidden Treasure

Let the Moon be in good aspect to Jupiter or Venus. If you erect a horoscope for this election, place the Moon in the fourth house.

Find Lost Articles

Search for lost articles during the first quarter and when your Sun sign is marked favorable. Also check to see that the planet ruling the lost item is trine, sextile, or conjunct the Moon. The Moon rules household utensils; Mercury rules letters and books; and Venus rules clothing, jewelry, and money.

Fishing

During the summer months, the best time of the day to fish is from sunrise to three hours after, and from two hours before sunset until one hour after. Fish do not bite in cooler months until the air is warm, from noon to 3 pm. Warm, cloudy days are good. The most favorable winds are from the south and southwest. Easterly winds are unfavorable. The best days of the month for fishing are when the Moon changes quarters, especially if the change occurs on a day when the Moon is in a water sign (Cancer, Scorpio, Pisces). The best period in any month is the day after the Full Moon.

Friendship

The need for friendship is greater when the Moon is in Aquarius or when Uranus aspects the Moon. Friendship prospers when Venus or Uranus is trine, sextile, or conjunct the Moon. The Moon in Gemini facilitates the chance meeting of acquaintances and friends.

Grafting or Budding

Grafting is the process of introducing new varieties of fruit on less desirable trees. For this process you should use the increasing phase of the Moon in fruitful signs such as Cancer, Scorpio, or Pisces. Capricorn may be used, too. Cut your grafts while trees are dormant, from December to March. Keep them in a cool, dark, not too dry or too damp place. Do the grafting before the sap starts to flow and while the Moon is waxing, and preferably while it is in Cancer, Scorpio, or Pisces. The type of plant should determine both cutting and planting times.

Habit (Breaking)

To end an undesirable habit, and this applies to ending everything from a bad relationship to smoking, start on a day when the Moon is in the fourth quarter and in the barren sign of Gemini, Leo, or Aquarius. Aries, Virgo, and Capricorn may be suitable as well, depending on the habit you want to be rid of. Make sure that your lunar cycle is favorable. Avoid lunar aspects to Mars or Jupiter. However, favorable aspects to Pluto are helpful.

Haircuts

Cut hair when the Moon is in Gemini, Sagittarius, Pisces, Taurus, or Capricorn, but not in Virgo. Look for favorable aspects to Venus. For faster growth, cut hair when the Moon is increasing in Cancer or Pisces. To make hair grow thicker, cut when the Moon is full in the signs of Taurus, Cancer, or Leo. If you want your hair to grow more slowly, have the Moon be decreasing in Aries, Gemini, or Virgo, and have the Moon square or opposing Saturn.

Permanents, straightening, and hair coloring will take well if the Moon is in Taurus or Leo and trine or sextile Venus. Avoid hair treatments if Mars is marked as square or in opposition, especially if heat is to be used. For permanents, a trine to Jupiter is helpful. The Moon also should be in the first quarter. Check the lunar cycle for a favorable day in relation to your Sun sign.

Harvest Crops

Harvest root crops when the Moon is in a dry sign (Aries, Leo, Sagittarius, Gemini, Aquarius) and waning. Harvest grain for storage just after Full Moon, avoiding Cancer, Scorpio, or Pisces. Harvest in the third and fourth quarters in dry signs. Dry crops in the third quarter in fire signs.

Health

A diagnosis is more likely to be successful when the Moon is in Aries, Cancer, Libra, or Capricorn; and less so when in Gemini, Sagittarius, Pisces, or Virgo. Begin a recuperation program when the Moon is in a cardinal or fixed sign and the day is favorable to your Sun sign. Enter hospitals at these times, too. For surgery, see "Surgical Procedures." Buy medicines when the Moon is in Virgo or Scorpio.

Home Furnishings (Buy new)

Saturn days (Saturday) are good for buying, and Jupiter days (Thursday) are good for selling. Items bought on days when Saturn is well aspected tend to wear longer and purchases tend to be more conservative.

Home (Buy new)

If you desire a permanent home, buy when the New Moon is in a fixed sign—Taurus or Leo—for example. Each sign will affect your decision in a different way. A house bought when the Moon is in Taurus is likely to be more practical and have a country look—right down to the split-rail fence. A house purchased when the Moon is in Leo will more likely be a real showplace.

If you're buying for speculation and a quick turnover, be certain that the Moon is in a cardinal sign (Aries, Cancer, Libra, Capricorn). Avoid buying when the Moon is in a fixed sign (Leo, Scorpio, Aquarius, Taurus).

Home (Make repairs)

In all repairs, avoid squares, oppositions, or conjunctions to the planet ruling the place or thing to be repaired. For example, bathrooms are ruled by Scorpio and Cancer. You would not want to start a project in those rooms when the Moon or Pluto is receiving hard aspects. The front entrance, hall, dining room, and porch are ruled by the Sun. So you would want to avoid times when Saturn or Mars are square, opposing, or conjunct the Sun. Also, let the Moon be waxing.

Home (Sell)

Make a strong effort to list your property for sale when the Sun is marked favorable in your sign and in good aspect to Jupiter. Avoid adverse aspects to as many planets as possible.

Job (Start new)

Jupiter and Venus should be sextile, trine, or conjunct the Moon. A day when your Sun is receiving favorable aspects is preferred.

Legal Matters

Good Moon-Jupiter aspects improve the outcome in legal decisions. To gain damages through a lawsuit, begin the process during the increasing Moon. To avoid paying damages, a court date during the decreasing Moon is desirable. Good Moon-Sun aspects strengthen your chance of success. A well-aspected Moon in Cancer or Leo, making good aspects to the Sun, brings the best results in custody cases. In divorce cases, a favorable Moon-Venus aspect is best.

Loan (Ask for)

A first and second quarter phase favors the lender, the third and fourth quarters favor the borrower. Good aspects of Jupiter and Venus to the Moon are favorable to both, as is having the Moon in Leo or Taurus.

Machinery, Appliances, or Tools (Buy)

Tools, machinery, and other implements should be bought on days when your lunar cycle is favorable and when Mars and Uranus are trine, sextile, or conjunct the Moon. Any quarter of the Moon is suitable. When buying gas or electrical appliances, the Moon should be in Aquarius.

Make a Will

Let the Moon be in a fixed sign (Taurus, Leo, Scorpio, or Aquarius) to ensure permanence. If the Moon is in a cardinal sign (Aries, Cancer, Libra, or Capricorn), the will could be altered. Let the Moon be waxing—increasing in light—and in good aspect to Saturn, Venus, or Mercury. In the case the will is made in an emergency during illness, and the Moon is slow in motion, void-of-course, combust, or under the sunbeams, the testator will die and the will remain unaltered. There is some danger that it will be lost or stolen, however.

Marriage

The best time for marriage to take place is when the Moon is increasing, but not yet full. Good signs for the Moon to be in are Taurus, Cancer, Leo, or Libra.

The Moon in Taurus produces the most steadfast marriages, but if the partners later want to separate, they may have a difficult time. Make sure that the Moon is well aspected, especially to Venus or Jupiter. Avoid aspects to Mars, Uranus, or Pluto, and the signs Aries, Gemini, Virgo, Scorpio, or Aquarius.

The values of the signs are as follows:

- Aries is not favored for marriage.
- Taurus from 0 to 19 degrees is good, the remaining degrees are less favorable.
- Cancer is unfavorable unless you are marrying a widow.
- Leo is favored, but it may cause one party to deceive the other as to his or her money or possessions.
- Virgo is not favored except when marrying a widow.
- Libra is good for engagements but not for marriage.
- Scorpio from 0 to 15 degrees is good, but the last fifteen degrees are entirely unfortunate. The woman may be fickle, envious, and quarrelsome.

- Sagittarius is neutral.
- Capricorn from 0 to 10 degrees are difficult for marriage, however, the remaining degrees are favorable, especially when marrying a widow.
- Aquarius is not favored
- Pisces is favored, although marriage under this sign can incline a woman to chatter a lot.

These effects are strongest when the Moon is in the sign. If the Moon and Venus are in a cardinal sign, happiness between the couple may not continue long.

On no account should the Moon apply to Saturn or Mars even by good aspect.

Medical Treatment for the Head

If possible, have Mars and Saturn free of hard aspects. Let the Moon be in Aries or Taurus, decreasing in light, in conjunction or aspect with Venus or Jupiter, and free of hard aspects. The Sun should not be in any aspect to the Moon when they are in Aries.

Medical Treatment for the Eyes

Let the Moon be increasing in light and motion and making favorable aspects to Venus or Jupiter, and unaspected by Mars. Keep the Moon out of Taurus, Capricorn, or Virgo. If an aspect between the Moon and Mars is unavoidable, let it be separating.

Medical Treatment for the Nose

Let the Moon be in Cancer, Leo, or Virgo, and not aspecting Mars or Saturn, and not in conjunction with a weak or retrograde planet.

Mining

Saturn rules mining. Begin work when Saturn is marked conjunct, trine, or sextile. Mine for gold when the Sun is marked conjunct, trine, or sextile. Mercury rules quicksilver, Venus rules copper, Jupiter rules tin, Saturn rules lead and coal, Uranus rules radioactive elements, Neptune rules oil, the Moon rules water. Mine for these items when the ruling planet is marked conjunct, trine, or sextile.

Mow Lawn

Mow in the first and second quarters (waxing phase) to increase growth and lushness, and in the third and fourth quarters (waning phase) to decrease growth.

Move to New Home

If you have a choice, and sometimes we don't, make sure that Mars is not aspecting the Moon. Move on a day favorable to your Sun sign, or when the Moon is conjunct, sextile, or trine the Sun.

Negotiate

When you are choosing a time to negotiate, consider what the meeting is about and what you want to have happen. If it is agreement or compromise between two parties that you desire, have the Moon be in the sign of Libra. When you are making contracts, it is best to have the Moon in the same element. For example, if your concern is communication, then elect a time when the Moon is in an air sign. If, on the other hand, your concern is about possessions, an earth sign would be more appropriate. Fixed signs are unfavorable, with the exception of Leo; so are cardinal signs, except for Capricorn. If you are negotiating the end of something, use the rules that apply to ending habits.

Occupational Training

When you begin training, see that your lunar cycle is favorable that day, and that the planet ruling your occupation is marked conjunct or trine.

Paint

Paint buildings during the waning Libra or Aquarius Moon. If the weather is hot, paint when the Moon is in Taurus. If the weather is cold, paint when the Moon is in Leo. Schedule the painting to start in the fourth quarter as the wood is drier and paint will penetrate wood better. Avoid painting around the New Moon, though, as the wood is likely to be damp, making the paint subject to scalding when hot weather hits it. If the temperature is below 70°F, it is not advisable to paint while the Moon is in Cancer, Scorpio, or Pisces as the paint is apt to creep, check, or run.

Party (Host or attend)

A party timed so the Moon is in Gemini, Leo, Libra, or Sagittarius, with good aspects to Venus and Jupiter, will be fun and well attended. There should be no aspects between the Moon and Mars or Saturn.

Pawn

Do not pawn any article when Jupiter is receiving a square or opposition from Saturn or Mars, or when Jupiter is within seventeen degrees of the Sun, for you will have little chance to redeem the items.

Pick Mushrooms

Mushrooms, one of the most promising traditional medicines in the world, should be gathered at the Full Moon.

Plant

Root crops, like carrots and potatoes, are best if planted in the sign Taurus or Capricorn. Beans, peas, tomatoes, peppers, and other fruit-bearing plants are best if planted in a sign that supports seed growth. Leaf plants, like lettuce, broccoli, or cauliflower, are best planted when the Moon is in a water sign.

It is recommended that you transplant during a decreasing Moon, when forces are streaming into the lower part of the plant. This helps root growth. For complete instructions on planting by the Moon, see Gardening by the Moon on page 256, A Guide to Planting (pages 265–70), Gardening Dates (page 308–15, and Companion Planting Guide (319–21).

Promotion (Ask for)

Choose a day favorable to your Sun sign. Mercury should be marked conjunct, trine, or sextile. Avoid days when Mars or Saturn is aspected.

Prune

Prune during the third and fourth quarter of a Scorpio Moon to retard growth and to promote better fruit. Prune when the Moon is in cardinal Capricorn to promote healing.

Reconcile People

If the reconciliation be with a woman, let Venus be strong and well aspected. If elders or superiors are involved, see that Saturn is receiving good aspects; if the reconciliation is between young people or between an older and younger person, see that Mercury is well aspected.

Roof a Building

Begin roofing a building during the third or fourth quarter, when the Moon is in Aries or Aquarius. Shingles laid during the New Moon have a tendency to curl at the edges.

Romance

There is less control of when a romance starts, but romances begun under an increasing Moon are more likely to be permanent or satisfying, while those begun during the decreasing Moon will tend to transform the participants. The tone of the relationship can be guessed from the sign the Moon is in. Romances begun with the Moon in Aries may be impulsive. Those begun in Capricorn will take greater effort to bring to a desirable conclusion, but they may be very rewarding. Good aspects between the Moon and Venus will have a positive influence on the relationship. Avoid unfavorable aspects to Mars, Uranus, and Pluto. A decreasing Moon, particularly the fourth quarter, facilitates ending a relationship, and causes the least pain.

Sauerkraut

The best-tasting sauerkraut is made just after the Full Moon in the fruitful signs of Cancer, Scorpio, or Pisces.

Select a Child's Sex

Count from the last day of menstruation to the first day of the next cycle and divide the interval between the two dates in half. Pregnancy in the first half produces females, but copulation should take place with the Moon in a feminine sign. Pregnancy in the latter half, up to three days before the beginning of menstruation, produces males, but copulation should take place with the Moon in a masculine sign. The three-day period before the next period again produces females.

Sell or Canvas

Begin these activities during a day favorable to your Sun sign. Otherwise, sell on days when Jupiter, Mercury, or Mars is trine, sextile, or conjunct the Moon. Avoid days when Saturn is square or opposing the Moon, for that always hinders business and causes discord. If the Moon is passing from the first quarter to full. It is best to have the Moon swift in motion and in good aspect with Venus and/or Jupiter.

Sign Papers

Sign contracts or agreements when the Moon is increasing in a fruitful sign and on a day when the Moon is making favorable aspects to Mercury. Avoid days when Mars, Saturn, or Neptune are square or opposite the Moon.

Spray and Weed

Spray pests and weeds during the fourth quarter when the Moon is in the barren sign Leo or Aquarius, and making favorable aspects to Pluto. Weed during a waning Moon in a barren sign. For the best days to kill weeds and pests, see pages 316–17.

Staff (Fire)

Have the Moon in the third or fourth quarter, but not full. The Moon should not be square any planets.

Staff (Hire)

The Moon should be in the first or second quarter, and preferably in the sign of Gemini or Virgo. The Moon should be conjunct, trine, or sextile Mercury or Jupiter.

Stocks (Buy)

The Moon should be in Taurus or Capricorn, and there should be a sextile or trine to Jupiter or Saturn.

Surgical Procedures

Blood flow, like ocean tides, appears to be related to Moon phases. To reduce hemorrhage after a surgery, schedule it within one week before or after a New Moon. Schedule surgery to occur during the increase of the Moon if possible, as wounds heal better and vitality is greater than during the decrease of the Moon. Avoid surgery within one week before or after the Full Moon.

Select a date when the Moon is past the sign governing the part of the body involved in the operation. For example, abdominal operations should be done when the Moon is in Sagittarius, Capricorn, or Aquarius. To find the signs and the body parts they rule, turn to the chart on page 31. The further removed the Moon sign is from the sign ruling the afflicted part of the body, the better.

For successful operations, avoid times when the Moon is applying to any aspect of Mars. (This tends to promote inflammation and complications). See the Lunar Aspectarian on pages 75–97 to find days with negative Mars aspects and positive Venus and Jupiter aspects. Never operate with the Moon in the same sign as a person's Sun sign or Ascendant. Let the Moon be in a fixed sign and avoid square or opposing aspects. The Moon should not be void-of-course.

Cosmetic surgery should be done in the increase of the Moon, when the Moon is not square or in opposition to Mars. Avoid days when the Moon is square or opposing Saturn or the Sun.

Travel (Air)

Start long trips when the Moon is making favorable aspects to the Sun. For enjoyment, aspects to Jupiter are preferable; for visiting, look for favorable aspects to Mercury. To prevent accidents, avoid squares or oppositions to Mars, Saturn, Uranus, or Pluto. Choose a day when the Moon is in Sagittarius or Gemini and well aspected to Mercury, Jupiter, or Uranus. Avoid adverse aspects of Mars, Saturn, or Uranus.

Travel (Automobile)

Start your journey on a day when the Moon is not in a fixed sign, and when it is marked favorable to your ruler, or to Mercury or Uranus. For automobile travels, choose a day when the Moon is in Gemini and making good aspects to Mercury.

If a speedy return from a journey is desired, have Jupiter square the Sun, and Venus in sextile to Jupiter, or place the Moon in Leo increasing in light and motion.

Visit

On setting out to visit a person, let the Moon be in aspect with any retrograde planet, for this ensures that the person you're visiting will be at home. If you desire to stay a long time in a place, let the Moon be in good aspect to Saturn. If you desire to leave the place quickly, let the Moon be in a cardinal sign.

Wean Children

To wean a child successfully, do so when the Moon is in Sagittarius, Capricorn, Aquarius, or Pisces—signs that do not rule vital human organs. By observing this astrological rule, much trouble for parents and child may be avoided.

Weight (Reduce)

If you want to lose weight, the best time to get started is when the Moon is in the third or fourth quarter, and in the barren sign of Virgo. Review the section on How to Use the Moon Tables and Lunar Aspectarian beginning on page 67 to help you select a date that is favorable to begin your weight-loss program.

Wine and Drink Other Than Beer

It is best to start brewing when the Moon is in Pisces or Taurus. Sextiles or trines to Venus are favorable, but avoid aspects to Mars or Saturn.

Write

Write for pleasure or publication when the Moon is in Gemini. Mercury should be making favorable aspects to Uranus and Neptune.

Medical Astrology

by Louise Riotte

In his book *Powerful Planets*, Llewellyn George, one of the great and most respected astrologers of all time, stated, "Medical astrology in its relation to diagnosis and the prevention and cure of disease, is a valuable adjunct to metaphysicians, doctors, surgeons, and dentists." What he said in 1931 is just as true today.

And physicians in the days of old, such as Hippocrates, "the Father of Medicine," used a knowledge of planetary influences to perform their wonders. They well knew the subject of sympathy and antipathy; they knew that the angle of crystallization at 60 degrees, called sextile, was creative; they knew that bodies in opposite points of the zodiac were disintegrative in their effects. They knew that sulphur corresponds to the planet Mercury, and being students of astrology, they knew many other facts that will not be clear to modern scientists until they, too, take up a serious study of planetary influences.

And so it may be seen that the subject of medical astrology takes in much more than the title implies. This fact is readily evidenced by many physicians, surgeons, non-drug-oriented practitioners, and dentists who are now using knowledge of astrology to enhance their skills and to assure more definite and satisfactory results by acting in harmony with the duly timed workings of nature.

By examining a person's natal chart, the physician skilled in medical astrology can see what disorders the patient is predisposed to at birth; by examining the progressed horoscope, he or she can see which tendencies are now coming into expression, whether complications are about to set in, or whether the sickness is about to break up. The doctor can calculate the time of crisis in advance, for he or she knows that in acute situations the crises come about on the seventh, fourteenth, twenty-first, and twenty-eighth days from the time the patient was taken sick. The Moon makes a revolution in her orbit in about twenty-eight and a half days, and the seventh, fourteenth, twenty-first days, and her return to her place at the time of the New Moon (twenty-eighth day) correspond to the quarters, adverse aspects, and crisis times in the illness. Therefore, the first, second, and third quarters of the Moon from the time the illness began are crisis days in diseases.

If the patient lives through these crises, and until the Moon returns to her place, the disease will dissolve itself. The crisis days are the dangerous ones. The most serious crisis day is the fourteenth, as a rule, when the Moon arrives at the opposite aspect to her place at the beginning of the illness. This crisis day is called the "Criticus Primus," the one of prime importance. More patients usually die on the fourteenth day of a serious illness than on the other crisis days, and if they survive, their chances for recovery are usually good.

One of the simple but potent rules that is interesting to surgeons is as follows: "Pierce not with steel that part of the body represented by the sign which the Moon occupies on that day." Another astrological rule may also be invoked: "To reduce the hazard of hemorrhage after a surgical operation, plan to have the surgery occur within one week before or after the New Moon; avoid, whenever possible, submitting to surgery with one week before or after the Full Moon."

These rules are best applied to cases where one can "elect" whether or not to have surgery at a given time; in emergency cases, of course, they cannot be applied as the delay of one or two weeks might prove fatal.

In his book, Llewellyn George tells a most interesting story of what occurred at the time when he was located in Portland, Oregon. "I was called upon frequently for some years by two prominent surgeons to make the charts of patients and determine the best date and time for surgical operations. During that period each of the operations was a success—and the patients recovered.

"I recall one extreme case of a lady who had already been operated on five times by other surgeons. Because she was in great distress on account of serious adhesions it was necessary to operate again. As she was very ill and weak, another operation would obviously be precarious.

"As usual, it became my duty to find the proper time for this operation. A task it proved to be. The lady had so many planetary afflictions that it was difficult to find a good place in her chart. I worked all night on it and at last found a spot wherein if the Moon was located it gave promise of success—but that time would be at midnight! Fortunately, the patient was willing to have the operation when the Moon was favorable if it promised relief.

"But midnight is a difficult time for securing the use of the operating room. However, the doctors went to the Good Samaritan hospital and frankly told the Sister Superior in charge the reason for wanting the operation at that unusual hour. Somewhat to their surprise she said, 'Certainly you may have the room, for we understand the importance of the Moon.'

"The operation proved satisfactory to all concerned. In fact, the patient was so delighted with the results that she became a student of astrology—and so did the surgeons; now they draw all such horoscopes themselves."

Dr. H.L. Cornell, author of the *Encyclopedia of Medical Astrology*, has stated that statistics show that surgical operations, including operations on the eyes, are apt to be most successful when the Moon is increasing in light, that is, between the New and Full Moons, and that the patients heal more rapidly and have fewer complications than when the Moon is decreasing.

During the decrease of the Moon, the vitality is usually less, and the bodily fluids at low ebb; these fluids rise and fill the vessels of the body to a greater fullness when the Moon is increasing.

Consideration of the Moon's phases is no less important in the practice of dentistry. Teeth should be extracted in either the first or second quarter (waxing Moon), which promotes healing.

The best signs for extraction are Gemini, Virgo, Sagittarius, Capricorn, and Pisces. Note that all these signs are some distance from the head. Mars and Saturn should be conjunct, trine, or sextile the Moon.

Avoid extractions when the Moon is passing through Aries, Cancer, Libra, Taurus, Leo, Scorpio, or Aquarius.

Fillings should be done when the Moon is waning in the third and fourth quarters, and in a fixed sign such as Taurus, Leo, Scorpio, or Aquarius.

Originally printed in Llewellyn's 1993 Moon Sign Book. Reprinted with permission.

How to Use the Moon Tables and Lunar Apectarian

Timing activities is one of the most important things you can do to ensure success. In many Eastern countries, timing by the planets is so important that practically no event takes place without first setting up a chart for it. Weddings have occurred in the middle of the night because the influences were best then. You may not want to take it that far, but you can still make use of the influences of the Moon whenever possible. It's easy and it works!

In the *Moon Sign Book* is information to help you plan just about any activity: weddings, fishing, making purchases, cutting your hair, traveling, and more. We provide the guidelines you need to pick the best day out of the several from which you have to choose. The Moon Tables are the *Moon Sign Book*'s primary method for choosing dates. Following are instructions, examples, and directions on how to read the Moon Tables. More advanced information on using the tables containing the Lunar Aspectarian and favorable and unfavorable days (found on odd-numbered pages opposite the Moon Tables), Moon void-of-course, and retrograde information to choose the dates best for you is also included.

We highly recommend reading the sections of this book called Why This Almanac is Different from Some Almanacs on page 7, How Important Is the Moon? on page 9, Moon Void-of-Course on page 100, and Retrograde Periods on page 109. It's not essential that you read these before you try the examples below, but reading them will deepen your understanding of the date-choosing process.

The Five Basic Steps

Step 1: Directions for Choosing Dates

Look up the directions for choosing dates for the activity that you wish to begin, then go to step 2.

Step 2: Check the Moon Tables

You'll find two tables for each month of the year beginning on page 74. The Moon Tables (on the left-hand pages) include the day, date, and sign the Moon is in; the element and nature of the sign; the Moon's phase; and when it changes sign or phase. If there is a time listed after a date, that time is the time when the Moon moves into that zodiac sign. Until then, the Moon is considered to be in the sign for the previous day.

The abbreviation Full signifies Full Moon and New signifies New Moon. The times listed with dates indicate when the Moon changes sign. The times listed after the phase indicate when the Moon changes phase.

Turn to the month you would like to begin your activity. You will be using the Moon's sign and phase information most often when you begin choosing your own dates. Use the Time Zone Conversions chart and table on pages 98–99 to convert time to your own time zone.

When you find dates that meet the criteria for the correct Moon phase and sign for your activity, you may have completed the process. For certain simple activities, such as getting a haircut, the phase and sign information is all that is needed. If the directions for your activity include information on certain lunar aspects, however, you should consult the Lunar Aspectarian. An example of this would be if the directions told you not to perform a certain activity when the Moon is square (Q) Jupiter.

Step 3: Check the Lunar Aspectarian

On the pages opposite the Moon Tables you will find tables containing the Lunar Aspectarian and Favorable and Unfavorable Days. The Lunar Aspectarian gives the aspects (or angles) of the Moon to the other planets. Some Moon-planets are favorable, while others are not. To use the Lunar Aspectarian, find the planet that the directions list as favorable for your activity, and run down the column to the date desired. For example, you should avoid aspects to Mars if you are planning surgery. So you would look for Mars across the top and then run down that column looking for days where there are no aspects to Mars (as signified by empty boxes). If you want to find a favorable aspect (sextile (X) or trine (T) to Mercury, run your finger down the column under Mercury until you find an X or T. Adverse aspects to planets are squares (Q) or oppositions (O). A conjunction (C) is sometimes beneficial, sometimes not, depending on the activity or planets involved.

Step 4: Favorable and Unfavorable Days

The tables listing favorable and unfavorable days are helpful when you want to choose your personal best dates because your Sun sign is taken into consideration. The twelve Sun signs are listed on the right side of the tables. Once you have determined which days meet your criteria for phase, sign, and aspects, you can determine whether or not those days are positive for you by checking the favorable and unfavorable days for your Sun sign.

To find out if a day is positive for you, find your Sun sign and then look down the column. If it is marked F, it is very favorable. The Moon is in the same sign as your Sun on a favorable day. If it is marked f, it is slightly favorable; U is very unfavorable; and u means slightly unfavorable. A day marked very unfavorable (U) indicates that the Moon is in the sign opposing your Sun.

Once you have selected good dates for the activity you are about to begin, you can go straight to the examples section beginning on the next page. To learn how to fine-tune your selections even further, read on.

Step 5: Void-of-Course Moon and Retrogrades

This last step is perhaps the most advanced portion of the procedure. It is generally considered poor timing to make decisions, sign important papers, or start special activities during a Moon void-of-course period or during a Mercury retrograde. Once you have chosen the best date for your activity based on steps one through four, you can check the Void-of-Course tables, beginning on page 101, to find out if any of the dates you have chosen have void periods.

The Moon is said to be void-of-course after it has made its last aspect to a planet within a particular sign, but before it has moved into the next sign. Put simply, the Moon is "resting" during the void-of-course period, so activities initiated at this time generally don't come to fruition. You will notice that there are many void periods during the year, and it is nearly impossible to avoid all of them. Some people choose to ignore these altogether and do not take them into consideration when planning activities.

Next, you can check the Retrograde Periods table on page 109 to see what planets are retrograde during your chosen date(s).

A planet is said to be retrograde when it appears to move backward in the sky as viewed from the Earth. Generally, the farther a planet is away from the Sun, the longer it can stay retrograde. Some planets will retrograde for several months at a time. Avoiding retrogrades is not as important in lunar planning as avoiding the Moon void-of-course, with the exception of the planet Mercury.

Mercury rules thought and communication, so it is advisable not to sign important papers, initiate important business or legal work, or make crucial decisions during these times. As with the Moon void-of-course, it is difficult to avoid all planetary retrogrades when beginning events, and you may choose to ignore this step of the process. Following are some examples using some or all of the steps outlined above.

Using What You've Learned

Let's say you want to have your hair cut. It's thin and you would like it to look fuller, so you find the directions for hair care and you see that for thicker hair you should cut hair while the Moon is Full and in the sign of Taurus, Cancer, or Leo. You should avoid the Moon in Aries, Gemini, or Virgo. Look up January in the Moon Tables. The Full Moon falls on January 25 at 5:32 am. The Moon moves into the sign of Leo January 24 at 6:21 pm, and remains in Leo until January 27 at 6:24 pm, so January 10 meets both the phase and sign criteria.

Let's move on to a more difficult example using the sign and phase of the Moon. You want to buy a permanent home. After checking the instructions for purchasing a house "Home (Buy new)," you'll read that it says you should buy a home when the Moon is in Taurus, Cancer, or Leo. You need to get a loan, so you should also look under "Loan (Ask for)." Here it says that the third and fourth Moon quarters favor the borrower (you). You are going to buy the house in August. Look up August in the Moon Tables. The Moon is in the third quarter August 20–25, the fourth quarter August 26–31. The Moon is in Taurus from 9:58 pm on August 23 until 4:43 am on August 26. The best days for obtaining a loan would be August 23–26, while the Moon is in Taurus.

Just match up the best sign and phase (quarter) to come up with the best date. With all activities, be sure to check the favorable and unfavorable days for your Sun sign in the table adjoining the Lunar Aspectarian. If there is a choice between several dates, pick the one most favorable for you. Because buying a home is an important business decision, you may also wish to see if there are Moon voids or a Mercury retrograde during these dates.

Now let's look at an example that uses signs, phases, and aspects. Our example is starting new home construction. We will use month of July. Looking under "Build (Start foundation)" you'll see that the Moon should be in the first quarter of fixed sign Taurus or Leo. You should select a time when the Moon is not making unfavorable aspects to Saturn. (Conjunctions are usually considered good if they are not to Mars, Saturn, or Neptune.) Look in the July Moon Table. You will see that the Moon is in the first quarter July 7–13. The Moon is in Leo between 3:11 pm on July 7 and 3:57 am on July 10. Now, look to the lunar aspectarian for July. We see that there are no squares or oppositions to Saturn on July 7–10. In addition, there are no negative aspects to Mars on these dates. If you wanted to start building your house in July, the best dates would be July 7–10.

A Note About Time and Time Zones

All tables in the *Moon Sign Book* use Eastern Time. You must calculate the difference between your time zone and the Eastern Time Zone. Please refer to the Time Zone Conversions chart on page 99 for help with time conversions.

How Does the Time Matter?

Due to the three-hour time difference between the east and west coasts of the United States, those of you living on the East Coast may be, for example, under the influence of a Virgo Moon, while those of you living on the West Coast will still have a Leo Moon influence.

We follow a commonly held belief among astrologers: whatever sign the Moon is in at the start of a day—12:00 am Eastern Time—is considered the dominant influence of the day. That sign is indicated in the Moon Tables. If the date you select for an activity shows the Moon changing signs, you can decide how important the sign change may be for your specific election and adjust your election date and time accordingly.

Use Common Sense

Some activities depend on outside factors. Obviously, you can't go out and plant when there is a foot of snow on the ground. You should adjust to the conditions at hand. If the weather was bad during the first quarter, when it was best to plant crops, do it during the second quarter while the Moon is in a fruitful sign. If the Moon is not in a fruitful sign during the first or second quarter, choose a day when it is in a semi-fruitful sign. The best advice is to choose either the sign or phase that is most favorable when the two don't coincide.

To Summarize

First, look up the activity under the proper heading, then look for the information given in the tables (the Moon Tables, Lunar Aspectarian, or Favorable and Unfavorable Days). Choose the best date considering the number of positive factors in effect. If most of the dates are favorable, there is no problem choosing the one that will fit your schedule. However, if there aren't any really good dates, pick the ones with the least number of negative influences. Please keep in mind that the information found here applies in the broadest sense to the events you want to plan or are considering. To be the most effective, when you use electional astrology, you should also consider your own birth chart in relation to a chart drawn for the time or times you have under consideration. The best advice we can offer you is: Read the entire introduction to each section.

January Moon Tables

Date	Sign	Element	Nature	Phase
1 Sat.	Virgo	Earth	Barren	3rd
2 Sun. 11:19 am	Libra	Air	Semi-fruitful	3rd
3 Mon.	Libra	Air	Semi-fruitful	4th 12:46 pm
4 Tue. 7:00 pm	Scorpio	Water	Fruitful	4th
5 Wed.	Scorpio	Water	Fruitful	4th
6 Thu. 10:44 pm	Sagittarius	Fire	Barren	4th
7 Fri.	Sagittarius	Fire	Barren	4th
8 Sat. 11:11 pm	Capricorn	Earth	Semi-fruitful	4th
9 Sun.	Capricorn	Earth	Semi-fruitful	4th
10 Mon. 10:07 pm	Aquarius	Air	Barren	New 7:03 am
11 Tue.	Aquarius	Air	Barren	1st
12 Wed. 9:50 pm	Pisces	Water	Fruitful	1st
13 Thu.	Pisces	Water	Fruitful	1st
14 Fri.	Pisces	Water	Fruitful	1st
15 Sat. 12:27 am	Aries	Fire	Barren	1st
16 Sun.	Aries	Fire	Barren	1st
17 Mon. 7:06 am	Taurus	Earth	Semi-fruitful	2nd 1:57 am
18 Tue.	Taurus	Earth	Semi-fruitful	2nd
19 Wed. 5:24 pm	Gemini	Air	Barren	2nd
20 Thu.	Gemini	Air	Barren	2nd
21 Fri.	Gemini	Air	Barren	2nd
22 Sat. 5:42 am	Cancer	Water	Fruitful	2nd
23 Sun.	Cancer	Water	Fruitful	2nd
24 Mon. 6:21 pm	Leo	Fire	Barren	2nd
25 Tue.	Leo	Fire	Barren	Full 5:32 am
26 Wed.	Leo	Fire	Barren	3rd
27 Thu. 6:24 am	Virgo	Earth	Barren	3rd
28 Fri.	Virgo	Earth	Barren	3rd
29 Sat. 5:13 pm	Libra	Air	Semi-fruitful	3rd
30 Sun.	Libra	Air	Semi-fruitful	3rd
31 Mon.	Libra	Air	Semi-fruitful	3rd

	Sun	Mercury	Venus	Mars	Jupiter	Saturn	Uranus	Neptune	Pluto	Aries	Taurus	Gemini	Cancer	Leo	Virgo	Libra	Scorpio	Sagittarius	Capricorn	Aquarius	Pisces
1		Q	Q						Q		f	u	f		F		f	u	f		U
2				X		X					f	u	f		F		f	u	f		U
3	Q				C			T		U	f	u	f			F		f	u	f	
4		X	X			Q			X	U	f	u	f			F		f	u	f	
5	X						T	Q			U	f	u	f			F		f	u	f
6							T				U	f	u	f			F		f	u	f
7				C			Q	X		f		U	f	u	f			F		f	u
8		C	C		X				C	f		U	f	u	f			F		f	u
9							X			u			U	f	u	f			F		f
10	C				Q	0				u			U	f	u	f			F		f
11				X				C		f	u	f		U	f	u	f			F	
12				T				X		f	u	f		U	f	u	f			F	
13		X	X	Q			C			f	u	f			U	f	u	f			F
14	X				T				Q	f	u	f			U	f	u	f			F
15		Q	Q							f	u	f			U	f	u	f			F
16				T	0	Q		X	T	F		f	u	f		U	f	u	f		
17	Q							X		F		f	u	f		U	f	u	f		
18		T	T					Q			F		f	u	f		U	f	u	f	
19	T					X					F		f	u	f		U	f	u	f	
20						Q	T			f		F		f	u	f		U	f	u	
21				0	T				0	f		F		f	u	f		U	f	u	
22						T				f		F		f	u	f		U	f	u	
23		0	0		Q					u	f		F		f	u	f		U	f	
24						C				u	f		F		f	u	f		U	f	
25	0							0		f	u	f		F		f	u	f		U	
26				T	X				T	f	u	f		F		f	u	f		U	
27						0				f	u	f		F		f	u	f		U	
28										f	u	f			F		f	u	f		U
29		T	T	Q		X			Q	f	u	f			F		f	u	f		U
30	T							T		U	f	u	f			F		f	u	f	
31			Q	X	C	Q			X	U	f	u	f			F		f	u	f	

February Moon Table

Date	Sign	Element	Nature	Phase
1 Tue. 1:51 am	Scorpio	Water	Fruitful	3rd
2 Wed.	Scorpio	Water	Fruitful	4th 2:27 am
3 Thu. 7:21 am	Sagittarius	Fire	Barren	4th
4 Fri.	Sagittarius	Fire	Barren	4th
5 Sat. 9:32 am	Capricorn	Earth	Semi-fruitful	4th
6 Sun.	Capricorn	Earth	Semi-fruitful	4th
7 Mon. 9:26 am	Aquarius	Air	Barren	4th
8 Tue.	Aquarius	Air	Barren	New 5:28 pm
9 Wed. 8:59 am	Pisces	Water	Fruitful	1st
10 Thu.	Pisces	Water	Fruitful	1st
11 Fri. 10:21 am	Aries	Fire	Barren	1st
12 Sat.	Aries	Fire	Barren	1st
13 Sun. 3:18 pm	Taurus	Earth	Semi-fruitful	1st
14 Mon.	Taurus	Earth	Semi-fruitful	1st
15 Tue.	Taurus	Earth	Semi-fruitful	2nd 7:16 pm
16 Wed. 12:18 am	Gemini	Air	Barren	2nd
17 Thu.	Gemini	Air	Barren	2nd
18 Fri. 12:13 pm	Cancer	Water	Fruitful	2nd
19 Sat.	Cancer	Water	Fruitful	2nd
20 Sun.	Cancer	Water	Fruitful	2nd
21 Mon. 12:54 am	Leo	Fire	Barren	2nd
22 Tue.	Leo	Fire	Barren	2nd
23 Wed. 12:44 pm	Virgo	Earth	Barren	Full 11:54 pm
24 Thu.	Virgo	Earth	Barren	3rd
25 Fri. 10:59 pm	Libra	Air	Semi-fruitful	3rd
26 Sat.	Libra	Air	Semi-fruitful	3rd
27 Sun.	Libra	Air	Semi-fruitful	3rd
28 Mon. 7:21 am	Scorpio	Water	Fruitful	3rd

Lunar Aspectarian   Favorable and Unfavorable Days

	Sun	Mercury	Venus	Mars	Jupiter	Saturn	Uranus	Neptune	Pluto	Aries	Taurus	Gemini	Cancer	Leo	Virgo	Libra	Scorpio	Sagittarius	Capricorn	Aquarius	Pisces
1		Q						T		U		f	u	f		F		f	u	f	
2	Q					T		Q		U		f	u	f		F		f	u	f	
3		X	X					Q		U		f	u	f		F		f	u	f	
4	X				X			X	C	f		U		f	u	f		F		f	u
5			C			X				f		U		f	u	f		F		f	u
6					Q	O				u	f		U		f	u	f		F		f
7			C							u	f		U		f	u	f		F		f
8	C	C				T		C	X	f	u	f		U		f	u	f		F	
9				X		C				f	u	f		U		f	u	f		F	
10						T					f	u	f		U		f	u	f		F
11			Q						Q		f	u	f		U		f	u	f		F
12			X		O			X		F		f	u	f		U		f	u	f	
13	X	X				Q			T	F		f	u	f		U		f	u	f	
14			Q	T				X	Q		F		f	u	f		U		f	u	f
15	Q	Q				X					F		f	u	f		U		f	u	f
16						Q					F		f	u	f		U		f	u	f
17			T		T			T		f		F		f	u	f		U		f	u
18	T	T							O	f		F		f	u	f		U		f	u
19			O			T				u	f		F		f	u	f		U		f
20					Q	C				u	f		F		f	u	f		U		f
21										u	f		F		f	u	f		U		f
22					X			O		f	u	f		F		f	u	f		U	
23	O		O						T	f	u	f		F		f	u	f		U	
24		O		T		O					f	u	f		F		f	u	f		U
25					X				Q		f	u	f		F		f	u	f		U
26										U		f	u	f		F		f	u	f	
27			Q	C	Q			T	X	U		f	u	f		F		f	u	f	
28			T					T		U		f	u	f		F		f	u	f	

March Moon Table

Date	Sign	Element	Nature	Phase
1 Tue.	Scorpio	Water	Fruitful	3rd
2 Wed. 1:29 pm	Sagittarius	Fire	Barren	3rd
3 Thu.	Sagittarius	Fire	Barren	4th 12:36 pm
4 Fri. 5:12 pm	Capricorn	Earth	Semi-fruitful	4th
5 Sat.	Capricorn	Earth	Semi-fruitful	4th
6 Sun. 6:49 pm	Aquarius	Air	Barren	4th
7 Mon.	Aquarius	Air	Barren	4th
8 Tue. 7:32 pm	Pisces	Water	Fruitful	4th
9 Wed.	Pisces	Water	Fruitful	4th
10 Thu. 9:03 pm	Aries	Fire	Barren	New 4:10 am
11 Fri.	Aries	Fire	Barren	1st
12 Sat.	Aries	Fire	Barren	1st
13 Sun. 1:05 am	Taurus	Earth	Semi-fruitful	1st
14 Mon.	Taurus	Earth	Semi-fruitful	1st
15 Tue. 8:44 am	Gemini	Air	Barren	1st
16 Wed.	Gemini	Air	Barren	1st
17 Thu. 7:44 pm	Cancer	Water	Fruitful	2nd 2:19 pm
18 Fri.	Cancer	Water	Fruitful	2nd
19 Sat.	Cancer	Water	Fruitful	2nd
20 Sun. 8:17 am	Leo	Fire	Barren	2nd
21 Mon.	Leo	Fire	Barren	2nd
22 Tue. 8:10 pm	Virgo	Earth	Barren	2nd
23 Wed.	Virgo	Earth	Barren	2nd
24 Thu.	Virgo	Earth	Barren	2nd
25 Fri. 6:00 am	Libra	Air	Semi-fruitful	Full 3:58 pm
26 Sat.	Libra	Air	Semi-fruitful	3rd
27 Sun. 1:29 pm	Scorpio	Water	Fruitful	3rd
28 Mon.	Scorpio	Water	Fruitful	3rd
29 Tue. 6:56 pm	Sagittarius	Fire	Barren	3rd
30 Wed.	Sagittarius	Fire	Barren	3rd
31 Thu. 10:48 pm	Capricorn	Earth	Semi-fruitful	3rd

Lunar Aspectarian — Favorable and Unfavorable Days

	Sun	Mercury	Venus	Mars	Jupiter	Saturn	Uranus	Neptune	Pluto	Aries	Taurus	Gemini	Cancer	Leo	Virgo	Libra	Scorpio	Sagittarius	Capricorn	Aquarius	Pisces
1	T			X		T		Q			U		f	u	f		F		f	u	f
2		T	Q								U		f	u.	f		F		f	u	f
3	Q			X			Q	X		f		U		f	u	f		F		f	u
4		Q							C	f		U		f	u	f		F		f	u
5	X		X		Q		X			u	f		U		f	u	f		F		f
6				C		0				u	f		U		f	u	f		F		f
7		X				T			C	f	u	f		U	f	u	f			F	
8								X		f	u	f		U	f	u	f			F	
9			C				C			f	u	f			U	f	u	f			F
10	C			X		T		Q		f	u	f			U	f	u	f			F
11		C								F		f		u	f		U	f	u	f	
12				Q	0	Q		X	T	F		f		u	f		U	f	u	f	
13							X			F		f		u	f		U	f	u	f	
14	X		X			X		Q			F		f	u	f		U		f	u	f
15				T				Q			F		f	u	f		U		f	u	f
16		X				T		T		f		F		f	u	f		U		f	u
17	Q		Q						0	f		F		f	u	f		U		f	u
18						T				u	f		F		f	u	f		U		f
19		Q			Q	C				u	f		F		f	u	f		U		f
20	T		T		0					u	f		F		f	u	f		U		f
21		T			X			0		f	u	f		F		f	u	f		U	
22								T		f	u	f		F		f	u	f		U	
23						0					f	u	f		F		f	u	f		U
24					X			Q			f	u	f		F		f	u	f		U
25	0		0	T							f	u	f		F		f	u	f		U
26		0			C	Q	T			U		f	u	f		F		f	u	f	
27			Q					X		U		f	u	f		F		f	u	f	
28						T	Q				U		f	u	f		F		f	u	f
29						T					U		f	u	f		F		f	u	f
30	T	T	T	X	X			Q		f		U		f	u	f		F		f	u
31							X	C		f		U		f	u	f		F		f	u

79

April Moon Table

Date	Sign	Element	Nature	Phase
1 Fri.	Capricorn	Earth	Semi-fruitful	4th 7:50 pm
2 Sat.	Capricorn	Earth	Semi-fruitful	4th
3 Sun. 1:31 am	Aquarius	Air	Barren	4th
4 Mon.	Aquarius	Air	Barren	4th
5 Tue. 4:45 am	Pisces	Water	Fruitful	4th
6 Wed.	Pisces	Water	Fruitful	4th
7 Thu. 7:28 am	Aries	Fire	Barren	4th
8 Fri.	Aries	Fire	Barren	New 4:32 pm
9 Sat. 11:50 am	Taurus	Earth	Semi-fruitful	1st
10 Sun.	Taurus	Earth	Semi-fruitful	1st
11 Mon. 6:55 pm	Gemini	Air	Barren	1st
12 Tue.	Gemini	Air	Barren	1st
13 Wed.	Gemini	Air	Barren	1st
14 Thu. 5:03 am	Cancer	Water	Fruitful	1st
15 Fri.	Cancer	Water	Fruitful	1st
16 Sat. 5:17 pm	Leo	Fire	Barren	2nd 10:37 am
17 Sun.	Leo	Fire	Barren	2nd
18 Mon.	Leo	Fire	Barren	2nd
19 Tue. 5:27 am	Virgo	Earth	Barren	2nd
20 Wed.	Virgo	Earth	Barren	2nd
21 Thu. 3:27 pm	Libra	Air	Semi-fruitful	2nd
22 Fri.	Libra	Air	Semi-fruitful	2nd
23 Sat. 10:25 pm	Scorpio	Water	Fruitful	2nd
24 Sun.	Scorpio	Water	Fruitful	Full 6:06 am
25 Mon.	Scorpio	Water	Fruitful	3rd
26 Tue. 2:46 am	Sagittarius	Fire	Barren	3rd
27 Wed.	Sagittarius	Fire	Barren	3rd
28 Thu. 5:33 am	Capricorn	Earth	Semi-fruitful	3rd
29 Fri.	Capricorn	Earth	Semi-fruitful	3rd
30 Sat. 7:54 am	Aquarius	Air	Barren	3rd

Lunar Aspectarian — Favorable and Unfavorable Days

	Sun	Mercury	Venus	Mars	Jupiter	Saturn	Uranus	Neptune	Pluto	Aries	Taurus	Gemini	Cancer	Leo	Virgo	Libra	Scorpio	Sagittarius	Capricorn	Aquarius	Pisces
1	Q	Q	Q		Q		X			u	f		U		f	u	f		F		f
2						0				u	f		U		f	u	f		F		f
3		X		C						u	f		U		f	u	f		F		f
4	X		X		T			C	X	f	u	f		U		f	u	f		F	
5						C				f	u	f		U		f	u	f		F	
6					T				Q		f	u	f		U		f	u	f		F
7		C									f	u	f		U		f	u	f		F
8	C		C	X	0	Q		X		F		f	u	f		U	f	u	f		
9									T	F		f	u	f		U	f	u	f		
10				Q			X	Q			F		f	u	f		U		f	u	f
11		X				X					F		f	u	f		U		f	u	f
12				T		Q				f		F		f	u	f		U		f	u
13	X			T				T	0	f		F		f	u	f		U		f	u
14		Q	X			T				f		F		f	u	f		U		f	u
15					Q	C				u	f		F		f	u	f		U		f
16	Q	T	Q							u	f		F		f	u	f		U		f
17				X						f	u	f		F		f	u	f		U	
18			0					0	T	f	u	f		F		f	u	f		U	
19	T		T			0				f	u	f		F		f	u	f		U	
20							X				f	u	f		F		f	u	f		U
21									Q		f	u	f		F		f	u	f		U
22		0		C			T			U		f	u	f		F		f	u	f	
23				T	Q				X	U		f	u	f		F		f	u	f	
24	0		0			T					U		f	u	f		F		f	u	f
25			Q		T		Q				U		f	u	f		F		f	u	f
26		T		X		Q					U		f	u	f		F		f	u	f
27								X	C	f		U		f	u	f		F		f	u
28	T			X	Q		X			f		U		f	u	f		F		f	u
29		Q	T			0				u	f		U		f	u	f		F		f
30										u	f		U		f	u	f		F		f

May Moon Table

Date	Sign	Element	Nature	Phase
1 Sun.	Aquarius	Air	Barren	4th 2:24 am
2 Mon. 10:43 am	Pisces	Water	Fruitful	4th
3 Tue.	Pisces	Water	Fruitful	4th
4 Wed. 2:36 pm	Aries	Fire	Barren	4th
5 Thu.	Aries	Fire	Barren	4th
6 Fri. 8:01 pm	Taurus	Earth	Semi-fruitful	4th
7 Sat.	Taurus	Earth	Semi-fruitful	4th
8 Sun.	Taurus	Earth	Semi-fruitful	New 4:45 am
9 Mon. 3:29 am	Gemini	Air	Barren	1st
10 Tue.	Gemini	Air	Barren	1st
11 Wed. 1:20 pm	Cancer	Water	Fruitful	1st
12 Thu.	Cancer	Water	Fruitful	1st
13 Fri.	Cancer	Water	Fruitful	1st
14 Sat. 1:17 am	Leo	Fire	Barren	1st
15 Sun.	Leo	Fire	Barren	1st
16 Mon. 1:46 pm	Virgo	Earth	Barren	2nd 4:57 am
17 Tue.	Virgo	Earth	Barren	2nd
18 Wed.	Virgo	Air	Semi-fruitful	2nd
19 Thu. 12:30 am	Libra	Air	Semi-fruitful	2nd
20 Fri.	Libra	Air	Semi-fruitful	2nd
21 Sat. 7:49 am	Scorpio	Water	Fruitful	2nd
22 Sun.	Scorpio	Water	Fruitful	2nd
23 Mon. 11:38 am	Sagittarius	Fire	Barren	Full 4:18 pm
24 Tue.	Sagittarius	Fire	Barren	3rd
25 Wed. 1:11 pm	Capricorn	Earth	Semi-fruitful	3rd
26 Thu.	Capricorn	Earth	Semi-fruitful	3rd
27 Fri. 2:10 pm	Aquarius	Air	Barren	3rd
28 Sat.	Aquarius	Air	Barren	3rd
29 Sun. 4:09 pm	Pisces	Water	Fruitful	3rd
30 Mon.	Pisces	Water	Fruitful	4th 7:47 am
31 Tue. 8:07 pm	Aries	Fire	Barren	4th

Lunar Aspectarian   Favorable and Unfavorable Days

	Sun	Mercury	Venus	Mars	Jupiter	Saturn	Uranus	Neptune	Pluto	Aries	Taurus	Gemini	Cancer	Leo	Virgo	Libra	Scorpio	Sagittarius	Capricorn	Aquarius	Pisces
1	Q	X	Q		T			C	X	f	u	f		U		f	u	f		F	
2			C							f	u	f		U		f	u	f		F	
3	X					T	C				f	u	f		U		f	u	f		F
4			X						Q		f	u	f		U		f	u	f		F
5					0		X			F		f	u	f		U		f	u	f	
6		C				Q			T	F		f	u	f		U		f	u	f	
7				X			X				F		f	u	f		U		f	u	f
8	C					X		Q			F		f	u	f		U		f	u	f
9			C	Q	T		Q				F		f	u	f		U		f	u	f
10								T		f		F		f	u	f		U		f	u
11		X							0	f		F		f	u	f		U		f	u
12				T	Q		T			u	f		F		f	u	f		U		f
13	X					C				u	f		F		f	u	f		U		f
14		Q	X	X						u	f		F		f	u	f		U		f
15							0			f	u	f		F		f	u	f		U	
16	Q								T	f	u	f		F		f	u	f		U	
17		T	Q	0			0				f	u	f		F		f	u	f		U
18	T					X			Q		f	u	f		F		f	u	f		U
19			T		C					U		f	u	f		F		f	u	f	
20						Q		T	X	U		f	u	f		F		f	u	f	
21										U		f	u	f		F		f	u	f	
22		0		T		T	T	Q			U		f	u	f		F		f	u	f
23	0										U		f	u	f		F		f	u	f
24			0	Q	X		Q	X		f		U		f	u	f		F		f	u
25									C	f		U		f	u	f		F		f	u
26				X	Q		X			u	f		U		f	u	f		F		f
27		T			0					u	f		U		f	u	f		F		f
28	T				T			C		f	u	f		U		f	u	f		F	
29		Q	T						X	f	u	f		U		f	u	f		F	
30	Q					C					f	u	f		U		f	u	f		F
31			Q	C		T			Q		f	u	f		U		f	u	f		F

June Moon Table

Date	Sign	Element	Nature	Phase
1 Wed.	Aries	Fire	Barren	4th
2 Thu.	Aries	Fire	Barren	4th
3 Fri. 2:20 am	Taurus	Earth	Semi-fruitful	4th
4 Sat.	Taurus	Earth	Semi-fruitful	4th
5 Sun. 10:36 am	Gemini	Air	Barren	4th
6 Mon.	Gemini	Air	Barren	New 5:55 pm
7 Tue. 8:46 pm	Cancer	Water	Fruitful	1st
8 Wed.	Cancer	Water	Fruitful	1st
9 Thu.	Cancer	Water	Fruitful	1st
10 Fri. 8:39 am	Leo	Fire	Barren	1st
11 Sat.	Leo	Fire	Barren	1st
12 Sun. 9:22 pm	Virgo	Earth	Barren	1st
13 Mon.	Virgo	Earth	Barren	1st
14 Tue.	Virgo	Earth	Barren	2nd 9:22 pm
15 Wed. 8:59 am	Libra	Air	Semi-fruitful	2nd
16 Thu.	Libra	Air	Semi-fruitful	2nd
17 Fri. 5:23 pm	Scorpio	Water	Fruitful	2nd
18 Sat.	Scorpio	Water	Fruitful	2nd
19 Sun. 9:45 pm	Sagittarius	Fire	Barren	2nd
20 Mon.	Sagittarius	Fire	Barren	2nd
21 Tue. 10:52 pm	Capricorn	Earth	Semi-fruitful	2nd
22 Wed.	Capricorn	Earth	Semi-fruitful	Full 12:14 am
23 Thu. 10:36 pm	Aquarius	Air	Barren	3rd
24 Fri.	Aquarius	Air	Barren	3rd
25 Sat. 11:03 pm	Pisces	Water	Fruitful	3rd
26 Sun.	Pisces	Water	Fruitful	3rd
27 Mon.	Pisces	Water	Fruitful	3rd
28 Tue. 1:51 am	Aries	Fire	Barren	4th 2:23 pm
29 Wed.	Aries	Fire	Barren	4th
30 Thu. 7:45 am	Taurus	Earth	Semi-fruitful	4th

Lunar Aspectarian   Favorable and Unfavorable Days

	Sun	Mercury	Venus	Mars	Jupiter	Saturn	Uranus	Neptune	Pluto	Aries	Taurus	Gemini	Cancer	Leo	Virgo	Libra	Scorpio	Sagittarius	Capricorn	Aquarius	Pisces
1	X	X			0					F		f	u	f		U		f	u	f	
2						Q		X	T	F		f	u	f		U		f	u	f	
3			X					X		F		f	u	f		U		f	u	f	
4								Q			F		f	u	f		U		f	u	f
5				X	X						F		f	u	f		U		f	u	f
6	C				T		Q	T		f		F		f	u	f		U		f		u
7		C		Q					0	f		F		f	u	f		U		f		u
8			C		Q		T			u	f		F		f	u	f		U		f
9						C				u	f		F		f	u	f		U		f
10				T						u	f		F		f	u	f		U		f
11				X				0		f	u	f		F		f	u	f		U	
12	X								T	f	u	f		F		f	u	f		U	
13		X	X				0				f	u	f		F		f	u	f		U
14	Q								Q		f	u	f		F		f	u	f		U
15			0		X						f	u	f		F		f	u	f		U
16		Q	Q		C			T		U		f	u	f		F		f	u	f	
17	T					Q			X	U		f	u	f		F		f	u	f	
18		T					T	Q			U		f	u	f		F		f	u	f
19			T			T					U		f	u	f		F		f	u	f
20				T	X		Q			f		U		f	u	f		F		f	u
21	0							X	C	f		U		f	u	f		F		f	u
22				Q	Q	X				u	f		U		f	u	f		F		f
23		0	0		0					u	f		U		f	u	f		F		f
24				X	T					f	u	f		U		f	u	f		F	
25							C	X		f	u	f		U		f	u	f		F	
26	T					C					f	u	f		U		f	u	f		F
27					T				Q		f	u	f		U		f	u	f		F
28	Q	T	T	C	0						f	u	f		U		f	u	f		F
29								X	T	F		f	u	f		U		f	u	f	
30		Q	Q			Q				F		f	u	f		U		f	u	f	

85

July Moon Table

Date	Sign	Element	Nature	Phase
1 Fri.	Taurus	Earth	Semi-fruitful	4th
2 Sat. 4:26 pm	Gemini	Air	Barren	4th
3 Sun.	Gemini	Air	Barren	4th
4 Mon.	Gemini	Air	Barren	4th
5 Tue. 3:07 am	Cancer	Water	Fruitful	4th
6 Wed.	Cancer	Water	Fruitful	New 8:02 am
7 Thu. 3:11 pm	Leo	Fire	Barren	1st
8 Fri.	Leo	Fire	Barren	1st
9 Sat.	Leo	Fire	Barren	1st
10 Sun. 3:57 am	Virgo	Earth	Barren	1st
11 Mon.	Virgo	Earth	Barren	1st
12 Tue. 4:09 pm	Libra	Air	Semi-fruitful	1st
13 Wed.	Libra	Air	Semi-fruitful	1st
14 Thu.	Libra	Air	Semi-fruitful	2nd 11:20 am
15 Fri. 1:51 am	Scorpio	Water	Fruitful	2nd
16 Sat.	Scorpio	Water	Fruitful	2nd
17 Sun. 7:35 am	Sagittarius	Fire	Barren	2nd
18 Mon.	Sagittarius	Fire	Barren	2nd
19 Tue. 9:26 am	Capricorn	Earth	Semi-fruitful	2nd
20 Wed.	Capricorn	Earth	Semi-fruitful	2nd
21 Thu. 8:55 am	Aquarius	Air	Barren	Full 7:00 am
22 Fri.	Aquarius	Air	Barren	3rd
23 Sat. 8:12 am	Pisces	Water	Fruitful	3rd
24 Sun.	Pisces	Water	Fruitful	3rd
25 Mon. 9:23 am	Aries	Fire	Barren	3rd
26 Tue.	Aries	Fire	Barren	3rd
27 Wed. 1:54 pm	Taurus	Earth	Semi-fruitful	4th 11:19 pm
28 Thu.	Taurus	Earth	Semi-fruitful	4th
29 Fri. 10:02 pm	Gemini	Air	Barren	4th
30 Sat.	Gemini	Air	Barren	4th
31 Sun.	Gemini	Air	Barren	4th

Lunar Aspectarian Favorable and Unfavorable Days

	Sun	Mercury	Venus	Mars	Jupiter	Saturn	Uranus	Neptune	Pluto	Aries	Taurus	Gemini	Cancer	Leo	Virgo	Libra	Scorpio	Sagittarius	Capricorn	Aquarius	Pisces
1	X						X	Q			F		f	u	f		U		f	u	f
2						X					F		f	u	f		U		f	u	f
3		X	X	X	T			Q		f		F		f	u	f		U		f	u
4								T	O	f		F		f	u	f		U		f	u
5					Q	T				f		F		f	u	f		U		f	u
6	C			Q						u	f		F		f	u	f		U		f
7							C			u	f		F		f	u	f		U		f
8		C	C		X					f	u	f		F		f	u	f		U	
9				T				O	T	f	u	f		F		f	u	f		U	
10										f	u	f		F		f	u	f		U	
11	X						O				f	u	f		F		f	u	f		U
12						X			Q		f	u	f		F		f	u	f		U
13				C						U		f	u	f		F		f	u	f	
14	Q	X	X	O				T	X	U		f	u	f		F		f	u	f	
15					Q	T				U		f	u	f		F		f	u	f	
16	T	Q	Q					Q			U		f	u	f		F		f	u	f
17						T					U		f	u	f		F		f	u	f
18		T		T	X		Q	X	C	f		U		f	u	f		F		f	u
19			T							f		U		f	u	f		F		f	u
20				Q		X				u	f		U		f	u	f		F		f
21	O			Q		O				u	f		U		f	u	f		F		f
22		O			T			C	X	f	u	f		U		f	u	f		F	
23			O	X						f	u	f		U		f	u	f		F	
24								Q			f	u	f		U		f	u	f		F
25	T					T					f	u	f		U		f	u	f		F
26		T			O			X	T	F		f	u	f		U		f	u	f	
27	Q			C	Q					F		f	u	f		U		f	u	f	
28		Q	T					X	Q		F		f	u	f		U		f	u	f
29											F		f	u	f		U		f	u	f
30	X		Q		T	X		Q		f		F		f	u	f		U		f	u
31		X						T	O	f		F		f	u	f		U		f	u

August Moon Table

Date	Sign	Element	Nature	Phase
1 Mon. 8:52 am	Cancer	Water	Fruitful	4th
2 Tue.	Cancer	Water	Fruitful	4th
3 Wed. 9:10 pm	Leo	Fire	Barren	4th
4 Thu.	Leo	Fire	Barren	New 11:05 pm
5 Fri.	Leo	Fire	Barren	1st
6 Sat. 9:54 am	Virgo	Earth	Barren	1st
7 Sun.	Virgo	Earth	Barren	1st
8 Mon. 10:08 pm	Libra	Air	Semi-fruitful	1st
9 Tue.	Libra	Air	Semi-fruitful	1st
10 Wed.	Libra	Air	Semi-fruitful	1st
11 Thu. 8:35 am	Scorpio	Water	Fruitful	1st
12 Fri.	Scorpio	Water	Fruitful	2nd 10:38 pm
13 Sat. 3:47 pm	Sagittarius	Fire	Barren	2nd
14 Sun.	Sagittarius	Fire	Barren	2nd
15 Mon. 7:13 pm	Capricorn	Earth	Semi-fruitful	2nd
16 Tue.	Capricorn	Earth	Semi-fruitful	2nd
17 Wed. 7:39 pm	Aquarius	Air	Barren	2nd
18 Thu.	Aquarius	Air	Barren	2nd
19 Fri. 6:52 pm	Pisces	Water	Fruitful	Full 1:53 pm
20 Sat.	Pisces	Water	Fruitful	3rd
21 Sun. 7:01 pm	Aries	Fire	Barren	3rd
22 Mon.	Aries	Fire	Barren	3rd
23 Tue. 9:58 pm	Taurus	Earth	Semi-fruitful	3rd
24 Wed.	Taurus	Earth	Semi-fruitful	3rd
25 Thu.	Taurus	Earth	Semi-fruitful	3rd
26 Fri. 4:43 am	Gemini	Air	Barren	4th 11:18 am
27 Sat.	Gemini	Air	Barren	4th
28 Sun. 2:57 pm	Cancer	Water	Fruitful	4th
29 Mon.	Cancer	Water	Fruitful	4th
30 Tue.	Cancer	Water	Fruitful	4th
31 Wed. 3:14 am	Leo	Fire	Barren	4th

Lunar Aspectarian   Favorable and Unfavorable Days

	Sun	Mercury	Venus	Mars	Jupiter	Saturn	Uranus	Neptune	Pluto	Aries	Taurus	Gemini	Cancer	Leo	Virgo	Libra	Scorpio	Sagittarius	Capricorn	Aquarius	Pisces
1				X						f		F		f	u	f			U		f	u
2			X		Q		T			u	f		F		f	u	f			U		f
3										u	f		F		f	u	f			U		f
4	C			Q		C				f	u	f		F		f	u	f		U	
5		C			X			0	T	f	u	f		F		f	u	f		U	
6			T							f	u	f		F		f	u	f		U	
7								0			f	u	f		F		f	u	f		U
8			C						Q	f	u	f			F		f	u	f		U
9		X				X				U		f	u	f		F		f	u	f	
10	X				C			T	X	U		f	u	f		F		f	u	f	
11			0			Q				U		f	u	f		F		f	u	f	
12	Q	Q						T	Q			U		f	u	f		F		f	u	f
13			X			T						U		f	u	f		F		f	u	f
14		T			X			Q	X	f			U	f	u	f		F	f	u	u
15	T		Q						C	f			U	f	u	f		F	f	u	u
16				T	Q	X				u	f		U	f	u	f			F		f
17			T							u	f		U	f	u	f			F		f
18		0		Q	T	0		C		f	u	f		U		f	u	f		F	
19	0								X	f	u	f		U		f	u	f		F	
20				X			C				f	u	f		U		f	u	f		F
21									Q		f	u	f		U		f	u	f		F
22		T	0		0	T		X		F		f	u	f		U		f	u	f	
23	T								T	F		f	u	f		U		f	u	f	
24		Q		C	Q	X					F		f	u	f		U		f	u	f
25						Q					F		f	u	f		U		f	u	f
26	Q				X	Q					F		f	u	f		U		f	u	f
27		X	T		T			T	0	f		F		f	u	f			U		f	u
28										f		F		f	u	f			U		f	u
29	X		Q	X			T			u	f		F		f	u	f			U		f
30				Q						u	f		F		f	u	f			U		f
31						C				u	f		F		f	u	f			U		f

September Moon Table

Date	Sign	Element	Nature	Phase
1 Thu.	Leo	Fire	Barren	4th
2 Fri. 3:56 pm	Virgo	Earth	Barren	4th
3 Sat.	Virgo	Earth	Barren	New 2:45 pm
4 Sun.	Virgo	Earth	Barren	1st
5 Mon. 3:52 am	Libra	Air	Semi-fruitful	1st
6 Tue.	Libra	Air	Semi-fruitful	1st
7 Wed. 2:10 pm	Scorpio	Water	Fruitful	1st
8 Thu.	Scorpio	Water	Fruitful	1st
9 Fri. 10:03 pm	Sagittarus	Fire	Barren	1st
10 Sat.	Sagittarus	Fire	Barren	1st
11 Sun.	Sagittarus	Fire	Barren	2nd 7:37 am
12 Mon. 2:56 am	Capricorn	Earth	Semi-fruitful	2nd
13 Tue.	Capricorn	Earth	Semi-fruitful	2nd
14 Wed. 5:02 am	Aquarius	Air	Barren	2nd
15 Thu.	Aquarius	Air	Barren	2nd
16 Fri. 5:24 am	Pisces	Water	Fruitful	2nd
17 Sat.	Pisces	Water	Fruitful	Full 10:01 pm
18 Sun. 5:43 am	Aries	Fire	Barren	3rd
19 Mon.	Aries	Fire	Barren	3rd
20 Tue. 7:47 am	Taurus	Earth	Semi-fruitful	3rd
21 Wed.	Taurus	Earth	Semi-fruitful	3rd
22 Thu. 1:07 pm	Gemini	Air	Barren	3rd
23 Fri.	Gemini	Air	Barren	3rd
24 Sat. 10:10 pm	Cancer	Water	Fruitful	3rd
25 Sun.	Cancer	Water	Fruitful	4th 2:41 am
26 Mon.	Cancer	Water	Fruitful	4th
27 Tue. 10:03 am	Leo	Fire	Barren	4th
28 Wed.	Leo	Fire	Barren	4th
29 Thu. 10:44 pm	Virgo	Earth	Barren	4th
30 Fri.	Virgo	Earth	Barren	4th

Lunar Aspectarian   Favorable and Unfavorable Days

	Sun	Mercury	Venus	Mars	Jupiter	Saturn	Uranus	Neptune	Pluto	Aries	Taurus	Gemini	Cancer	Leo	Virgo	Libra	Scorpio	Sagittarius	Capricorn	Aquarius	Pisces
1			X	Q	X			0	T	f	u	f		F		f	u	f		U	
2		C								f	u	f		F		f	u	f		U	
3	C						0				f	u	f		F		f	u	f		U
4				T					Q		f	u	f		F		f	u	f		U
5						X					f	u	f		F		f	u	f		U
6					C			T	X	U		f	u	f		F		f	u	f	
7			C							U		f	u	f		F		f	u	f	
8	X	X				Q	T	Q		U		f	u	f		F		f	u	f	
9			0							U		f	u	f		F		f	u	f	
10		Q					T	Q		f		U		f	u	f		F		f	u
11	Q				X			X	C	f		U		f	u	f		F		f	u
12			X				X			f		U		f	u	f		F		f	u
13	T	T			T	Q				u	f		U		f	u	f		F		f
14		Q			0					u	f		U		f	u	f		F		f
15			Q	T				C	X	f	u	f		U		f	u	f		F	
16			T				C			f	u	f		U		f	u	f		F	
17	0	0		X					Q		f	u	f		U		f	u	f		F
18						T					f	u	f		U		f	u	f		F
19					0			X	T	F		f	u	f		U		f	u	f	
20						Q	X			F		f	u	f		U		f	u	f	
21			0	C				Q			F		f	u	f		U		f	u	f
22	T	T									F		f	u	f		U		f	u	f
23						X	Q	T		f		F		f	u	f		U		f	u
24				T					0	f		F		f	u	f		U		f	u
25	Q	Q						T		u	f		F		f	u	f		U		f
26			T	X	Q					u	f		F		f	u	f		U		f
27	X									u	f		F		f	u	f		U		f
28		X				C		0		f	u	f		F		f	u	f		U	
29			Q	Q	X				T	f	u	f		F		f	u	f		U	
30							0			f	u	f		F		f	u	f		U

October Moon Table

Date	Sign	Element	Nature	Phase
1 Sat.	Virgo	Earth	Barren	4th
2 Sun. 10:24 am	Libra	Air	Semi-fruitful	4th
3 Mon.	Libra	Air	Semi-fruitful	New 6:28 am
4 Tue. 8:03 pm	Scorpio	Water	Fruitful	1st
5 Wed.	Scorpio	Water	Fruitful	1st
6 Thu.	Scorpio	Water	Fruitful	1st
7 Fri. 3:28 am	Sagittarius	Fire	Barren	1st
8 Sat.	Sagittarius	Fire	Barren	1st
9 Sun. 8:43 am	Capricorn	Earth	Semi-fruitful	1st
10 Mon.	Capricorn	Earth	Semi-fruitful	2nd 3:01 pm
11 Tue. 12:05 pm	Aquarius	Air	Barren	2nd
12 Wed.	Aquarius	Air	Barren	2nd
13 Thu. 2:05 pm	Pisces	Water	Fruitful	2nd
14 Fri.	Pisces	Water	Fruitful	2nd
15 Sat. 3:39 pm	Aries	Fire	Barren	2nd
16 Sun.	Aries	Fire	Barren	2nd
17 Mon. 6:04 pm	Taurus	Earth	Semi-fruitful	Full 8:14 am
18 Tue.	Taurus	Earth	Semi-fruitful	3rd
19 Wed. 10:44 pm	Gemini	Air	Barren	3rd
20 Thu.	Gemini	Air	Barren	3rd
21 Fri.	Gemini	Air	Barren	3rd
22 Sat. 6:41 am	Cancer	Water	Fruitful	3rd
23 Sun.	Cancer	Water	Fruitful	3rd
24 Mon. 5:48 pm	Leo	Fire	Barren	4th 9:17 pm
25 Tue.	Leo	Fire	Barren	4th
26 Wed.	Leo	Fire	Barren	4th
27 Thu. 6:28 am	Virgo	Earth	Barren	4th
28 Fri.	Virgo	Earth	Barren	4th
29 Sat. 6:15 pm	Libra	Air	Semi-fruitful	4th
30 Sun.	Libra	Air	Semi-fruitful	4th
31 Mon.	Libra	Air	Semi-fruitful	4th

	Sun	Mercury	Venus	Mars	Jupiter	Saturn	Uranus	Neptune	Pluto	Aries	Taurus	Gemini	Cancer	Leo	Virgo	Libra	Scorpio	Sagittarius	Capricorn	Aquarius	Pisces
1			X	T					Q		f	u	f		F		f	u	f		U
2											f	u	f		F		f	u	f		U
3	C					X		T		U		f	u	f		F		f	u	f	
4		C			C				X	U		f	u	f		F		f	u	f	
5						Q	T	Q		U		f	u	f		F		f	u	f	
6				0							U		f	u	f		F		f	u	f
7			C			T	Q				U		f	u	f		F		f	u	f
8	X							X	C	f		U		f	u	f		F		f	u
9		X			X		X			f		U		f	u	f		F		f	u
10	Q			T						u	f		U		f	u	f		F		f
11		Q	X	Q						u	f		U		f	u	f		F		f
12	T				0			C		f	u	f		U		f	u	f		F	
13				Q	T				X	f	u	f		U		f	u	f		F	
14		T	Q				C				f	u	f		U		f	u	f		F
15				X					Q		f	u	f		U		f	u	f		F
16			T		T			X		F		f	u	f		U		f	u	f	
17	0				0			T		F		f	u	f		U		f	u	f	
18		0				Q	X	Q			F		f	u	f		U		f	u	f
19			C								F		f	u	f		U		f	u	f
20						X	Q			f		F		f	u	f		U		f	u
21			0					T	0	f		F		f	u	f		U		f	u
22	T				T		T			f		F		f	u	f		U		f	u
23				X						u	f		F		f	u	f		U		f
24	Q	T			Q					u	f		F		f	u	f		U		f
25						C	0			f	u	f		F		f	u	f		U	
26		Q	T	Q					T	f	u	f		F		f	u	f		U	
27	X			X			0			f	u	f		F		f	u	f		U	
28				T							f	u	f		F		f	u	f		U
29		X	Q						Q		f	u	f		F		f	u	f		U
30						X		T		U		f	u	f		F		f	u	f	
31			X						X	U		f	u	f		F		f	u	f	

November Moon Table

Date	Sign	Element	Nature	Phase
1 Tue. 2:29 am	Scorpio	Water	Fruitful	New 8:25 pm
2 Wed.	Scorpio	Water	Fruitful	1st
3 Thu. 8:55 am	Sagittarius	Fire	Barren	1st
4 Fri.	Sagittarius	Fire	Barren	1st
5 Sat. 1:17 pm	Capricorn	Earth	Semi-fruitful	1st
6 Sun.	Capricorn	Earth	Semi-fruitful	1st
7 Mon. 4:31 pm	Aquarius	Air	Barren	1st
8 Tue.	Aquarius	Air	Barren	2nd 8:57 pm
9 Wed. 7:22 pm	Pisces	Water	Fruitful	2nd
10 Thu.	Pisces	Water	Fruitful	2nd
11 Fri. 10:22 pm	Aries	Fire	Barren	2nd
12 Sat.	Aries	Fire	Barren	2nd
13 Sun.	Aries	Fire	Barren	2nd
14 Mon. 2:02 am	Taurus	Earth	Semi-fruitful	2nd
15 Tue.	Taurus	Earth	Semi-fruitful	Full 7:58 pm
16 Wed. 7:10 am	Gemini	Air	Barren	3rd
17 Thu.	Gemini	Air	Barren	3rd
18 Fri. 2:42 pm	Cancer	Water	Fruitful	3rd
19 Sat.	Cancer	Water	Fruitful	3rd
20 Sun.	Cancer	Water	Fruitful	3rd
21 Mon. 1:10 am	Leo	Fire	Barren	3rd
22 Tue.	Leo	Fire	Barren	3rd
23 Wed. 1:41 pm	Virgo	Earth	Barren	4th 5:11 pm
24 Thu.	Virgo	Earth	Barren	4th
25 Fri.	Virgo	Earth	Barren	4th
26 Sat. 1:58 am	Libra	Air	Semi-fruitful	4th
27 Sun.	Libra	Air	Semi-fruitful	4th
28 Mon. 11:33 am	Scorpio	Water	Fruitful	4th
29 Tue.	Scorpio	Water	Fruitful	4th
30 Wed. 5:32 pm	Sagittarius	Fire	Barren	4th

Lunar Aspectarian   Favorable and Unfavorable Days

	Sun	Mercury	Venus	Mars	Jupiter	Saturn	Uranus	Neptune	Pluto	Aries	Taurus	Gemini	Cancer	Leo	Virgo	Libra	Scorpio	Sagittarius	Capricorn	Aquarius	Pisces
1	C				C	Q	T			U		f	u	f		F		f	u	f	
2				O				Q		U		f	u	f		F		f	u	f	
3		C					Q			U		f	u	f		F		f	u	f	
4						T		X		f		U		f	u	f		F		f	u
5			C		X				C	f		U		f	u	f		F		f	u
6	X			T			X			u	f		U		f	u	f		F		f
7						Q				u	f		U		f	u	f		F		f
8	Q	X		Q		O			C	f	u	f		U		f	u	f		F	
9									X	f	u	f		U		f	u	f		F	
10		Q	X	X	T		C				f	u	f		U		f	u	f		F
11	T								Q		f	u	f		U		f	u	f		F
12		T	Q			T		X		F		f	u	f		U		f	u	f	
13									T	F		f	u	f		U		f	u	f	
14			T	C	O	Q	X			F		f	u	f		U		f	u	f	
15	O							Q		F		f	u	f		U		f	u	f	
16								Q		F		f	u	f		U		f	u	f	
17		O				X	T			f		F		f	u	f		U		f	u
18									O	f		F		f	u	f		U		f	u
19			O	X	T	T				u	f		F		f	u	f		U		f
20	T									u	f		F		f	u	f		U		f
21		T		Q	Q	C				u	f		F		f	u	f		U		f
22								O		f	u	f		F		f	u	f		U	
23	Q	Q							T	f	u	f		F		f	u	f		U	
24				T	X	O				f	u	f		F		f	u	f		U	
25			T						Q	f	u	f		F		f	u	f		U	
26	X	X								f	u	f		F		f	u	f		U	
27			Q			X		T	X	U		f	u	f		F		f	u	f	
28										U		f	u	f		F		f	u	f	
29				O	C	Q	T	Q		U		f	u	f		F		f	u	f	
30		C	X							U		f	u	f		F		f	u	f	

December Moon Table

Date	Sign	Element	Nature	Phase
1 Thu.	Sagittarius	Fire	Barren	New 10:01 am
2 Fri. 8:42 pm	Capricorn	Earth	Semi-fruitful	1st
3 Sat.	Capricorn	Earth	Semi-fruitful	1st
4 Sun. 10:36 pm	Aquarius	Air	Barren	1st
5 Mon.	Aquarius	Air	Barren	1st
6 Tue.	Aquarius	Air	Barren	1st
7 Wed. 12:44 am	Pisces	Water	Fruitful	1st
8 Thu.	Pisces	Water	Fruitful	2nd 4:36 am
9 Fri. 4:02 am	Aries	Fire	Barren	2nd
10 Sat.	Aries	Fire	Barren	2nd
11 Sun. 8:46 am	Taurus	Earth	Semi-fruitful	2nd
12 Mon.	Taurus	Earth	Semi-fruitful	2nd
13 Tue. 2:59 pm	Gemini	Air	Barren	2nd
14 Wed.	Gemini	Air	Barren	2nd
15 Thu. 11:01 pm	Cancer	Water	Fruitful	Full 11:16 am
16 Fri.	Cancer	Water	Fruitful	3rd
17 Sat.	Cancer	Water	Fruitful	3rd
18 Sun. 9:18 am	Leo	Fire	Barren	3rd
19 Mon.	Leo	Fire	Barren	3rd
20 Tue. 9:39 pm	Virgo	Earth	Barren	3rd
21 Wed.	Virgo	Earth	Barren	3rd
22 Thu.	Virgo	Earth	Barren	3rd
23 Fri.10:26 am	Libra	Air	Semi-fruitful	4th 2:36 pm
24 Sat.	Libra	Air	Semi-fruitful	4th
25 Sun. 9:04 pm	Scorpio	Water	Fruitful	4th
26 Mon.	Scorpio	Water	Fruitful	4th
27 Tue.	Scorpio	Water	Fruitful	4th
28 Wed. 3:43 am	Sagittarius	Fire	Barren	4th
29 Thu.	Sagittarius	Fire	Barren	4th
30 Fri. 6:35 am	Capricorn	Earth	Semi-fruitful	New 10:12 pm
31 Sat.	Capricorn	Earth	Semi-fruitful	1st

	Sun	Mercury	Venus	Mars	Jupiter	Saturn	Uranus	Neptune	Pluto	Aries	Taurus	Gemini	Cancer	Leo	Virgo	Libra	Scorpio	Sagittarius	Capricorn	Aquarius	Pisces
1	C					T	Q	X		f		U		f	u	f		F		f	u
2									C	f		U		f	u	f		F		f	u
3				T	X		X			u	f		U	f	u	f			F		f
4		X	C							u	f		U	f	u	f			F		f
5	X				Q	Q	0			f	u	f		U	f	u	f			F	
6		Q						C	X	f	u	f		U	f	u	f			F	
7				X	T			C		f	u	f		U	f	u	f			F	
8	Q	T	X						Q		f	u	f		U	f	u	f			F
9						T					f	u	f		U	f	u	f			F
10	T							X	T	F		f	u	f		U		f	u	f	
11			Q	C			X			F		f	u	f		U		f	u	f	
12				0	Q		Q				F		f	u	f		U		f	u	f
13		0	T								F		f	u	f		U		f	u	f
14						X	Q	T		f		F		f	u	f		U		f	u
15	0								0	f		F		f	u	f		U		f	u
16			X		T		T			u	f		F	f	u	f			U		f
17										u	f		F	f	u	f			U		f
18			0							u	f		F	f	u	f			U		f
19		T			Q	Q	C	0		f	u	f		F	f	u	f			U	
20	T								T	f	u	f		F	f	u	f			U	
21		Q		T	X		0				f	u	f		F	f	u	f			U
22								Q			f	u	f		F	f	u	f			U
23	Q		T								f	u	f		F	f	u	f			U
24		X				X		T		U		f	u	f		F		f	u	f	
25			Q						X	U		f	u	f		F		f	u	f	
26	X			0	C	Q	T				U		f	u	f		F		f	u	f
27						Q					U		f	u	f		F		f	u	f
28			X		T	Q					U		f	u	f		F		f	u	f
29		C					X		C	f		U		f	u	f		F		f	u
30	C						X			f		U		f	u	f		F		f	u
31				T	X					u	f		U	f	u	f			F		f

Time Zone Map

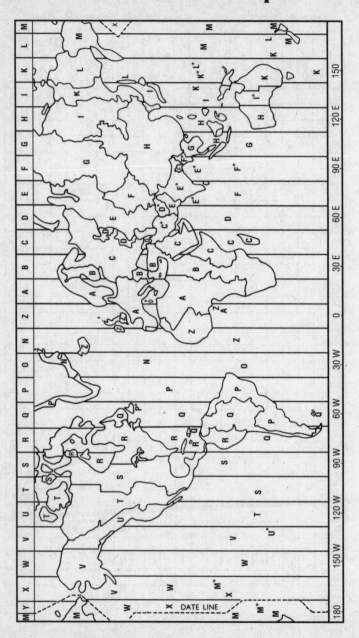

Time Zone Conversions

World Time Zones Compared to Eastern Time

(R)	EST—Used	(C*)	Add 8½ hours
(S)	CST—Subtract 1 hour	(D)	Add 9 hours
(T)	MST—Subtract 2 hours	(D*)	Add 9½ hours
(U)	PST—Subtract 3 hours	(E)	Add 10 hours
(V)	Subtract 4 hours	(E*)	Add 10½ hours
(V*)	Subtract 4½ hours	(F)	Add 11 hours
(W)	Subtract 5 hours	(F*)	Add 11½ hours
(X)	Subtract 6 hours	(G)	Add 12 hours
(Y)	Subtract 7 hours	(H)	Add 13 hours
(Q)	Add 1 hour	(I)	Add 14 hours
(P)	Add 2 hours	(I*)	Add 14½ hours
(P*)	Add 2½ hours	(K)	Add 15 hours
(O)	Add 3 hours	(K*)	Add 15½ hours
(N)	Add 4 hours	(L)	Add 16 hours
(Z)	Add 5 hours	(L*)	Add 16½ hours
(A)	Add 6 hours	(M)	Add 17 hours
(B)	Add 7 hours	(M*)	Add 17½ hours
(C)	Add 8 hours		

Important!

All times given in the *Moon Sign Book* are set in Eastern Time. The conversions shown here are for standard times only. Use the time zone conversions chart and table to calculate the difference in your time zone. You must make the adjustment for your time zone and adjust for Daylight Saving Time where applicable.

Moon Void-of-Course

by Kim Rogers-Gallagher

The Moon circles the Earth in about twenty-eight days, moving through each sign in two and a half days (or so). As she passes through the thirty degrees of each sign, she "visits" with the planets in numerical order, forming aspects with them. Because she moves one degree in just two to two-and-a-half hours, her influence on each planet lasts only a few hours. She eventually reaches the planet that's in the highest degree of any sign, and forms what will be her final aspect before leaving the sign. From this point until she enters the next sign, she is referred to as void-of-course.

Think of it this way: The Moon is the emotional "tone" of the day, carrying feelings with her particular to the sign she's "wearing" at the moment. After she has contacted each of the planets, she symbolically "rests" before changing her costume, so her instinct is temporarily on hold. It's during this time that many people feel "fuzzy" or "vague." Plans or decisions made now often do not pan out. Without the instinctual "knowing" the Moon provides as she touches each planet, we tend to be unrealistic or exercise poor judgment. The traditional definition of the void Moon is that "nothing will come of this." Actions initiated under a void Moon are often wasted, irrelevant, or incorrect—usually because information is hidden, missing, or has been overlooked.

Although it's not a good time to initiate plans, routine tasks seem to go along just fine. This period is ideal for reflection. On the lighter side, remember there are good uses for the void Moon. It is the period when the universe seems to be most open to loopholes. It's a great time to make plans you don't want to fulfill or schedule things you don't want to do. See the table on pages 101–06 for a schedule of the 2005 Moon void-of-course times.

Moon Void-of-Course Tables

Last Aspect   **Moon enters New Sign**

		January		
2	1:23 am	2	Libra	11:19 am
4	9:20 am	4	Scorpio	7:00 pm
6	1:29 pm	6	Sagittarius	10:44 pm
8	10:02 pm	8	Capricorn	11:11 pm
10	12:58 pm	10	Aquarius	10:07 pm
12	10:44 am	12	Pisces	9:50 pm
14	3:22 pm	15	Aries	12:27 am
17	1:57 am	17	Taurus	7:06 am
19	5:19 pm	19	Gemini	5:24 pm
21	4:26 pm	22	Cancer	5:42 am
24	4:17 am	24	Leo	6:21 pm
26	5:39 pm	27	Virgo	6:24 am
29	4:07 pm	29	Libra	5:13 pm
31	10:21 pm	2/1	Scorpio	1:51 am
		February		
2	5:56 pm	3	Sagittarius	7:21 am
5	8:07 am	5	Capricorn	9:32 am
6	8:47 pm	7	Aquarius	9:26 am
8	11:19 pm	9	Pisces	8:59 am
11	12:14 am	11	Aries	10:21 am
13	5:53 am	13	Taurus	3:18 pm
15	10:07 pm	16	Gemini	12:18 am
18	12:23 am	18	Cancer	12:13 pm
20	7:06 am	21	Leo	12:54 am
23	4:47 am	23	Virgo	12:44 pm
25	12:00 pm	25	Libra	10:59 pm
27	8:49 pm	28	Scorpio	7:21 am
		March		
2	5:25 am	2	Sagittarius	1:29 pm
4	4:45 pm	4	Capricorn	5:12 pm

Last Aspect   Moon enters New Sign

6	3:28 am	6	Aquarius	6:49 pm
8	10:28 am	8	Pisces	7:32 pm
10	11:44 am	10	Aries	9:03 pm
12	3:13 pm	13	Taurus	1:05 am
15	1:10 am	15	Gemini	8:44 am
17	2:19 pm	17	Cancer	7:44 pm
20	7:59 am	20	Leo	8:17 am
22	9:20 am	22	Virgo	8:10 pm
24	7:36 pm	25	Libra	6:00 am
27	3:30 am	27	Scorpio	1:29 pm
29	2:06 am	29	Sagittarius	6:56 pm
31	1:24 pm	31	Capricorn	10:48 pm
		April		
2	9:34 am	3	Aquarius	1:31 am
4	7:32 pm	5	Pisces	4:45 am
6	10:03 pm	7	Aries	7:28 am
9	2:00 am	9	Taurus	11:50 am
11	1:37 am	11	Gemini	6:55 pm
14	1:01 am	14	Cancer	5:03 am
16	10:37 am	16	Leo	5:17 pm
19	4:13 am	19	Virgo	5:27 am
21	4:45 am	21	Libra	3:27 pm
23	12:46 pm	23	Scorpio	10:25 pm
25	8:24 pm	26	Sagittarius	2:46 am
28	2:02 am	28	Capricorn	5:33 am
29	6:00 pm	30	Aquarius	7:54 am
		May		
2	12:47 am	2	Pisces	10:43 am
4	4:22 am	4	Aries	2:36 pm
6	9:22 am	6	Taurus	8:01 pm
9	1:15 am	9	Gemini	3:29 am

Last Aspect   Moon enters New Sign

11	10:58 am	11	Cancer	1:20 pm
13	11:04 am	14	Leo	1:17 am
16	4:57 am	16	Virgo	1:46 pm
18	9:00 pm	19	Libra	12:30 am
20	8:40 pm	21	Scorpio	7:49 am
23	12:54 am	23	Sagittarius	11:38 am
25	2:52 am	25	Capricorn	1:11 pm
27	11:22 am	27	Aquarius	2:10 pm
29	5:19 am	29	Pisces	4:09 pm
31	1:53 pm	31	Aries	8:07 pm
		June		
3	1:24 am	3	Taurus	2:20 am
5	1:25 am	5	Gemini	10:36 am
7	2:50 pm	7	Cancer	8:46 pm
10	6:18 am	10	Leo	8:39 am
12	7:40 am	12	Virgo	9:22 pm
15	1:24 am	15	Libra	8:59 am
17	11:02 am	17	Scorpio	5:23 pm
19	4:06 pm	19	Sagittarius	9:45 pm
21	11:34 am	21	Capricorn	10:52 pm
23	6:04 pm	23	Aquarius	10:36 pm
25	11:23 am	25	Pisces	11:03 pm
28	1:51 am	28	Aries	1:51 am
30	3:57 am	30	Taurus	7:45 am
		July		
2	1:02 pm	2	Gemini	4:26 pm
4	12:36 pm	5	Cancer	3:07 am
7	12:54 pm	7	Leo	3:11 pm
9	12:49 pm	10	Virgo	3:57 am
12	3:12 pm	12	Libra	4:09 pm
15	1:32 am	15	Scorpio	1:51 am
16	10:15 pm	17	Sagittarius	7:35 am

Last Aspect   Moon enters New Sign

19	2:03 am	19	Capricorn	9:26 am
21	7:00 am	21	Aquarius	8:55 am
23	3:33 am	23	Pisces	8:12 am
24	8:19 pm	25	Aries	9:23 am
27	1:23 pm	27	Taurus	1:54 pm
29	12:59 am	29	Gemini	10:02 pm
31	5:10 pm	8/1	Cancer	8:52 am
		August		
2	11:59 am	3	Leo	9:10 pm
5	5:45 pm	6	Virgo	9:54 am
8	6:10 am	8	Libra	10:08 pm
10	5:10 pm	11	Scorpio	8:35 am
13	8:06 am	13	Sagittarius	3:47 pm
15	4:43 pm	15	Capricorn	7:13 pm
16	9:02 pm	17	Aquarius	7:39 pm
19	1:53 pm	19	Pisces	6:52 pm
21	5:45 am	21	Aries	7:01 pm
23	7:46 am	23	Taurus	9:58 pm
25	2:14 am	26	Gemini	4:43 am
27	10:49 pm	28	Cancer	2:57 pm
30	3:22 am	31	Leo	3:14 am
		September		
2	7:44 am	2	Virgo	3:56 pm
4	11:40 am	5	Libra	3:52 am
7	4:33 am	7	Scorpio	2:10 pm
9	3:31 am	9	Sagittarius	10:03 pm
11	12:52 pm	12	Capricorn	2:56 pm
13	2:22 pm	14	Aquarius	5:02 am
15	4:23 pm	16	Pisces	5:24 am
17	10:01 pm	18	Aries	5:43 am
19	6:36 pm	20	Taurus	7:47 am

Last Aspect   Moon enters New Sign

22	12:41 pm	22	Gemini	1:07 pm
24	8:57 am	24	Cancer	10:10 pm
26	9:24 pm	27	Leo	10:03 am
29	11:12 am	29	Virgo	10:44 pm
		October		
1	9:22 pm	2	Libra	10:24 am
4	11:15 am	4	Scorpio	8:03 pm
7	1:51 am	7	Sagittarius	3:28 am
9	2:20 am	9	Capricorn	8:43 am
11	6:42 am	11	Aquarius	12:05 pm
13	9:34 am	13	Pisces	2:05 pm
15	2:55 am	15	Aries	3:39 pm
17	2:58 pm	17	Taurus	6:04 pm
19	6:50 am	19	Gemini	10:44 pm
22	5:07 am	22	Cancer	6:41 am
24	5:16 pm	24	Leo	5:48 pm
26	10:23 pm	27	Virgo	6:28 am
29	5:06 pm	29	Libra	6:15 pm
31	6:17 pm	11/1	Scorpio	2:29 am
		November		
2	9:05 am	3	Sagittarius	8:55 am
5	12:58 am	5	Capricorn	1:17 pm
6	3:18 pm	7	Aquarius	4:31 pm
9	7:31 am	9	Pisces	7:22 pm
11	10:33 am	11	Aries	10:22 pm
13	2:07 pm	14	Taurus	2:02 am
15	7:58 pm	16	Gemini	7:10 am
18	2:02 am	18	Cancer	2:42 pm
20	11:03 pm	21	Leo	1:10 am
23	12:25 am	23	Virgo	1:41 pm
25	1:10 pm	26	Libra	1:58 am

Last Aspect   Moon enters New Sign

27	11:38 pm	28	Scorpio	11:33 am
30	10:16 am	30	Sagittarius	5:32 pm
		December		
2	10:17 am	2	Capricorn	8:42 pm
4	1:56 pm	4	Aquarius	10:36 pm
6	4:58 pm	7	Pisces	12:44 am
8	11:16 pm	9	Aries	4:02 am
11	5:50 am	11	Taurus	8:46 am
13	1:46 pm	13	Gemini	2:59 pm
15	12:11 pm	15	Cancer	11:01 pm
16	7:33 pm	18	Leo	9:18 am
20	8:09 pm	20	Virgo	9:39 pm
22	11:30 pm	23	Libra	10:26 am
25	10:53 am	25	Scorpio	9:04 pm
27	2:26 am	28	Sagittarius	3:43 am
29	10:01 pm	30	Capricorn	6:35 am
31	4:09 am	1/1	Aquarius	7:14 am

Eclipse Dates in 2005

Dates are given in parentheses for eclipses that fall across two days due to time zone differences. Times are in Eastern Time and are rounded off to the nearest minute. The exact time of an eclipse generally differs from the exact time of a New or Full Moon. For solar eclipses, "greatest eclipse" represents the time (converted from Local Mean Time) of the Moon's maximum obscuration of the Sun as viewed from the Earth. For lunar eclipses, "middle of eclipse" represents the time at which the Moon rests at the centermost point of its journey through the shadow cast by the Earth passing between it and the Sun. Data is from *Astronomical Phenomena for the Year 2005*, prepared by the United States Naval Observatory and Her Majesty's Nautical Almanac Office (United Kingdom).

April 8

Total solar eclipse at 4:37 pm EDT: 19° ♈ 6'

Eclipse begins	1:51 pm	171° E	41° S
Greatest eclipse	4:16 pm	123° E	16° S
Eclipse ends	7:20 pm	78° E	15° N

April 24

Penumbral lunar eclipse at 5:56 am EDT: 4° ♏ 20'

Eclipse enters penumbra	3:50 am	119° E	13° S
Middle of eclipse	5:55 am		
Eclipse leaves penumbra	8:00 am	180° E	14° S

October 3

Annular solar eclipse at 6:33 am EDT: 10° ♎ 19'

Eclipse begins	3:36 am	23° E	41° N
Greatest eclipse	6:11 am	25° W	18° N
Eclipse ends	9:28 am	67° W	17° S

October 17

Partial lunar eclipse at 8:04 am EDT: 24° ♈ 13'

Eclipse enters penumbra	5:51 am	178° E	10° N
Middle of eclipse	8:04 am		
Eclipse leaves penumbra	10:15 am	168° W	10° N

Retrograde Periods

Eastern Time (ET) in regular type, **Pacific Time (PT)** in bold type

Planet	Begin	ET	PT	End	ET	PT
Saturn	11/07/04		**10:54 pm**	03/21/05	9:54 pm	**6:54 pm**
	11/08/04	1:54 am				
Jupiter	02/01/05	9:26 pm	**6:26 pm**	06/05/05	3:20 am	**12:20 am**
Mercury	03/19/05	7:13 pm	**4:13 pm**	04/12/05	3:45 am	**12:35 am**
Pluto	03/26/05	9:29 pm	**6:29 pm**	09/02/05	6:52 am	**3:52 am**
Chiron	05/08/05	9:47 pm	**6:47 pm**	10/04/05		**10:32 pm**
				10/05/05	1:32 am	
Neptune	05/19/05	7:36 pm	**4:36 pm**	10/26/05	7:24 pm	**4:24 pm**
Uranus	06/14/05	6:38 pm	**3:38 pm**	11/15/05	7:07 pm	**4:07 pm**
Mercury	07/22/05	10:59 pm	**7:59 pm**	08/15/05	11:49 pm	**8:49 pm**
Mars	10/01/05	6:04 pm	**3:04 pm**	12/09/05	11:03 pm	**8:03 pm**
Mercury	11/13/05		**9:42 pm**	12/03/05	9:22 pm	**6:22 pm**
	11/14/05	12:42 am				
Saturn	11/22/05	4:01 am	**1:01 am**	04/05/06	8:54 am	**5:54 am**
Venus	12/24/05	4:36 am	**1:36 am**	02/03/06	4:18 am	**1:18 am**

	04 Dec	05 Jan	Feb	Mar	Apr	May	Jun	Jul	Aug	Sep	Oct	Nov	05 Dec	06 Jan
☿				▓	▓				▓			▓		
♀														▓
♂											▓	▓		
♃			▓	▓	▓	▓								
♄	▓	▓	▓	▓								▓	▓	▓
♅							▓	▓	▓	▓	▓			
♆						▓	▓	▓	▓	▓				
♇				▓	▓	▓	▓	▓	▓					
⚷						▓	▓	▓	▓	▓				

Find Your Moon Sign

Every year we give tables for the position of the Moon during that year, but it is more complicated to provide tables for the Moon's position in any given year because of its continuous movement. However, the problem was solved by Grant Lewi in *Astrology for the Millions*, which is available from Llewellyn Worldwide.

Grant Lewi's System

Step 1:
Find your birth year in the tables on pages 114–23.

Step 2:
Run down the left-hand column and see if your birth date is there. If your birth date is in the left-hand column, run over this line until you come to the column under your birth year. Here you will find a number. This is your base number. Write it down, and go directly to the direction under the heading "What to Do with Your Base Number" on page 112.

Step 3:
If your birth date is not in the left-hand column, get a pencil and paper. Your birth date falls between two numbers in the left-hand column. Look at the date closest after your birth date; run across this line to your birth year. Write down the number you find there, and label it "top number." Directly beneath it on your

piece of paper write the number printed just above it in the table. Label this "bottom number." Subtract the bottom number from the top number. If the top number is smaller, add 360 and subtract. The result is your difference.

Step 4:
Go back to the left-hand column and find the date before your birth date. Determine the number of days between this date and your birth date. Write this down and label it "intervening days."

Step 5:
Note which group your difference falls in.

Difference	Daily Motion
80–87	12 degrees
88–94	13 degrees
95–101	14 degrees
102–106	15 degrees

Note: If you were born in a leap year and use the difference between February 26 and March 5, then the daily motion is slightly different. If you fall into this category use the figures below.

Difference	Daily Motion
94–99	12 degrees
100–108	13 degrees
109–115	14 degrees
115–122	15 degrees

Step 6:
Write down the "daily motion" corresponding to your place in the proper table of difference above. Multiply daily motion by the number labeled "intervening days" (found at step 5).

Step 7:
Add the result of step 6 to your bottom number. This is your base number. If it is more than 360, subtract 360 from it and call the result your base number.

What to Do with Your Base Number

Locate your base number in the Table of Base Numbers. At the top of the column you will find the sign your Moon was in. In the far left-hand column you will find the degree the Moon occupied at 7:00 am of your birth date if you were born under Eastern Standard Time (EST). Refer to the Time Zone Conversions chart and table on page 99 to adjust information for your time zone.

If you don't know the hour of your birth, accept this as your Moon's sign and degree. If you do know the hour of your birth, get the exact degree as follows:

If you were born after 7:00 am EST, determine the number of hours after the time that you were born. Divide this by two, rounding up if necessary. Add this to your base number, and the result in the table will be the exact degree and sign of the Moon on the year, month, date, and hour of your birth.

If you were born before 7:00 am EST, determine the number of hours before the time that you were born. Divide this by two. Subtract this from your base number, and the result in the table will be the exact degree and sign of the Moon on the year, month, date, and hour of your birth.

Table of Base Numbers

	♈ (13)	♉ (14)	♊ (15)	♋ (16)	♌ (17)	♍ (18)	♎ (19)	♏ (20)	♐ (21)	♑ (22)	♒ (23)	♓ (24)
0°	0	30	60	90	120	150	180	210	240	270	300	330
1°	1	31	61	91	121	151	181	211	241	271	301	331
2°	2	32	62	92	122	152	182	212	242	272	302	332
3°	3	33	63	93	123	153	183	213	243	273	303	333
4°	4	34	64	94	124	154	184	214	244	274	304	334
5°	5	35	65	95	125	155	185	215	245	275	305	335
6°	6	36	66	96	126	156	186	216	246	276	306	336
7°	7	37	67	97	127	157	187	217	247	277	307	337
8°	8	38	68	98	128	158	188	218	248	278	308	338
9°	9	39	69	99	129	159	189	219	249	279	309	339
10°	10	40	70	100	130	160	190	220	250	280	310	340
11°	11	41	71	101	131	161	191	221	251	281	311	341
12°	12	42	72	102	132	162	192	222	252	282	312	342
13°	13	43	73	103	133	163	193	223	253	283	313	343
14°	14	44	74	104	134	164	194	224	254	284	314	344
15°	15	45	75	105	135	165	195	225	255	285	315	345
16°	16	46	76	106	136	166	196	226	256	286	316	346
17°	17	47	77	107	137	167	197	227	257	287	317	347
18°	18	48	78	108	138	168	198	228	258	288	318	248
19°	19	49	79	109	139	169	199	229	259	289	319	349
20°	20	50	80	110	140	170	200	230	260	290	320	350
21°	21	51	81	111	141	171	201	231	261	291	321	351
22°	22	52	82	112	142	172	202	232	262	292	322	352
23°	23	53	83	113	143	173	203	233	263	293	323	353
24°	24	54	84	114	144	174	204	234	264	294	324	354
25°	25	55	85	115	145	175	205	235	265	295	325	355
26°	26	56	86	116	146	176	206	236	266	296	326	356
27°	27	57	87	117	147	177	207	237	267	297	327	357
28°	28	58	88	118	148	178	208	238	268	298	328	358
29°	29	59	89	119	149	179	209	239	269	299	329	359

Month	Date	1911	1912	1913	1914	1915	1916	1917	1918	1919	1920
Jan.	1	289	57	211	337	100	228	23	147	270	39
Jan.	8	20	162	299	61	192	332	110	231	5	143
Jan.	15	122	251	23	158	293	61	193	329	103	231
Jan.	22	214	335	120	256	23	145	290	68	193	316
Jan.	29	298	66	221	345	108	237	32	155	278	49
Feb.	5	31	170	308	69	203	340	118	239	16	150
Feb.	12	130	260	32	167	302	70	203	338	113	239
Feb.	19	222	344	128	266	31	154	298	78	201	325
Feb.	26	306	75	231	353	116	248	41	164	286	60
Mar.	5	42	192	317	77	214	2	127	248	26	172
Mar.	12	140	280	41	176	311	89	212	346	123	259
Mar.	19	230	5	136	276	39	176	308	87	209	346
Mar.	26	314	100	239	2	124	273	49	173	294	85
Apr.	2	52	200	326	86	223	10	135	257	35	181
Apr.	9	150	288	51	184	321	97	222	355	133	267
Apr.	16	238	14	146	286	48	184	318	96	218	355
Apr.	23	322	111	247	11	132	284	57	181	303	96
Apr.	30	61	208	334	96	232	19	143	267	43	190
May	7	160	296	60	192	331	105	231	4	142	275
May	14	246	22	156	294	56	192	329	104	227	3
May	21	331	122	255	20	141	294	66	190	312	105
May	28	69	218	342	106	240	29	151	277	51	200
Jun.	4	170	304	69	202	341	114	240	14	151	284
Jun.	11	255	30	167	302	65	200	340	112	235	11
Jun.	18	340	132	264	28	151	304	74	198	322	114
Jun.	25	78	228	350	115	249	39	159	286	60	209
Jul.	2	179	312	78	212	349	122	248	25	159	293
Jul.	9	264	39	178	310	74	209	350	120	244	20
Jul.	16	349	141	273	36	161	312	84	206	332	123
Jul.	23	87	237	358	125	258	48	168	295	70	218
Jul.	30	187	321	86	223	357	131	256	36	167	302
Aug.	6	272	48	188	319	82	219	360	129	252	31
Aug.	13	359	150	282	44	171	320	93	214	342	131
Aug.	20	96	246	6	133	268	57	177	303	81	226
Aug.	27	195	330	94	234	5	140	265	46	175	310
Sep.	3	281	57	198	328	90	229	9	138	260	41
Sep.	10	9	158	292	52	180	329	102	222	351	140
Sep.	17	107	255	15	141	279	65	186	312	91	234
Sep.	24	203	339	103	244	13	149	274	56	184	319
Oct.	1	288	68	206	337	98	240	17	148	268	52
Oct.	8	18	167	301	61	189	338	111	231	360	150
Oct.	15	118	263	24	149	290	73	195	320	102	242
Oct.	22	212	347	113	254	22	157	284	65	193	326
Oct.	29	296	78	214	346	106	250	25	157	276	61
Nov.	5	26	177	309	70	197	348	119	240	7	161
Nov.	12	129	271	33	158	300	81	203	329	112	250
Nov.	19	221	355	123	262	31	164	295	73	202	334
Nov.	26	305	88	223	355	115	259	34	165	285	70
Dec.	3	34	187	317	79	205	359	127	249	16	171
Dec.	10	138	279	41	168	310	89	211	340	120	259
Dec.	17	230	3	134	270	40	172	305	81	211	343
Dec.	24	313	97	232	3	124	267	44	173	294	78
Dec.	31	42	198	325	87	214	9	135	257	25	181

Month	Date	1921	1922	1923	1924	1925	1926	1927	1928	1929	1930
Jan.	1	194	317	80	211	5	127	250	23	176	297
Jan.	8	280	41	177	313	90	211	349	123	260	22
Jan.	15	4	141	275	41	175	312	86	211	346	123
Jan.	22	101	239	3	127	272	51	172	297	83	222
Jan.	29	203	325	88	222	13	135	258	34	184	306
Feb.	5	289	49	188	321	99	220	359	131	269	31
Feb.	12	14	149	284	49	185	320	95	219	356	131
Feb.	19	110	249	11	135	281	60	181	305	93	230
Feb.	26	211	334	96	233	21	144	266	45	191	314
Mar.	5	297	58	197	343	107	230	8	153	276	41
Mar.	12	23	157	294	69	194	328	105	238	6	140
Mar.	19	119	258	19	157	292	68	190	327	104	238
Mar.	26	219	343	104	258	29	153	275	70	200	323
Apr.	2	305	68	205	352	115	240	16	163	284	51
Apr.	9	33	166	304	77	204	337	114	247	14	149
Apr.	16	130	266	28	164	303	76	198	335	115	246
Apr.	23	227	351	114	268	38	161	285	79	208	331
Apr.	30	313	78	214	1	123	250	25	172	292	61
May	7	42	176	313	85	212	348	123	256	23	160
May	14	141	274	37	173	314	84	207	344	125	254
May	21	236	359	123	277	47	169	295	88	217	339
May	28	321	88	222	11	131	259	34	181	301	70
Jun.	4	50	186	321	94	220	358	131	264	31	171
Jun.	11	152	282	45	182	324	93	215	354	135	263
Jun.	18	245	7	134	285	56	177	305	96	226	347
Jun.	25	330	97	232	20	139	268	44	190	310	78
Jul.	2	58	197	329	103	229	9	139	273	40	181
Jul.	9	162	291	54	192	333	101	223	4	144	272
Jul.	16	254	15	144	294	65	185	315	104	236	355
Jul.	23	338	106	242	28	148	276	54	198	319	87
Jul.	30	67	208	337	112	238	20	147	282	49	191
Aug.	6	171	300	62	202	341	110	231	15	152	281
Aug.	13	264	24	153	302	74	194	324	114	244	4
Aug.	20	347	114	253	36	157	285	65	206	328	95
Aug.	27	76	218	346	120	248	29	156	290	59	200
Sep.	3	179	309	70	213	350	119	239	25	161	290
Sep.	10	273	32	162	312	83	203	332	124	252	13
Sep.	17	356	122	264	44	166	293	75	214	337	105
Sep.	24	86	227	354	128	258	38	165	298	70	208
Oct.	1	187	318	78	223	358	128	248	35	169	298
Oct.	8	281	41	170	322	91	212	340	134	260	23
Oct.	15	5	132	274	52	175	303	85	222	345	115
Oct.	22	97	235	3	136	269	46	174	306	81	216
Oct.	29	196	327	87	232	7	137	257	44	179	307
Nov.	5	289	50	178	332	99	221	349	144	268	31
Nov.	12	13	142	283	61	183	313	93	231	353	126
Nov.	19	107	243	12	144	279	54	183	315	91	225
Nov.	26	206	335	96	241	17	145	266	52	189	314
Dec.	3	297	59	187	343	107	230	359	154	276	39
Dec.	10	21	152	291	70	191	324	101	240	1	137
Dec.	17	117	252	21	153	289	63	191	324	99	234
Dec.	24	216	343	105	249	28	152	275	60	199	322
Dec.	31	305	67	197	352	115	237	9	162	285	47

Month	Date	1931	1932	1933	1934	1935	1936	1937	1938	1939	1940
Jan.	1	60	196	346	107	231	8	156	277	41	181
Jan.	8	162	294	70	193	333	104	240	4	144	275
Jan.	15	257	20	158	294	68	190	329	104	239	360
Jan.	22	342	108	255	32	152	278	67	202	323	88
Jan.	29	68	207	353	116	239	19	163	286	49	191
Feb.	5	171	302	78	203	342	113	248	14	153	284
Feb.	12	267	28	168	302	78	198	339	113	248	8
Feb.	19	351	116	266	40	161	286	78	210	332	96
Feb.	26	77	217	1	124	248	29	171	294	59	200
Mar.	5	179	324	86	213	350	135	256	25	161	306
Mar.	12	276	48	176	311	86	218	347	123	256	29
Mar.	19	360	137	277	48	170	308	89	218	340	119
Mar.	26	86	241	10	132	258	52	180	302	69	223
Apr.	2	187	334	94	223	358	144	264	34	169	315
Apr.	9	285	57	185	321	95	227	355	133	264	38
Apr.	16	9	146	287	56	178	317	99	226	349	128
Apr.	23	96	250	18	140	268	61	189	310	80	231
Apr.	30	196	343	102	232	7	153	273	43	179	323
May	7	293	66	193	332	103	237	4	144	272	47
May	14	17	155	297	64	187	327	108	235	357	139
May	21	107	258	28	148	278	69	198	318	90	239
May	28	205	351	111	241	17	161	282	51	189	331
Jun.	4	301	75	201	343	111	245	13	154	280	55
Jun.	11	25	165	306	73	195	337	117	244	5	150
Jun.	18	117	267	37	157	288	78	207	327	99	248
Jun.	25	215	360	120	249	28	169	291	60	200	339
Jul.	2	309	84	211	353	119	254	23	164	289	64
Jul.	9	33	176	315	82	203	348	125	253	13	160
Jul.	16	126	276	46	165	297	87	216	336	108	258
Jul.	23	226	8	130	258	38	177	300	69	210	347
Jul.	30	317	92	221	2	128	262	33	173	298	72
Aug.	6	41	187	323	91	211	359	133	261	21	170
Aug.	13	135	285	54	175	305	97	224	346	116	268
Aug.	20	237	16	138	267	49	185	308	78	220	355
Aug.	27	326	100	232	10	136	270	44	181	307	80
Sep.	3	49	197	331	100	220	8	142	270	31	179
Sep.	10	143	295	62	184	314	107	232	355	125	278
Sep.	17	247	24	147	277	58	194	317	89	228	4
Sep.	24	335	108	243	18	145	278	55	189	316	88
Oct.	1	58	206	341	108	229	17	152	278	40	188
Oct.	8	151	306	70	193	322	117	240	4	134	288
Oct.	15	256	32	155	287	66	203	324	100	236	13
Oct.	22	344	116	253	27	154	287	64	198	324	98
Oct.	29	68	214	350	116	239	25	162	286	49	196
Nov.	5	161	316	78	201	332	126	248	12	145	297
Nov.	12	264	41	162	298	74	212	333	111	244	22
Nov.	19	353	125	262	36	162	296	73	207	332	108
Nov.	26	77	222	0	124	248	33	172	294	58	205
Dec.	3	171	325	87	209	343	135	257	19	156	305
Dec.	10	272	50	171	309	82	220	341	120	253	30
Dec.	17	1	135	271	45	170	306	81	217	340	118
Dec.	24	86	231	10	132	256	43	181	302	66	214
Dec.	31	182	333	95	217	354	142	265	27	167	313

Month	Date	1941	1942	1943	1944	1945	1946	1947	1948	1949	1950
Jan.	1	325	88	211	353	135	258	22	165	305	68
Jan.	8	50	176	315	85	219	348	126	256	29	160
Jan.	15	141	276	50	169	312	87	220	340	123	258
Jan.	22	239	12	133	258	52	182	303	69	224	352
Jan.	29	333	96	221	2	143	266	32	174	314	75
Feb.	5	57	186	323	95	227	358	134	265	37	170
Feb.	12	150	285	58	178	320	96	228	349	131	268
Feb.	19	250	20	142	267	62	190	312	78	234	359
Feb.	26	342	104	231	11	152	274	43	182	323	83
Mar.	5	65	196	331	116	236	8	142	286	46	179
Mar.	12	158	295	66	199	328	107	236	10	139	279
Mar.	19	261	28	150	290	72	198	320	102	243	8
Mar.	26	351	112	242	34	161	281	53	204	332	91
Apr.	2	74	205	340	125	244	16	152	294	55	187
Apr.	9	166	306	74	208	337	117	244	19	148	289
Apr.	16	270	36	158	300	81	206	328	112	252	17
Apr.	23	360	120	252	42	170	290	63	212	340	100
Apr.	30	83	214	350	133	254	25	162	302	64	195
May	7	174	316	82	217	346	127	252	27	158	299
May	14	279	45	166	311	90	215	336	123	260	26
May	21	9	128	261	50	179	299	72	221	349	110
May	28	92	222	1	141	263	33	173	310	73	204
Jun.	4	184	326	91	226	356	137	261	36	168	307
Jun.	11	287	54	174	322	98	224	344	134	268	34
Jun.	18	17	137	270	60	187	308	81	231	357	119
Jun.	25	102	231	11	149	272	42	183	318	82	213
Jul.	2	194	335	99	234	7	145	269	44	179	316
Jul.	9	296	63	183	332	106	233	353	144	277	43
Jul.	16	25	147	279	70	195	318	89	241	5	129
Jul.	23	110	240	21	157	280	52	192	327	91	224
Jul.	30	205	343	108	242	18	153	278	52	190	324
Aug.	6	304	71	192	341	115	241	3	153	286	51
Aug.	13	33	156	287	80	203	327	98	251	13	138
Aug.	20	119	250	30	165	289	63	201	336	99	235
Aug.	27	216	351	117	250	28	162	287	61	200	332
Sep.	3	314	80	201	350	125	249	13	161	296	59
Sep.	10	41	165	296	90	211	336	108	260	21	146
Sep.	17	127	261	39	174	297	74	209	345	107	246
Sep.	24	226	359	126	259	38	170	295	70	209	341
Oct.	1	323	88	211	358	135	257	22	170	306	67
Oct.	8	49	174	306	99	220	344	118	269	30	154
Oct.	15	135	272	47	183	305	84	217	353	116	256
Oct.	22	236	8	134	269	47	180	303	80	217	351
Oct.	29	333	95	220	7	144	265	31	179	315	75
Nov.	5	58	181	317	107	229	352	129	277	39	162
Nov.	12	143	283	55	192	314	94	225	1	125	265
Nov.	19	244	18	141	279	55	189	311	90	225	0
Nov.	26	343	104	229	16	153	274	39	189	323	84
Dec.	3	67	189	328	115	237	360	140	284	47	171
Dec.	10	153	292	64	200	324	103	234	9	136	274
Dec.	17	252	28	149	289	63	199	319	100	234	9
Dec.	24	351	112	237	27	161	282	47	199	331	93
Dec.	31	76	198	338	123	246	9	150	293	55	180

Month	Date	1951	1952	1953	1954	1955	1956	1957	1958	1959	1960
Jan.	1	194	336	115	238	6	147	285	47	178	317
Jan.	8	297	67	199	331	107	237	9	143	278	47
Jan.	15	30	150	294	70	200	320	104	242	9	131
Jan.	22	114	240	35	161	284	51	207	331	94	223
Jan.	29	204	344	124	245	17	155	294	55	189	325
Feb.	5	305	76	207	341	116	246	18	152	287	56
Feb.	12	38	159	302	80	208	330	112	252	17	140
Feb.	19	122	249	45	169	292	61	216	340	102	233
Feb.	26	215	352	133	253	27	163	303	63	199	333
Mar.	5	314	96	216	350	125	266	27	161	297	75
Mar.	12	46	180	310	91	216	351	121	262	25	161
Mar.	19	130	274	54	178	300	86	224	349	110	259
Mar.	26	225	14	142	262	37	185	312	72	208	356
Apr.	2	324	104	226	358	135	274	37	169	307	83
Apr.	9	54	189	319	100	224	360	131	271	34	170
Apr.	16	138	285	62	187	308	97	232	357	118	269
Apr.	23	235	23	150	271	46	194	320	82	217	5
Apr.	30	334	112	235	6	146	282	48	177	317	91
May	7	62	197	330	109	232	8	142	279	42	177
May	14	146	296	70	196	316	107	240	6	127	279
May	21	243	32	158	280	54	204	328	91	225	15
May	28	344	120	244	15	155	290	55	187	326	100
Jun.	4	71	205	341	117	241	16	153	288	51	186
Jun.	11	155	306	79	204	325	117	249	14	137	288
Jun.	18	252	42	166	290	63	214	336	101	234	25
Jun.	25	354	128	253	26	164	298	63	198	335	109
Jul.	2	80	214	351	125	250	24	164	296	60	195
Jul.	9	164	315	88	212	335	126	259	22	147	297
Jul.	16	260	52	174	299	72	223	344	110	243	34
Jul.	23	3	137	261	37	173	307	71	209	343	118
Jul.	30	89	222	2	134	258	33	174	304	68	205
Aug.	6	174	324	97	220	345	134	268	30	156	305
Aug.	13	270	62	182	308	82	232	353	118	254	42
Aug.	20	11	146	269	48	181	316	79	220	351	126
Aug.	27	97	232	11	143	267	43	183	314	76	215
Sep.	3	184	332	107	228	355	143	278	38	166	314
Sep.	10	280	71	191	316	92	241	2	127	265	50
Sep.	17	19	155	278	58	189	325	88	230	359	135
Sep.	24	105	242	20	152	274	54	191	323	84	225
Oct.	1	193	341	116	237	4	152	287	47	174	324
Oct.	8	291	79	200	324	103	249	11	135	276	58
Oct.	15	27	163	287	68	198	333	98	239	8	143
Oct.	22	113	252	28	162	282	64	199	332	92	235
Oct.	29	201	350	125	245	12	162	295	56	182	334
Nov.	5	302	87	209	333	114	256	19	144	286	66
Nov.	12	36	171	297	76	207	341	109	247	17	150
Nov.	19	121	262	37	171	291	73	208	341	101	244
Nov.	26	209	0	133	254	20	173	303	65	190	345
Dec.	3	312	95	217	342	124	265	27	154	295	75
Dec.	10	45	179	307	84	216	348	119	255	27	158
Dec.	17	129	271	46	180	299	82	218	350	110	252
Dec.	24	217	11	141	263	28	184	311	73	199	355
Dec.	31	321	103	225	352	132	273	35	164	303	84

Month	Date	1961	1962	1963	1964	1965	1966	1967	1968	1969	1970
Jan.	1	96	217	350	128	266	27	163	298	76	197
Jan.	8	179	315	89	217	350	126	260	27	161	297
Jan.	15	275	54	179	302	86	225	349	112	257	36
Jan.	22	18	141	264	35	189	311	74	207	359	122
Jan.	29	105	225	1	136	275	35	173	306	85	206
Feb.	5	188	323	99	225	360	134	270	35	171	305
Feb.	12	284	64	187	310	95	235	357	121	267	45
Feb.	19	26	150	272	46	197	320	81	218	7	130
Feb.	26	113	234	11	144	283	45	182	315	93	216
Mar.	5	198	331	109	245	9	142	280	54	180	313
Mar.	12	293	73	195	332	105	244	5	142	277	54
Mar.	19	34	159	280	71	205	329	90	243	15	139
Mar.	26	122	243	19	167	291	54	190	338	101	226
Apr.	2	208	340	119	253	18	151	290	63	189	323
Apr.	9	303	82	204	340	116	252	14	150	288	62
Apr.	16	42	167	288	81	213	337	99	253	23	147
Apr.	23	130	253	28	176	299	64	198	347	109	235
Apr.	30	216	349	128	261	27	161	298	71	197	333
May	7	314	90	213	348	127	260	23	158	299	70
May	14	51	176	298	91	222	345	109	262	32	155
May	21	137	263	36	186	307	74	207	357	117	245
May	28	225	359	137	270	35	172	307	80	205	344
Jun.	4	325	98	222	357	137	268	31	168	309	78
Jun.	11	60	184	308	99	231	353	119	270	42	163
Jun.	18	146	272	45	195	315	82	217	6	126	253
Jun.	25	233	10	145	279	43	183	315	89	214	355
Jul.	2	336	106	230	6	147	276	40	178	318	87
Jul.	9	70	191	318	108	241	1	129	279	51	171
Jul.	16	154	281	56	204	324	91	227	14	135	261
Jul.	23	241	21	153	288	52	193	323	98	223	5
Jul.	30	345	115	238	16	156	286	47	188	327	97
Aug.	6	79	200	327	116	250	10	138	288	60	180
Aug.	13	163	289	66	212	333	99	238	22	144	270
Aug.	20	250	32	161	296	61	203	331	106	233	14
Aug.	27	353	124	246	27	164	295	55	199	335	106
Sep.	3	88	208	336	126	259	19	147	297	68	189
Sep.	10	172	297	77	220	342	108	249	30	152	279
Sep.	17	260	41	170	304	72	212	340	114	244	23
Sep.	24	1	134	254	37	172	304	64	208	344	115
Oct.	1	97	217	344	136	267	28	155	308	76	198
Oct.	8	180	306	88	228	351	117	259	38	161	289
Oct.	15	270	50	179	312	82	220	350	122	254	31
Oct.	22	10	143	262	47	182	313	73	217	353	123
Oct.	29	105	226	352	146	275	37	163	318	84	207
Nov.	5	189	315	97	237	359	127	268	47	168	299
Nov.	12	281	58	188	320	93	228	359	130	264	39
Nov.	19	19	151	271	55	191	321	82	225	3	131
Nov.	26	113	235	1	157	282	45	172	328	92	215
Dec.	3	197	326	105	245	7	138	276	55	176	310
Dec.	10	291	66	197	328	102	237	7	139	273	48
Dec.	17	30	159	280	63	202	329	91	234	13	139
Dec.	24	121	243	11	167	291	53	183	337	101	223
Dec.	31	204	336	113	254	14	149	284	64	184	320

Month	Date	1971	1972	1973	1974	1975	1976	1977	1978	1979	1980
Jan.	1	335	109	246	8	147	279	56	179	318	90
Jan.	8	71	197	332	108	243	6	144	278	54	176
Jan.	15	158	283	69	207	328	93	240	18	139	263
Jan.	22	244	20	169	292	54	192	339	102	224	4
Jan.	29	344	117	255	17	156	288	64	188	327	99
Feb.	5	81	204	342	116	253	14	153	287	63	184
Feb.	12	167	291	79	216	337	101	251	26	147	271
Feb.	19	252	31	177	300	62	203	347	110	233	14
Feb.	26	353	126	263	27	164	297	72	199	334	109
Mar.	5	91	224	351	124	262	34	162	296	72	204
Mar.	12	176	312	90	224	346	122	262	34	156	203
Mar.	19	261	55	185	309	72	226	356	118	243	37
Mar.	26	1	149	270	37	172	320	80	208	343	130
Apr.	2	100	233	360	134	270	43	170	307	80	213
Apr.	9	184	320	101	232	355	131	273	42	164	302
Apr.	16	271	64	194	317	82	235	5	126	254	46
Apr.	23	9	158	278	47	181	329	88	217	352	139
Apr.	30	109	242	8	145	278	52	178	318	88	222
May	7	193	329	111	240	3	141	282	50	173	312
May	14	281	73	203	324	92	243	14	134	264	54
May	21	19	167	287	55	191	337	97	226	3	147
May	28	117	251	16	156	286	61	187	328	96	231
Jun.	4	201	339	120	249	11	151	291	59	180	323
Jun.	11	291	81	213	333	102	252	23	143	273	63
Jun.	18	29	176	296	64	201	346	106	234	13	155
Jun.	25	125	260	25	167	295	69	196	338	105	239
Jul.	2	209	349	129	258	19	162	299	68	188	334
Jul.	9	300	90	222	341	111	261	32	152	282	72
Jul.	16	40	184	305	72	212	354	115	243	24	163
Jul.	23	133	268	35	176	303	78	206	347	114	248
Jul.	30	217	0	137	267	27	172	308	77	197	344
Aug.	6	309	99	230	350	120	271	40	161	290	83
Aug.	13	51	192	314	81	223	2	124	252	34	171
Aug.	20	142	276	45	185	312	86	217	356	123	256
Aug.	27	225	10	146	276	36	182	317	86	206	353
Sep.	3	317	109	238	360	128	281	48	170	299	93
Sep.	10	61	200	322	90	232	10	132	262	43	180
Sep.	17	151	284	56	193	321	94	228	4	132	264
Sep.	24	234	20	155	284	45	191	326	94	215	2
Oct.	1	325	120	246	9	136	291	56	179	308	103
Oct.	8	70	208	330	101	241	19	140	273	51	189
Oct.	15	160	292	66	202	330	102	238	12	140	273
Oct.	22	243	28	165	292	54	199	336	102	225	10
Oct.	29	334	130	254	17	146	301	64	187	318	112
Nov.	5	79	217	338	112	249	27	148	284	59	197
Nov.	12	169	300	76	210	339	111	247	21	148	282
Nov.	19	253	36	175	300	63	207	347	110	234	18
Nov.	26	344	139	262	25	156	310	73	195	329	120
Dec.	3	87	226	346	122	257	36	157	294	67	206
Dec.	10	177	310	84	220	347	121	255	31	156	292
Dec.	17	261	45	185	308	72	216	356	118	242	28
Dec.	24	355	148	271	33	167	318	81	203	340	128
Dec.	31	95	235	355	132	265	44	166	303	76	214

Month	Date	1981	1982	1983	1984	1985	1986	1987	1988	1989	1990
Jan.	1	226	350	129	260	36	162	300	71	205	333
Jan.	8	315	89	225	346	126	260	36	156	297	72
Jan.	15	53	188	309	73	225	358	119	243	37	168
Jan.	22	149	272	35	176	319	82	206	348	129	252
Jan.	29	234	0	137	270	43	172	308	81	213	343
Feb.	5	324	98	234	354	135	270	44	164	306	82
Feb.	12	64	196	317	81	236	6	128	252	48	175
Feb.	19	157	280	45	185	328	90	217	356	138	260
Feb.	26	242	10	145	279	51	182	316	90	222	353
Mar.	5	332	108	242	15	143	280	52	185	313	93
Mar.	12	74	204	326	104	246	14	136	275	57	184
Mar.	19	166	288	55	208	337	97	227	19	147	268
Mar.	26	250	20	154	300	60	191	326	111	230	1
Apr.	2	340	119	250	24	151	291	60	194	322	103
Apr.	9	84	212	334	114	255	22	144	286	66	192
Apr.	16	175	296	66	216	346	106	237	27	156	276
Apr.	23	259	28	164	309	69	199	336	119	240	9
Apr.	30	349	130	258	33	160	302	68	203	331	113
May	7	93	221	342	124	264	31	152	297	75	201
May	14	184	304	75	225	355	114	246	36	165	285
May	21	268	36	175	317	78	207	347	127	249	18
May	28	358	140	266	41	170	311	76	211	341	122
Jun.	4	102	230	350	135	272	40	160	307	83	210
Jun.	11	193	313	84	234	3	123	255	45	173	294
Jun.	18	277	45	185	325	87	216	357	135	258	27
Jun.	25	8	149	275	49	180	320	85	219	352	130
Jul.	2	110	239	359	146	281	49	169	317	92	219
Jul.	9	201	322	93	244	11	133	263	55	181	304
Jul.	16	286	54	196	333	96	225	7	143	266	37
Jul.	23	19	158	284	57	191	328	94	227	3	138
Jul.	30	119	248	7	155	290	57	178	327	101	227
Aug.	6	210	331	101	254	19	142	272	66	189	313
Aug.	13	294	64	205	341	104	236	16	152	274	48
Aug.	20	30	166	293	66	202	337	103	236	13	147
Aug.	27	128	256	17	164	299	65	187	335	111	235
Sep.	3	218	340	110	264	27	151	281	75	197	321
Sep.	10	302	75	214	350	112	247	24	160	282	59
Sep.	17	40	174	302	74	212	345	112	245	23	156
Sep.	24	138	264	26	172	309	73	197	343	121	243
Oct.	1	226	349	119	274	36	159	292	84	206	329
Oct.	8	310	86	222	359	120	258	32	169	291	70
Oct.	15	50	183	310	84	220	354	120	255	31	165
Oct.	22	148	272	35	181	319	81	206	352	130	251
Oct.	29	234	357	130	282	44	167	303	92	214	337
Nov.	5	318	96	230	8	129	268	40	178	300	79
Nov.	12	58	193	318	93	229	4	128	265	39	175
Nov.	19	158	280	44	190	329	90	214	2	139	260
Nov.	26	243	5	141	290	53	175	314	100	223	345
Dec.	3	327	106	238	16	139	277	49	185	310	88
Dec.	10	66	203	326	103	237	14	136	274	48	185
Dec.	17	167	288	52	200	337	98	222	12	147	269
Dec.	24	252	13	152	298	62	184	324	108	232	355
Dec.	31	337	114	248	24	149	285	59	193	320	96

Month	Date	1991	1992	1993	1994	1995	1996	1997	1998	1999	2000
Jan.	1	111	242	15	145	281	53	185	317	92	223
Jan.	8	206	326	108	244	16	136	279	56	186	307
Jan.	15	289	54	210	337	99	225	21	147	270	37
Jan.	22	18	158	299	61	190	329	110	231	2	140
Jan.	29	119	252	23	155	290	62	193	326	101	232
Feb.	5	214	335	116	254	24	145	287	66	193	315
Feb.	12	298	63	220	345	108	235	31	155	278	47
Feb.	19	29	166	308	69	201	337	119	239	12	148
Feb.	26	128	260	32	164	299	70	202	335	111	240
Mar.	5	222	356	124	265	32	166	295	76	201	337
Mar.	12	306	87	229	354	116	259	39	164	285	72
Mar.	19	39	189	317	77	211	360	128	248	22	170
Mar.	26	138	280	41	172	310	90	212	343	121	260
Apr.	2	230	5	133	275	40	175	305	86	210	345
Apr.	9	314	98	237	3	123	270	47	173	294	83
Apr.	16	49	198	326	86	220	9	136	257	31	180
Apr.	23	148	288	50	180	320	98	221	351	132	268
Apr.	30	238	13	143	284	48	183	315	95	218	353
May	7	322	109	245	12	132	281	55	182	302	93
May	14	57	207	335	95	228	18	144	267	39	190
May	21	158	296	59	189	330	106	230	1	141	276
May	28	247	21	154	292	57	191	326	103	227	1
Jun.	4	330	119	253	21	141	291	64	190	311	102
Jun.	11	66	217	343	105	236	28	152	276	48	199
Jun.	18	168	304	68	199	340	114	238	11	150	285
Jun.	25	256	29	165	300	66	199	337	111	236	10
Jul.	2	339	129	262	29	150	300	73	198	321	111
Jul.	9	74	227	351	114	245	38	160	285	57	209
Jul.	16	177	313	76	210	348	123	246	22	158	293
Jul.	23	265	38	175	309	75	208	347	120	245	19
Jul.	30	349	137	272	37	160	308	83	206	331	119
Aug.	6	83	237	359	123	255	48	169	293	67	218
Aug.	13	186	322	84	221	356	132	254	33	166	302
Aug.	20	273	47	185	318	83	218	356	129	253	29
Aug.	27	358	146	282	45	169	317	93	214	340	128
Sep.	3	93	246	7	131	265	56	177	301	78	226
Sep.	10	194	331	92	231	4	141	263	43	174	311
Sep.	17	281	56	194	327	91	228	5	138	261	39
Sep.	24	8	154	292	53	178	326	102	223	349	137
Oct.	1	104	254	16	139	276	64	186	310	89	234
Oct.	8	202	339	101	241	13	149	273	53	183	319
Oct.	15	289	66	202	337	99	238	13	148	269	49
Oct.	22	16	164	301	61	187	336	111	231	357	148
Oct.	29	115	262	25	148	287	72	195	318	100	242
Nov.	5	211	347	111	250	22	157	283	61	193	326
Nov.	12	297	76	211	346	107	247	22	157	277	58
Nov.	19	24	174	309	70	194	346	119	240	5	159
Nov.	26	126	270	33	156	297	80	203	328	109	251
Dec.	3	220	355	121	258	31	165	293	69	202	334
Dec.	10	305	85	220	355	115	256	31	165	286	67
Dec.	17	32	185	317	79	203	357	127	249	13	169
Dec.	24	135	278	41	166	306	89	211	338	117	260
Dec.	31	230	3	131	266	41	173	303	78	211	343

Month	Year	2001	2002	2003	2004	2005	2006	2007	2008	2009	2010
Jan.	1	355	128	263	33	165	300	74	203	336	111
Jan.	8	89	228	355	117	260	39	165	288	71	211
Jan.	15	193	317	79	209	4	127	249	20	174	297
Jan.	22	280	41	174	310	91	211	346	121	261	21
Jan.	29	4	137	273	42	175	308	84	211	345	119
Feb.	5	97	238	3	126	268	49	173	296	80	221
Feb.	12	202	326	87	219	12	136	257	31	182	306
Feb.	19	289	49	184	319	99	220	356	130	269	31
Feb.	26	13	145	283	49	184	316	94	219	355	127
Mar.	5	106	248	11	147	278	59	181	317	90	229
Mar.	12	210	334	95	244	20	145	265	56	190	315
Mar.	19	298	58	193	342	107	229	4	153	277	40
Mar.	26	23	153	293	69	193	325	104	239	4	136
Apr.	2	116	257	20	155	289	67	190	325	101	237
Apr.	9	218	343	104	255	28	154	274	67	198	323
Apr.	16	306	68	202	351	115	239	12	162	285	50
Apr.	23	32	162	303	77	202	334	114	247	12	146
Apr.	30	127	265	29	163	300	75	199	333	112	245
May	7	226	352	113	264	37	162	284	76	207	331
May	14	314	77	210	1	123	248	21	172	293	59
May	21	40	173	312	86	210	345	122	256	20	157
May	28	138	273	38	171	311	83	207	342	123	254
Jun.	4	235	0	122	273	46	170	294	84	217	339
Jun.	11	322	87	219	11	132	257	30	181	302	68
Jun.	18	48	183	320	95	218	356	130	265	29	168
Jun.	25	149	281	46	181	321	92	216	352	132	262
Jul.	2	245	8	132	281	56	178	304	93	227	347
Jul.	9	330	95	229	20	140	266	41	190	310	76
Jul.	16	56	195	328	104	227	7	138	274	38	179
Jul.	23	158	290	54	191	330	101	224	2	140	272
Jul.	30	254	16	142	290	65	186	313	101	236	356
Aug.	6	339	103	239	28	149	274	52	198	319	84
Aug.	13	65	205	336	112	236	17	147	282	47	188
Aug.	20	167	299	62	201	338	110	232	12	149	281
Aug.	27	264	24	151	299	74	194	321	111	245	5
Sep.	3	348	112	250	36	158	282	63	206	328	93
Sep.	10	74	215	345	120	246	26	156	290	58	197
Sep.	17	176	309	70	211	347	120	240	22	157	290
Sep.	24	273	33	159	309	83	203	330	122	253	14
Oct.	1	356	120	261	44	167	291	73	214	336	103
Oct.	8	84	224	354	128	256	34	165	298	68	205
Oct.	15	184	318	78	220	355	129	248	31	167	299
Oct.	22	281	42	167	320	91	212	338	132	261	23
Oct.	29	5	129	271	52	175	301	82	222	344	113
Nov.	5	95	232	4	136	266	42	174	306	78	213
Nov.	12	193	327	87	229	5	137	257	40	177	307
Nov.	19	289	51	176	331	99	221	346	143	268	31
Nov.	26	13	139	280	61	183	312	91	231	352	123
Dec.	3	105	240	13	144	276	51	183	315	87	223
Dec.	10	203	335	96	237	15	145	267	48	188	315
Dec.	17	297	59	185	341	107	229	356	152	277	39
Dec.	24	21	150	288	70	190	322	98	240	0	134
Dec.	31	114	249	22	153	285	60	191	324	96	232

Dates to Hunt or Fish

Dates to Hunt or Fish	Qtr.	Sign
Jan. 4, 7:00 pm-Jan. 6, 10:44 pm	4th	Scorpio
Jan. 12, 9:50 pm-Jan. 15, 12:27 am	1st	Pisces
Jan. 22, 5:42 am-Jan. 24, 6:21 pm	2nd	Cancer
Feb. 1, 1:51 am-Feb. 3, 7:21 am	3rd	Scorpio
Feb. 9, 8:59 am-Feb. 11, 10:21 am	1st	Pisces
Feb. 18, 12:13 pm-Feb. 21, 12:54 am	2nd	Cancer
Feb. 28, 7:21 am-Mar. 2, 1:29 pm	3rd	Scorpio
Mar. 2, 1:29 pm-Mar. 4, 5:12 pm	3rd	Sagittarius
Mar. 8, 7:32 pm-Mar. 10, 9:03 pm	4th	Pisces
Mar. 17, 7:44 pm-Mar. 20, 8:17 am	2nd	Cancer
Mar. 27, 1:29 pm-Mar. 29, 6:56 pm	3rd	Scorpio
Mar. 29, 6:56 pm-Mar. 31, 10:48 pm	3rd	Sagittarius
Apr. 5, 4:45 am-Apr. 7, 7:28 am	4th	Pisces
Apr. 14, 5:03 am-Apr. 16, 5:17 pm	1st	Cancer
Apr. 23, 10:25 pm-Apr. 26, 2:46 am	2nd	Scorpio
Apr. 26, 2:46 am-Apr. 28, 5:33 am	3rd	Sagittarius
May 2, 10:43 am-May 4, 2:36 pm	4th	Pisces
May 11, 1:20 pm-May 14, 1:17 am	1st	Cancer
May 21, 7:49 am-May 23, 11:38 am	2nd	Scorpio
May 23, 11:38 am-May 25, 1:11 pm	2nd	Sagittarius
May 29, 4:09 pm-May 31, 8:07 pm	3rd	Pisces
Jun. 7, 8:46 pm-Jun. 10, 8:39 am	1st	Cancer
Jun. 17, 5:23 pm-Jun. 19, 9:45 pm	2nd	Scorpio
Jun. 19, 9:45 pm-Jun. 21, 10:52 pm	2nd	Sagittarius
Jun. 25, 11:03 pm-Jun. 28, 1:51 am	3rd	Pisces
Jun. 28, 1:51 am-Jun. 30, 7:45 am	3rd	Aries
Jul. 5, 3:07 am-Jul. 7, 3:11 pm	4th	Cancer

Jul. 15, 1:51 am-Jul. 17, 7:35 am	2nd	Scorpio
Jul. 17, 7:35 am-Jul. 19, 9:26 am	2nd	Sagittarius
Jul. 23, 8:12 am-Jul. 25, 9:23 am	3rd	Pisces
Jul. 25, 9:23 am-Jul. 27, 1:54 pm	3rd	Aries
Aug. 1, 8:52 am-Aug. 3, 9:10 pm	4th	Cancer
Aug. 11, 8:35 am-Aug. 13, 3:47 pm	1st	Scorpio
Aug. 13, 3:47 pm-Aug. 15, 7:13 pm	2nd	Sagittarius
Aug. 19, 6:52 pm-Aug. 21, 7:01 pm	3rd	Pisces
Aug. 21, 7:01 pm-Aug. 23, 9:58 pm	3rd	Aries
Aug. 28, 2:57 pm-Aug. 31, 3:14 am	4th	Cancer
Sep. 7, 2:10 pm-Sep. 9, 10:03 pm	1st	Scorpio
Sep. 16, 5:24 am-Sep. 18, 5:43 am	2nd	Pisces
Sep. 18, 5:43 am-Sep. 20, 7:47 am	3rd	Aries
Sep. 24, 10:10 pm-Sep. 27, 10:03 am	3rd	Cancer
Oct. 4, 8:03 pm-Oct. 7, 3:28 am	1st	Scorpio
Oct. 13, 2:05 pm-Oct. 15, 3:39 pm	2nd	Pisces
Oct. 15, 3:39 pm-Oct. 17, 6:04 pm	2nd	Aries
Oct. 22, 6:41 am-Oct. 24, 5:48 pm	3rd	Cancer
Nov. 1, 2:29 am-Nov. 3, 8:55 am	4th	Scorpio
Nov. 9, 7:22 pm-Nov. 11, 10:22 pm	2nd	Pisces
Nov. 11, 10:22 pm-Nov. 14, 2:02 am	2nd	Aries
Nov. 18, 2:42 pm-Nov. 21, 1:10 am	3rd	Cancer
Nov. 28, 11:33 am-Nov. 30, 5:32 pm	4th	Scorpio
Dec. 7, 12:44 am-Dec. 9, 4:02 am	1st	Pisces
Dec. 9, 4:02 am-Dec. 11, 8:46 am	2nd	Aries
Dec. 15, 11:01 pm-Dec. 18, 9:18 am	3rd	Cancer
Dec. 25, 9:04 pm-Dec. 28, 3:43 am	4th	Scorpio

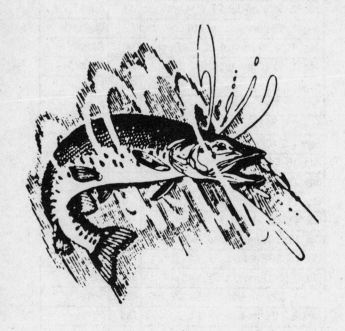

Fishing by the Moon

by Louise Riotte

Hundreds of books have been written about the art of fishing since Izaak Walton penned the first edition of the *Compleat Angler* in 1653. The serious fisherperson has probably read a number of these books, and most of us have studied something of the creature that we pursue. We know that fish are creatures of instinct and habit. The problem is that anglers, too, are creatures of habit. We also develop patterns of behavior, and most of us are painfully aware of how seldom our patterns coincide with the fish's pattern.

Owning the best equipment and reading the best books will not improve anyone's fishing unless that person knows how to use that equipment and knowledge. It becomes evident to the student of astrology that most anglers need to forget some of their unproductive fishing habits and learn a variety of new approaches. In the final analysis, being successful at fishing means being versatile. What is written here is for everyone who pursues fish not only for the pure joy of relaxing in the outdoors but also in the hopes that someday he or she will catch the lunker of a lifetime.

As creatures captive to their environment, fish are closely attuned to changes in weather and water conditions, and they respond to these changes by moving around in lakes and rivers. Season, time of day, and many other factors have a bearing on whether or not you will catch a fish at a particular time.

From sunset to one hour after during the summer months, fishing should be great. In the cooler months, fishing is best from noon to three in the afternoon. The best day to fish is a warm, close, and cloudy day that follows a bright moonlit night. This is because fish have no eyelids. On a cloudy day, there is no light to distress them so they feed near the surface.

Winds, too, have a bearing on these matters with the most favorable winds from the south, southwest, and west. East winds are unfavorable.

*When the wind is in the north
The skilful fisher goes not forth,
When the wind is in the south
It blows the bait in the fish's mouth,
When the wind is in the east
'Tis neither good for man nor beast,
When the wind is in the west
Then fishing's at its very best.*

The concept of fish movement is really very simple. Most game fish spawn in the spring of the year, migrating into shallow waters. This migration is triggered by water temperature. Each species also prefers a certain set of bottom conditions over which to spawn. Walleyes, for instance, like hard gravel bottoms while northern pike prefer shallow, weedy sloughs. After spawning, fish begin movement into a summer location pattern, often choosing another area of the lake. Again, this movement is triggered by water temperature and is in response to locating prey that the game fish will feed on all summer long. Once this pattern is established, fish location will be fairly predictable throughout the summer.

With the arrival of the first cold nights that come in the fall, lakes and rivers cool off rather quickly, and once more the fish move to a new location. In the north, where lakes and rivers ice over, ice fishermen usually find a gradual movement of game fish from shallow to deeper waters as the winter progresses. In southern waters, fish also move deeper and become less active, but daily weather conditions can make dramatic changes if a warm spell sends the water temperature soaring.

There are many who believe that fish can sense weather changes and are particularly active three days before a storm. But on the day of the actual weather change, the fish will not bite. This may be because the winds often stir up the water, inducing the smaller fish to come out, and small fish are followed by big fish that consider them their lawful prey. In turn, anglers follow big fish with the same idea.

A wise old fisherman once told me to watch out for a storm if insects were flying low and fish were jumping out of the water to catch them. Insects fly lower to avoid the thin atmosphere above due to the lowering air pressure. He also said to take note of the variety of insect that was flying and to set flies for bait accordingly.

After heavy rains fish may not bite since plenty of food has been washed into the lake. They are also hard to catch when fresh snow water is in a stream. Generally speaking, June is usually the best fishing month and July the worst.

It is generally conceded that the best days of the month for fishing are those on which the Moon changes quarters (plus the day before and day after), especially if the change occurs on a day when the Moon is in a water sign (Cancer, Scorpio, or Pisces). The best period in any month is the day after the Full Moon. Three days before and after the Full Moon are also favorable.

My friend and fishing expert Lucy Hagan, who works by day and often fishes at night, says she has her best luck when she fishes "down the moonbeam."

And which sign of the three water signs is the best? An experienced fisherman took a day off from his job, and it happened to fall under the sign of Scorpio. He caught the fish he had been after for so long but was so delighted to win the fight of wills that he put the fish back. His theory was that fish are hungrier, less cautious, and more likely to be caught in the sign of Scorpio.

He also told me that he had his best luck when using an active lure. "With live bait," he said, "attach the hook so the bait will have natural movements. With artificial lures, jig or pop the bait and vary the pace of the retrieve. Present the lure to the water in a manner that will be interesting to the fish both in location and in action. Fish the shady sides of logs and rocks, the down current sides of boulders and large stumps, and the windless side of ledges and cliffs. Let the bait sink and keep it moving all the time."

You must polish your techniques to fit the fish. Their pattern is not likely to change, so your pattern must if you are to be successful.

Although they don't have eyelids, fish possess remarkable sight. Sensitive to light, they adjust their eyesight to the rhythms of the natural night and day cycle. Any sudden light thrown on them will cause them to quit the area rapidly. Because of the

placement of their eyes, it is impossible for them to see objects on the same level or directly under them. However, they can see all that is occurring above and around them for distances of 50 feet or more.

They also have a keen sense of smell and don't like strong aromas. Certain odors can be attractive, however. Many fisherpersons believe that bait rubbed with oil of anise will draw the fish. Others swear by the juice of smallage or lovage.

According to Clarence Meyer in the *Herbalist Almanac*, the Chinese use the following method for catching fish: "Take *Cocculous indicus*, pulverize and mix with dough, then scatter it broadcast over the water, as you would with seed. The fish will seize it with great avidity, and they will instantly become so intoxicated that they will turn belly up on top of the water by dozens, hundreds, or even thousands, as the case may be. All that you have to do, is to have a boat, gather them up and put them in a tub of clean water, and presently they will be as lively and healthy as ever." Some American Indian tribes also used herbs, such as blue-curls, camphorweed, vinegarweed, and wild cucumber, in a similar fashion.

Remember that fish have very good hearing as evidenced by their sensitivity to vibrations. Be as quiet in your movements as possible—talking does not seem to bother them as much as walking about or dropping something heavy.

As previously indicated, fish are usually on three levels of most lakes, ponds, and streams. Some, according to season, time of day, etc., are near the surface, some midwater, and some on the bottom. Work the various levels to find the area of biting fish.

Troll whenever possible. This enables you to cover large or otherwise inaccessible areas to locate fish. Furthermore, you learn more about the water you are working.

Position yourself with your back to the wind and don't let your shadow fall on the water. If fishing in moving water, cast upstream and let your bait drift down with the flow.

Fish are greedy by nature. They also have a built-in sense as to the size of an object they can swallow and they will go for larger baits up to their maximum swallowing capacity.

Fishing for an abundant catch will be most rewarding in the sign of Cancer. Big ones may be caught in the sign of Scorpio, but they do tend to slack off a little bit when the Moon is in Pisces, although this is still a good fishing sign. Other possibilities are the most signs of Taurus, Virgo, Libra, and Capricorn.

A fishing guide states: "The best time to catch fish is when the Moon is directly overhead and the two hours before and after. The next best time is the hour before and after the Moon is straight down on the other side of the earth." The author insists these periods work every time.

Fish usually feed on a regular time schedule. If they feed in the early morning, they will be likely to feed again in the late afternoon and again early the next morning. Night feeders are just as regular.

Often fish will feed on only one insect or food for quite lengthy periods. When this happens, it is almost impossible to lure them with any other bait.

Before and after spawning season, fish will eagerly take a variety of baits. Brook trout and many other species will absolutely refuse food during spawning.

The larger the fish, the faster its swimming ability. It has been calculated that fish can swim about eight miles per hour for each foot of body length, but after striking a bait or making any other sudden move, a fish can accelerate up to about 50 percent over its usual cruising speed.

During the summer months, black bass go in pairs—if you catch one, try for its mate. Don't try to catch black bass when the water is smooth; it's a waste of time.

There are other water creatures besides fish that deserve honorable mention. When the Moon is full, residents of Chatham on Cape Cod head for the beach where they dig up bushels of giant sea clams, which are about four times as big as the quahogs favored by most New Englanders. Clams are ruled by the Moon. An experienced clam digger says they should be dug at the entrance of the wet Sun sign in Libra—its first week is thought to be its best time. She says she marks special spots that look good for digging and then uses this Libra week for harvesting. She, too, thinks they are best and most plentiful during the Full Moon.

According to Louisiana folk, crabs (ruled by the Moon and Cancer) are best caught when the Moon is full. They use a chicken neck for bait, and the crabs bite quickly. They claim the meat at this time is full and juicy, but at other times the crabs are mostly shell.

Originally printed in Llewellyn's 1993 Moon Sign Book. Reprinted with permission.

Home, Health, and Leisure

Water and the
Art of Submission

by Robin Antepara

How do we get what we want in life? In astrology, Mars is designated the god of war, and the primary agent of our desires. In Western astrology, Mars rules Aries, a fire sign associated with the will and energy needed to assert oneself in the competitive world. These qualities are synonymous with Western culture. Mars is direct and to the point. He knows what he wants and fights for it if need be. Eastern cultures offer an alternative way to get what you want, though.

Using the Feminine Energy in Your Chart to Get What You Want

Eastern cultures have very different ideas about this. In tai chi and other martial arts, self-assertion is not actuated through outward aggression but by giving in to an opponent's force. In yielding to a punch or kick, the martial artist causes an adversary to fall forward on his or her own energy. We can understand the philosophical foundation underlying this approach through the Chinese classic *The Art of War*. By remaining passive and formless, the ancient text tells us "no one can formulate a strategy against you." Maintaining formlessness allows the martial artist to conserve her energy "while inducing others to dissipate theirs."

The late Hong Kong–born martial artist Bruce Lee echoed these sentiments in his film *Enter the Dragon*. "Be formless, shapeless, like water," he tells his students. "You put water into a cup, it becomes the cup; you put water into a bottle, it becomes the bottle. Now water can flow, or it can crash. Be water, my friend."

It would be difficult for astrologers, as in tune as they are with the four elements, not to resonate with this. Water and earth signs are the feminine or "yin" energies of the universe, fire and air the masculine or "yang" energies. Water and earth feel and receive and intuit; they absorb information from the environment and react to it. Fire and air, on the other hand, act and manifest outward.

In this article, we will explore the yin characteristics of Cancer, Scorpio, and Pisces—the three water signs. More than any other element, water is associated with emotional intelligence, what psychologist Daniel Goleman calls the ability to empathize and "get on with other people." Water is also associated with the need for nurturing and connection.

Western culture in general, and American culture in particular, are fiery and masculine by nature. As a result, there is tremendous pressure on Americans to assert themselves in fiery ways—something that's true irrespective of gender or astrological type. This naturally presents a handicap for those earthy and watery personalities who prefer other modes of assertion.

However, you don't have to be swept up in the psycho-social biases of the mainstream culture. With self-awareness gained through your natal chart you can accommodate to your culture of birth and learn how to cultivate your own unique style of self expression. By examining Asian-inspired modes of assertion we'll see how Westerners with a water emphasis in their charts can honor their feminine natures. Following is an account of how two Easterners (one famous, one not) tapped into the water in their charts. Then we'll turn the spotlight back on Western culture and look at how two prominent Americans utilized their water planets.

Imagine this: You are a thirty-two-year-old woman who is eager to marry and raise a family. You have been going out with the same guy for almost six years and are ready to make a commitment. However, your boyfriend is from a foreign country and your mother violently opposes the union. She threatens to cut you off, she accuses the guy of underworld dealings, and she says she will call the police and have him put under investigation. Her hysteria is baseless—all hallucinations of a xenophobic and fearful parent. Your father agrees with your mother, but not quite as stridently.

What do you do? You are in love with your boyfriend and anxious to marry. You want to have a baby before it's too late.

If you are like most Western women, you fight back. You argue with your mother and defend your boyfriend. You tell about all the noteworthy things he's done. You even consider defying your mother's wishes and marrying your boyfriend.

This case actually involves a Japanese woman I'll call Kyoko. With Sun, Venus, and Mercury in Pisces, Kyoko is the personification of the watery, empathetic personality type. In her chart, the mutable Piscean energy is bolstered by a friendly sextile from Mars in Taurus, an earth sign.

What did Kyoko do? In a nutshell, she did nothing. After her mother's initial outburst, the incident (and the relationship) were never mentioned again. Her boyfriend reacted angrily to this. He wanted his girlfriend to defend him and defy her parent's wishes, but Kyoko did nothing.

Two years later, the relationship was still miraculously intact, but not without its scars. Kyoko was sitting with her parents one Sunday morning, and the father said to his now thirty-four-year-old daughter, "It's time you thought about getting married. Would you like us to find someone for you?"

"I already have someone," Kyoko said calmly.

"Oh?" said the father, at which point his daughter mentioned the maligned American boyfriend.

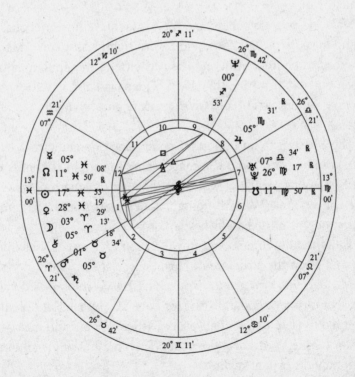

Kyoko's chart. (Birth data withheld to protect privacy.)

There was a moment of silence while her father poured himself another cup of tea. "Oh, is that still going on?" he said. "Well, I suppose you know what you want," at which point her parents agreed to the marriage.

Kyoko had gotten exactly what she wanted, but how did she do it? By doing nothing and yielding to her parents.

But she was "yielding" only on the surface. On the inside, she was holding fast to her goals and sticking with her boyfriend—despite his anger, and despite several affairs he'd had along the way in protest to Kyoko's apparent submission to her mother. Note that Kyoko did not bring up the topic of marriage. Her parents were the ones who reinitiated it. This echoes another principle from *The Art of War*, which is: Make your enemies come to you.

Make no mistake, there is a bit of Machiavelli in this chart. With Pluto opposing Venus, and Saturn tightly conjoining Mars, the need to be in control and the capacity for manipulation are high. But you'll notice that Kyoko managed the situation by drawing on her essentially watery nature and "giving in" to her parent's wishes.

This leads us to an important point: Don't romanticize water. We should be wary about romanticizing the submissiveness of the East. What's really at work is a different paradigm of power. The conventional Western notion about "losers/weak" and "winners/strong" is turned on its head.

To more fully understand this, let's consider recent sociological studies on the structure of Japanese society. In Japan, people are divided into two groups: *senpai* and *kohai*. The senpai group has seniority, and kohai do not (or have less of it.) The kohai is required to yield to a senpai's every wish and command, just as a Japanese wife must kneel down and fetch her husband's slippers and draw his bath at night.

But is she as subservient as she seems? Although the wife and the kohai bow down, behind the scenes they are pulling strings and adroitly controlling the situation.[5] This is the essence of water: It gives way to every stone and obstacle in its path, all the while wearing down boulders until they become infinitesimal grains of sand. It has tremendous power but, unlike fire, you don't see it at work.

In the West, the guy with the most money, status, or prestige—the corporate CEO, the political king-maker—has the most power. While the situation in the East looks similar, it is anything but. The kohai appears to yield but remains invisible and unknown and thus extremely powerful. Conversely, the senpai is loud and known and open to attack.

Mohandas Gandhi

We can see this dynamic at work in the chart of Mohandas Gandhi. Gandhi's Sun was in airy Libra but he had a Mars-Venus conjunction in Scorpio. Gandhi was the father of passive resistance—a school of political protest that preaches non-violence coupled with non-cooperation. But, the Mahatma appeared passive, he was willful and intense. One could make the case that passive resistance is the archetype of watery self-assertion.

This watery self-assertion is apparent throughout Gandhi's life. In the beginning of his career in South Africa, he helped Indian migrant workers fight discriminatory laws, organizing a campaign to burn the passes that only Indians and other "coloreds" had to carry. However, he refused to fight back when the police beat him and meekly accepted the blows that landed him in the hospital. Years later, Gandhi seemed to withdrew from all action when he used fasting as an instrument of political protest. On the surface, a fast is devoid of action. The person who fasts doesn't eat. In the later stages he doesn't even have the energy to move. But, while Gandhi was lying in bed, his kidneys failing

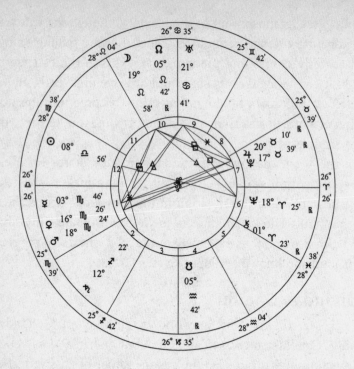

Mohandas Gandhi was born October 2, 1869, at 7:11 am LMT in Porbandar, India.

and on the edge of death, the British Empire was crumbling. On the surface Gandhi was doing nothing; in fact, he was harnessing the watery intensity of Scorpio. As we can see from this example, water is seemingly devoid of action and form, but devastating when directed toward a goal.

Don't think that Asians are the only ones who can use the water in their charts to get what they want. We'll now take a look at the horoscopes of two American presidents and see how one used the water in his chart to great effect while the other drowned in it.

Franklin Delano Roosevelt

Franklin Delano Roosevelt held office during the 1930s at the height of the Great Depression. He was in power at a time when people were fearful of the future and hungry for guidance and support. The banking system was on the verge of collapse and the economy at an all-time low. Americans yearned for a mother figure who would tell them everything was going to be all right.

Sadly, they did not get the nurturing and support they needed from Herbert Hoover. As the Depression got worse, the outgoing president withdrew into a defiant shell and refused to take responsibility for what was happening in the country, let alone provide emotional support to the millions who needed it.

Roosevelt, who had Sun conjunct Venus in Aquarius, reversed that process. He took hold of the reins and instituted massive public works projects. FDR ushered in the era of big government, transforming the presidency from what was a small, personalized office into a sprawling bureaucracy, increasing staff and opening new departments.

How was FDR able to push through such far-reaching projects and so drastically alter the face of the federal government? The answer is complex, but one factor was his Cancer Moon. The Moon is a symbol of the feminine qualities, of instincts, and of nurturing. Roosevelt's Moon is particularly strong because it is in its own sign. It is also one of the most elevated planets in his chart, a factor that gives it added power.

FDR utilized his Cancer Moon to the full, giving the American public the nurturing they so desperately needed. One measure of this can be seen through the number of press conferences he gave: an average of 330 per year during his terms in office. Contrast this with the paltry twelve that Hoover gave during his last year.

But Roosevelt did not just go up to the lectern and spout facts and statistics. Press conferences were far from his most important mode of communication. He was open and accessible in a way that was unprecedented in American history. He invited reporters into his inner chambers, held impromptu press conferences, and even played poker with them. He hobnobbed with

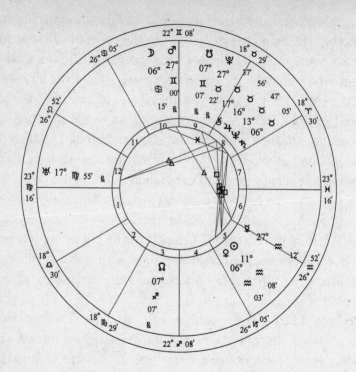

Franklin D. Roosevelt was born January 30, 1882, at 8:45 PM LMT in Hyde Park, New York.

celebrities, cultivating a celebrity image himself. "What a charmer!" Katharine Hepburn exclaimed in her memoir, recalling a visit with him during the 1930s. "Warm. Funny. Franklin Delano Roosevelt had the gift of laughter. And a great gift it is."

Another manifestation of watery sensitivity was FDR's pioneering use of radio. Most politicians were scared of the new media, retreating to more conventional forms of communication. However, FDR immediately realized its potential, taking to the microphone with relish. He established a deeply emotional connection with his audience during his legendary "fireside chats," talking about his family, even his dog. If it was hot in the studio he would stop to take a drink of water, announcing to his listeners that his throat was dry.

This simple gesture was his way of reaching out—a great and powerful man appearing vulnerable. In fact, he was vulnerable: bound to a wheelchair, paralyzed from the waist down. The important point is that he didn't fight his vulnerability. On the contrary, some have speculated that it helped him empathize with the hardships and woes of the average citizen. Here again we see the power of water, in this case expressed through Roosevelt's acceptance of his own vulnerability, and his compassion for others who were weak and in pain.

Richard Nixon

Contrast this with the chart of Richard Nixon, a man whose name has become synonymous with paranoia and suspicion. It was Nixon's profound distrust of others that generated the Watergate break-in at the Democratic Party headquarters—an event that ultimately led to his resignation. This earned Nixon the dubious distinction of being the only president in U.S. history to be forced out of office.

Nixon distrusted just about everyone: the Democrats, the press, and all but two of his top aides at the White House. Unlike FDR, he had precious little respect or affection for his constituency. "You've got to be a little evil to understand those people out there," Nixon once said.

On one level this is understandable based on his chart. His Sun, Mercury, and Jupiter were in Capricorn, and he had a nearly exact Mars-Pluto opposition. His control needs were way above average. But what most people don't know is that this control freak also had one of the most empathetic placements in the zodiac: Venus in Pisces.

Venus is the planet of love and intimacy. She indicates our style of relating. Pisces, a mutable water sign, is symbolic of deep

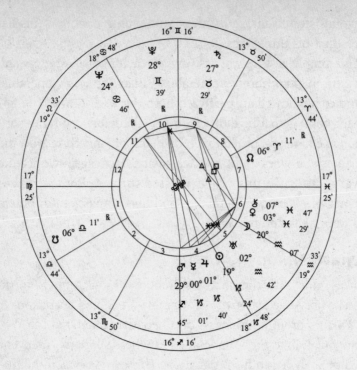

Richard Nixon was born January 9, 1913, at 9:35 pm in Yorba Linda, California.

sensitivity. People with strong placements in Pisces are often known for their compassion and altruism. Venus is "exalted"—at the height of her power—in the sign of the fish. In the positive expression of this placement, Venus is exquisitely attuned to other people's moods and emotional needs.

So what was going on with Nixon? Not only did he not exhibit any of these qualities, it was as though he were trying to shut out any possibility of emotional connection. More than any other president, Nixon worked alone, cloistering himself in a remote room in the Old Executive Office Building.

In fact, Nixon was manifesting the shadow side of Pisces. There was deep sensitivity to feelings, yes, but not to other people's. He was petulant and vindictive when he felt that his own deep, sensitive feelings were not being honored. Where FDR used the water in his chart to draw people to him, Nixon (unconsciously) used it to push people away. This cold, remote man, once condescendingly referred to as "Tricky Dicky," had a soft side, but one that he never came to terms with. Nixon fought against the watery aspect of his being tooth and nail. And because he denied it in himself, he recoiled whenever he encountered it in the outer world, refusing to let any softness or vulnerability creep into his relationships.

In such a fiery culture as America's, we perhaps shouldn't be surprised if there is a certain macho fear of water in the mainstream culture. It's a fear that men in particular fall prey to. But water is water. It always flows; it always has the potential to heal. And all of us have it somewhere in our charts. If we don't have planets in water signs, then at least water is found on a cusp or through a house placement.

Before we close, a parting caveat: Just as we should be wary of superficial labels such as "winner-loser," "weak-strong," so, too, should we be careful of making easy distinctions between the merits of the fire-air versus the water-earth temperament. There is light and shadow to every astrological energy, and the elements are no exception. Looked at positively, fire and air are immensely useful. They are direct and above board; people with generous helpings of fire in their chart are more often than not honest and direct in their dealings with others. On the shadow side, though, the masculine elements—fire in particular—can be headstrong and impetuous, even violent.

Watery types, on the other hand, are empathetic and intuitive. On the shadow side, this same element can be manipulative and self-serving. It's up to us to cultivate the constructive side of these energies and to create a positive environment for both ourselves and others.

Bibliography

Sun Tzu. *The Art of War*, Shambhala Publications,1988.

Enter the Dragon, 1973, Warner Video.

Goleman, Daniel. *Emotional Intelligence*, 1995, Bantam Books.

Halberstam, David. *The Powers That Be*, Dell Books, 1979

Hepburn, Katharine. *Me*, Random House, 1991.

Gould, Lewis. *The Modern American Presidency*, University Press of Kansas, 2003.

About the Author

Robin Antepara, M.A., is an astrologer and free-lance writer who has lived in Japan for over fifteen years. She is working on a Ph.D. in depth psychology and is interested in archetypal psychology and cross-cultural studies. She is available for consultations and may be reached at: robina@gol.com.

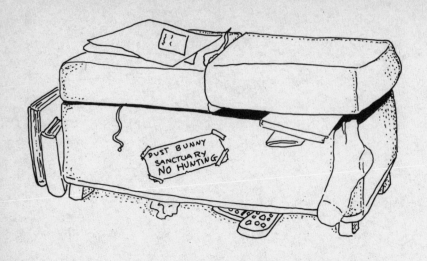

Housekeeping by Phases of the Moon

by Daniel B. Brawner

Before I begin, let me explain something. I am not an expert on housekeeping, and if anyone wants to dispute that, I can provide references, including my mother, my neighbors, and several womenfriends. The list goes on and on. I write murder mysteries—nice ones, without a lot of blood (too messy). But after spending most of my adult life in a state of self-induced squalor, I finally did what good detectives are supposed to do—I got a clue.

I discovered that if you really must clean, you should make the time count. And the best way to accomplish that is to clean according to the phases of the Moon.

Why Clean?

An obsessive-compulsive (neat) woman of my acquaintance insists that living in a clean home bestows on her a sense of inner calm. "I can't concentrate on anything else when the house is messy," she once said, glancing significantly around at my cluttered living room.

Her revelation left me conflicted. On one hand, I was sorry for her because I had always possessed what I imagined was an enviable talent for being perfectly serene in the midst of any mess. On the other hand, if my messy house meant that my woman friend really couldn't concentrate on anything else, then my hopes for a romantic evening were out the window. This alone would be a good enough reason to clean thoroughly and often. But there are other reasons, too.

Keeping an orderly house means that you can find things you're looking for. If you could get back all the time during the year you spent looking in vain for stuff that was misplaced or covered up by other stuff, you could learn Greek or build a gazebo. If, in the course of looking for the telephone, you move the couch and find, not only a mummified cheese sandwich, but two of the replacements you bought for the television remote control you lost, then you know it's time to clean.

A clean house is a healthy house. Any environmentalist will tell you that a staggering amount of dust, pollen, mold, dried-up bug parts, and regular garden-variety dirt ends up in the air and on the horizontal surfaces of your home. Not to mention the hair and sloughed-off skin and other debris that periodically falls off human beings. Fortunately, routine cleaning, especially, if it's done at the proper lunar cycle, will make your home a healthier place to live.

I'm not sure that cleanliness is natural, considering that Nature is untidy by its very—well, nature. But cleanliness is certainly civilized. It helps separate us from the lower animals that lack real estate agents A clean, orderly house is a manifestation of our orderly *Homo sapiens* brain—a model for the universe as it was meant to be: in harmony with the celestial music of the spheres. We are not pigs. We're not!

Dust Bunnies and Other Wild Beasts

The term "dust bunny" sounds cute, almost cuddly, unless you consider that each one probably carries countless toothy, microscopic dust mites that look like something out of a science-fiction "creature feature" movie and feed on tiny bits of human skin. And then there's the fact that mothers consider their children's dust bunnies to be a sign of their maternal failure. And women tend to think of them as emblematic of deep-rooted problems like fear of commitment.

Dust bunnies, like real live bunnies, are prolific and will keep coming back no matter what you do. But to cut down on their quick reappearance, you should remove dust bunnies while the Moon is waning. Disturbing them during the fertility of a waxing Moon only invigorates adolescent dust bunnies and encourages them to develop into huge, hulking dirt rabbits. Like pruning roses in the spring, sweeping out dust bunnies under a waxing Moon will only make them grow.

Refrigerator mold, on the other hand, should be removed under a waxing Moon. Refrigerator mold is accustomed to growing in the dark. Extensive scientific experiments have been conducted which conclude that when the door is closed, the refrigerator light actually does go out. In fact, opening the door alarms the mold, causing it to send out spores into the kitchen like tiny lifeboats, hoping to colonize some dark spot in case the refrigerator becomes permanently polluted with light. These Robinson Crusoe molds sometimes become marooned in dark bread wrappers or under the microwave where they cultivate crops of vile green fuzz.

Washing wooden floors should be done when the Moon is waning and when it is not in a water sign like Pisces because the water is likely to oversaturate the wood and cause it to warp. Waxing floors should be done when the Moon is—well, you figure it out.

Cleaning windows is a dreaded chore. You'd think it would be advisable to clean windows during the sign of Virgo because of the need for meticulous detail. But, concentrated attention to detail can send an otherwise well-adjusted individual dashing first inside then outside to remove real and imagined streaks from first one side of the glass, then the other. This manic behavior can go on until help arrives and the window washer is obliged to take a long, quiet vacation under close supervision.

Therefore, it is preferable to wash windows under the sign of Sagittarius, which will foster feelings of barely restrained optimism. If you follow this advice, you may find that your anxiety about this onerous task disappears and that you are thoroughly satisfied with having done a pretty good job.

You will not want to change your cat's litter box under the sign of Aries, which engenders rapid response to a problem, or you could find yourself ready to pounce on the litter box, standing over your poor cat while he tries to do his business. Pisces, with its compassion and sensitivity to the environment, is an appropriate sign under which to change the litter box. But honestly, when it comes to litter boxes, if you wait for a sign, you have waited too long.

With laundry, like litter boxes, there is no time like the present. Unless you make your own soap out of lye and pound your dirty laundry on rocks by the river, doing the washing is one of the easiest and most satisfying housekeeping jobs there is. It is the perfect task for a multitasking person. Washing clothes under a water sign will ensure that your laundry gets wetter than wet. Just one note of caution: Washing under the sign of Cancer may help suds flow around every fold and inside every pocket, but Cancer's tendency to absorb their surroundings like a sponge may leave you feeling washed out and smelling like All-Temperature Cheer.

The Other Kind of Cleaning

One kind of cleaning involves rubber gloves, bleach, and buckets of hot, soapy water. You can do this kind of cleaning while you fantasize about vacationing in Fiji, or rehearsing how you will ask your boss for a raise. The other kind of cleaning is more like exorcism.

After a particularly messy divorce, you may want to completely cleanse your home of any reminder of that former member of your household. This can include items of clothing, photographs, address books, and those little personal items like handkerchiefs, their BMW, the bed they slept in, and the wallpaper they defiled with their breath. Before proceeding, be sure to check your local fire ordinances. If your neighbors see you dancing naked around a bonfire on your lawn, hooting and laughing and casting incantations, I'm sure they'll understand.

For clearing negative energy from your home, burning sage will work wonders. Of course, it does smell suspiciously like marijuana and you might not want to push your luck with the neighbors.

Alternatively, you could try forming thoughts of positive intention while drumming. Wind chimes and finger cymbals clear the air with their celestial resonance. And if that doesn't cut it, try a couple of gallons of pure ammonia and a power washer.

When To Call it Quits

Let's be honest about this: Housekeeping is no fun. Cleaning is most enjoyable if somebody else does it. If you can get away with it, get your mother to clean for you, or your friend, or pay a maid, or let a couple of especially fluffy sheep dogs chase each other around your floor for a while.

Okay, clean your house, but get a life. The idea is to feel good about the place you live. A messy house will not let you rest. But an immaculate house won't either. So set yourself a time limit and clean your little heart out. And when your time's up, stop. Then turn out all the lights, open the curtains, and let the Moon shine in. Now, doesn't that look good!

About the Author

Daniel B. Brawner is an award-winning humor columnist and the author of a New Age mystery novel, *Employment Is Murder*. He lives in Iowa.

Inspire and Motivate Yourself

by Stephanie Clement, Ph.D.

Alll too often we look outside ourselves to find motivation for our activities. This is especially true for extroverts, who spend much of their mental and emotional energy out in the world. (Even the most introverted personality gets out there some of the time.) If you're like most people, you tend to wait for inspiration to come to you, instead of finding it within yourself.

In this article I have focused on understanding your own internal process to discover self-motivational techniques. Sometimes you have to be the one to start something new. You need to come up with the way to make things happen in your career, your social life, and within your family. Moon signs offer ways to make this happen.

The Moon represents our internal functions and how it affects us in every area of our lives. When we consider the Moon's placement in our charts, we delve into the less conscious areas of life. For example, the Moon is associated with physical digestion, fertility, and body fluids; and with subconscious thought, emotions, and core beliefs.

Those subconscious lunar thoughts can coalesce around ideas and ideals to show us our direction. When that happens, the Moon can be a source of profound motivation and inspiration. The Moon sign in the birth chart indicates your natural motivational direction. This means that you can most easily motivate yourself, or others can motivate you, through the sign of your Moon.

The sign opposite your own Moon can also provide motivation, so be sure to read about that sign, too. Opposite signs provide insight about how you project your inner sensitivity into the world. The opposite sign also indicates something about the people and things out in the world that get your attention and hold it. We are most easily motivated when we have a clear perception of who is asking and what they want. This is just as true for the inner voice coming from within you—if you can hear it clearly, you can respond effectively.

A third way to use the Moon for motivation is to check out its sign each day and read about that sign. This works because the Moon's location in the zodiac each day reveals the current energy around you. If you are an introvert, this method may work well because it takes you outside yourself to engage with the world. Extroverts will like this method because the Moon is so obvious and easy to connect with.

Self-Motivation

Be sure to read the opposite sign to get both sides of your personal motivational story.

Moon Signs and their Opposite Sign

♈	Aries	♎	Libra
♉	Taurus	♏	Scorpio
♊	Gemini	♐	Sagittarius
♋	Cancer	♑	Capricorn
♌	Leo	♒	Aquarius
♍	Virgo	♓	Pisces

I begin the discussion of each sign by stating the most basic need of the sign. This is a good place to start because it indicates the most fundamental motivation within the individual. Once that need is grasped, then you can explore ways to motivate yourself successfully. You will also find simple ways to motivate others, if you know their Moon sign.

Motivation can lead you toward both constructive activity and less positive actions. When we feel pressured, we defend ourselves. Sometimes we fight back with destructive means. If you understand yourself better, you can develop positive responses and practice them when you are not under pressure. Sooner or later those responses become habits that kick in even when the pressure is on. You still retain the ability to respond less constructively, but you enhance your choices through constructive practice.

Moon Signs

Aries: Need to be "Numero Uno"

What sort of Number One do you want to be? Do you want to come out on top no matter what? Would you like for others to be happy when you win? Would you like your coworkers and friends to accompany you into win/win situations? Does anyone really have to lose for you to still be Numero Uno? (Hint: I believe the answers to these questions are as follows: great, probably, yes, definitely, and no.)

So how do you take that urge to be Number One and turn it into a self-motivational tool that works for you? You define what it means to be first as concisely and completely as possible. Here are some ideas:

- Always a winner: You can do this by making an effort to help others to be winners. Then you find yourself among winners, which is a good place for you to be.

- Best friend: Treat all your friends as well as you want to be treated.

- Best partner: Go way beyond halfway with your partner in every way.
- Best at planning: Show that you know where you are headed and how to get there safely and successfully.
- Best at encouraging others: Spread your natural enthusiasm around! (This one should become very easy for you to do.)
- Best parent: Care for your children each day. Treat them like the precious jewels they are. Listen to their conversational gems intently.

For each of these areas, the definition of "best" varies, which means that skillful action in each area is different. The physical actions that help you win the kung fu competition may not be useful in motivating your children as you will not want to beat them up. The underlying mental and emotional strengths that the martial art teaches you will be valuable in every area I have listed.

By redefining what being Number One means in terms of the situation, you give yourself a wide range of motivational possibilities. All you really need to do is add on a word or two to your thought: I want to be the Number One ____ (fill in the blank). Then seek ways to make that become reality.

Taurus: Need to Maintain Security

Do you occasionally find yourself doing something really strange just to avoid a problem or a person you don't want to face? Sure there's a problem, but not really all that big a difficulty. Yet you go way out of your way to skirt the issues before you. This may be because you are using a tried-and-true method that you developed in the past for dealing with problems that made you feel insecure.

When security is your most basic need, how can you use that to motivate yourself? First, it's important to recognize that being secure is a good thing. Without security we would not put down roots. Our families could never be comfortable. And without a secure base we would never be willing to take a risk! We would be too busy trying to shore up whatever situation arises, moment to moment.

You can use your security needs as a basis for self-motivation. All you need is to reframe what security means to you at this stage of your life. For children, security needs are defined in terms of food, clothing, and a safe home. They need car seats, suitable clothing for weather conditions, and protection from physical and emotional harm. Teens might define security as belonging to the peer group, managing school and extracurricular activities well, and finding that first love. Adults will have yet another set of definitions. Here are a few frames for your definition of security:

- A "good" job: You might have to take a risk and apply for a different position to get a better job.

- Adequate income: You have to define "adequate" for you and stop accepting someone else's idea of what enough is.

- Committed romantic relationship: You seek someone who fulfills your unique ideal of a partner, not necessarily what your parents or friends want for you.

- Intellectual stimulation: Something to keep you thinking is important because when the insecure times arrive—and they do—you fare better if you have sharpened your cognitive skills. That way you don't have to fall back on emotionally charged childhood security strategies.

- Plans for the future: Retirement may be a long way off. However, planning for your own future and for your family's future is a good thing. You don't have to have a ton of money in the bank right now, for example, but you will want to have a plan for how you will provide for yourself and your family five, ten, or twenty years from now. Then you want to make steady progress toward those goals.

Gemini: Need to be Clever and Informed

The need to be informed is pretty much universal. For you, however, it is the central mission. You always want to know everything that is going on with everyone. What if it's none of your business? Your emotional drive may cause you to interfere with other people's privacy because you simply must know. The need to be clever is connected to the need for information. After all, how can you make the best jokes if you don't have the complete story? The new frame you need to expand your repertoire of clever behavior may include the following:

- Listen: The cleverest people at a party are the ones who get other people talking. First of all, they acquire more information that way. Pretty obvious. In addition, they seem very clever when they respond to what has been said, instead of inserting witty comments that have little to do with the topic of conversation.

- Offer suggestions: Not everyone will want to do things just the way you do. Knowing when to make a suggestion is half the picture. Knowing how is the other half. You will seem a lot more clever if you make suggestions in a way that each person can understand and implement.

- Be truthful: This doesn't mean being blunt or rude. It means telling it like it is, not like you want it to be. It includes acknowledging the facts, the emotions that accompany them, and even the spiritual basis for your own decisions.

- Demonstrate compassion: We often feel angry or sad or glad for another person. It's important for you to sort out your own mad/sad/glad from what the other person may be experiencing. Then you can truly feel compassion for that individual.

- Experience the moment: Sometimes glad just isn't the appropriate feeling. We need to be able to feel sad or mad, and we need to help others to feel these emotions when appropriate. We also can help ourselves and others over rough spots by recognizing the feelings and determining choices for how to deal with them.

Cancer: Need for Emotional Security

Emotional security is one step up from the security mentioned for Taurus Moons. If you are entangled in providing the most basic security, then you really don't have the time or energy to figure out your feelings. When the basic needs are satisfied, then emotional security needs become clearer.

For young children, the parents are the most influential sources of emotional security. Consistency is a huge component of security in a child's life. Teens go through massive physical and emotional changes, and they need support from parents, teachers, and other authority figures as they learn to manage emotional needs. Adults are not immune to emotional challenges either. They need to use adult methods to achieve adult emotional goals. Childhood methods for finding emotional security were fine in childhood but may not work well now.

Here are some suggestions for additional choices when you seek to motivate yourself, based on your need for emotional security:

- Picture safe places: Identify settings (locations) in which you generally experience emotional well-being. Spend a few minutes each day picturing yourself in these safe places.

- Identify unsafe settings: Spend some time thinking about them. Don't get into your feelings. Just think about what in these situations makes you feel uncomfortable.

- Develop a "safe" mentality: Devise scenarios for times when you are in the uncomfortable place. Imagine that feeling "morphing" into a feeling of emotional security and safety. Practice this morphing mentality.

You will find that this mental practice makes it easier for you to modify circumstances so they feel more secure. You will identify the one or two things that, if changed, would make the situation feel better. You also learn to identify factors early in the game that are simply not acceptable to you. In this way you exit untenable situations quickly and skillfully, thereby boosting your feelings of emotional security. The motivation is greater security, and the method is to imagine (think without engaging emotion) what needs to happen to make the situation safer.

Leo: Need to be Respected and Loved

You will say that everyone needs to be respected and loved. However, you probably know plenty of people who override this need with some other more pressing need. For example, Gemini Moons need to have all the information. This need could easily get in the way of love and respect, particularly if the Gemini Moon person betrays confidences. The Leo Moon person requires love and respect in order to feel adequate.

The strategies for earning love and respect of parents and teachers are vastly different from those required in romantic or business partnerships. As a child you may have learned to curb your own desires in order to receive positive emotional strokes. In extreme cases this strategy could lead you to commit illegal acts in order to feel you belong.

How can you satisfy the need for love and respect better? How can you use this need for self-motivation? Here are some ideas:

- Honesty: Encourage others to pursue their passions, just as you hope to be encouraged in your own. Don't suck up. Just be honest. Honesty is a central factor in all your relationships.

- Intuition: Work to develop your intuition. It can be your best ally in figuring out complex situations with other people. But don't just blurt out your intuition. Research it a little bit to test its validity. People will love the demonstration of sensitivity; you actually spent the time to help them.

- Luxury: On another tack completely, you like nice things. You surround yourself with quality to gain the respect of others. People will not love you for this. However, they will love how generous you are with your time and energy. You don't have to give away the store to gain respect and love. In fact, people will respect you more if you are moderate and sensible.

- Ambition: In leadership positions you work best with others when you recognize their ambitions. Cultivate the attitude that if your coworkers and employees are successful, you are more successful. They will love you when you toot their horns for them.

Virgo: Need to be Correct and Insightful

The need to be accurate and the need to be insightful can be at odds with each other. You will find that you tend to one or the other, but you don't have to sacrifice one for the other. Instead you can use the two tendencies as motivational factors in your life.

I like to think of being insightful as a process similar to the creative act of writing. Paying attention to details is similar to the

act of editing. When I write, I let the creative part take over, and give the editor a rest—or even a vacation! The words don't have to be perfect, they just need to be on the paper (or on the hard drive of my computer). I will have time later to reread and revise. When I am editing, I make sure the creative part is on vacation. That part doesn't have to sit around and observe the editing process.

You may feel the division of work I am describing is a bit artificial. You may not be comfortable thinking about having different parts. However, we all play different roles in life, and the precisely accurate role is different from the insightful one. These two roles are different, but you can master them both. Here are some suggestions for how to do that:

- Be practical: You may find that you ignore some of the details in favor of achieving necessary movement. There will be time enough later to tie up the loose ends.

- Imagine the outcome: When you begin any project, no matter how tedious, try to imagine the future results. If you see that what you are doing just won't matter much in the end, you can reduce the amount of energy put into today's activities.

- Exercise good manners: You don't have to become Miss Manners, the excruciatingly correct matron of social grace. If you understand social rules, you will know when they can be broken. For example, if you really want to serve fried chicken, provide extra napkins for each guest and show them you are not afraid to use your fingers.

Libra: Need to be Appreciated and Popular

Libra, like Virgo, has two needs that can be incompatible. Often we want to be appreciated for the work we do, but we don't really care about being popular. We just want to get the job done well, and we want to be compensated appropriately. Money is often the goal, not popularity.

On the other hand, popularity is our goal sometimes, and price is no object. We are willing to put in the time, energy, and cash to achieve the goal. Elected office has some of these characteristics. The problem with getting elected to a position is that we then have to perform—we have to get the job done. What gains us appreciation may not be what made us popular in the first place. Here are some ways to motivate yourself to balance popularity with appreciation in your life:

- Express your feelings: It's fairer to others that you tell them how you feel instead of hiding your feelings and developing resentments.

- Do things for others: It's really fun to do things for other people just because you can. You don't expect anything back, really. Yes, you need to be appreciated. But you don't need to be paid in cash, and you don't necessarily expect the favor to be returned. In fact, you even say, "I know you will do something nice for someone else."

- Be a true partner: You don't have to depend on your partner for every little thing. The two of you support each other but need not lean on each other until you become co-dependent. Instead, you encourage one another and help each other in a pinch. You are each other's biggest fans.

Scorpio: Need to be in Control, Significant, and Right

Scorpio is another sign with conflicting needs. If you need to be in control, you may be willing to sacrifice being right. Sometimes we get out of control when we are arguing a point that really matters to us. I feel that the urge to do something significant can be the motivation to balance out the other two. It's mostly a matter of how you define these three needs.

Sometimes we maintain control over a difficult situation by compromising. We don't give in completely, as that would feel out of control. Instead, like balancing the hot and cold water when we take a shower, we balance a sense of adequate control with a feeling that what we are doing is right or proper. Out of that balanced position comes the likelihood that we can achieve results, and that sometimes those results will be significant for us and for others. I have learned to measure my results in smaller units. That way I feel a sense of accomplishment as I am going along, not just when a big project is complete.

- Be tough when it matters: You can be hard as nails when you need to be, but you don't need to be that all the time. If you are tough, you can save it for the clinches.

- Stand up for what is right when it matters: You don't have to win every argument. Save up being right for moments when you really care. That way you don't exhaust yourself with petty issues.

- Maintain control when it matters: You can let your friends or your children choose their own flavor of ice cream. In addition, you can practice good self-control. If you are not in control of yourself, it's tough to control others, and it's even tougher to be right.

Remember that tough people do cry, and to cry is not to lose control. To show your feelings is to show that you are human. The bottom line here is self-control, not utter control.

Sagittarius: Need to Have Opinions Respected

In order for your opinions to be respected, they need to have substance. This means that you can motivate yourself by seeking the kinds of information sources that hold up to your standards of accuracy and excitement.

- Respect yourself: Think through new ideas and goals. Be sure they suit your internal sense of balance and value before you begin. It's easier to decide now to go forward or to stop. Later, when things are already in motion, you won't want to change your mind and look bad in front of others.

- Understand your own changeable moods: Just because your mood changes doesn't mean you have to give up respect. If you understand yourself, you are more than halfway to gaining understanding from others.
- Recognize your ideals: To paint a clear picture of how to achieve them, and then to strive for them even when others are not very supportive, you must first recognize them. If it's important enough to you to do something, it's important to do it well. Then your self-respect is mirrored in the admiration you receive from others.
- Gain understanding on the philosophical level: Just knowing the nuts and bolts will never be enough to satisfy you.

Capricorn: Need to Make Progress

You are like the wrangler trying to keep his cattle moving in the right direction and in a group. You have lots of goals, and the same twenty-four-hour day allotted to you as the rest of us do. You have to have a definite plan if you are to continue to make progress in every area.

- Acknowledge feelings: You do have feelings underneath your tough exterior, and you may not want other people to be aware of them, but those feelings are part of your progress measurement equipment. Dark moods lighten as you recognize change in your life.
- Be responsible for self first: Examine your sense of duty to see if it includes anything extra, like your parents' idea of what you should be: By being responsible to yourself and for yourself first, you become a better friend, parent, or partner.
- Take daily personal inventory: Even if you only spend five minutes on it, assess your progress in small increments, and you will identify progress even when things are moving very

slowly. Such an assessment actually feeds your desire for progress while chalking up those small successes. You may want to have a rather detailed list of things to do so that you can check off items every day.

Aquarius: Need to be Socially Significant or Unusual

You have so many ideas and seemingly so little time. You want everything you do to matter to the world, not just to yourself or a small group of acquaintances. You also like to stand out in a crowd, and it's important to stand out for positive reasons.

- Think things through: You can become known for your clarity. People will appreciate the fact that you know what the score is throughout the game.
- Practice understanding human nature: The Mother Theresas of the world are known for their good works, but they also have strong ideas about how to achieve them. They are not wishy-washy personalities, that's for sure. They understand how to motivate others because they have been motivating themselves for so long.
- Practice compassion: If you lack compassion for others, you have not hit the highest mark. Use your thinking ability to figure out the most compassionate response that will work in a given situation.

You love change and independence. These strong desires can become part of your desire for significance when you are able to take an unusual approach to solve an ordinary problem. Sometimes your simple willingness to help will be a powerful force in another person's life.

Pisces: Need to Identify the Ideal, to Understand Psychic Impressions

You seek to understand life on a deeper level than many people. You want to know the inner meaning of everything around you. To do this you have to reach out, and when you reach out, you are sometimes overwhelmed by the emotions you encounter. Learning to sort through the psychic input is essential to your ability to remain motivated to seek the ideal. Without this capacity you feel you have to retreat to the safety of solitude. What to do?

- Recognize your own moods and seek an ideal level. You don't have to maintain it all the time, but it helps to know where it is. Then you can return to it quickly and easily.

- Meditation to focus your thoughts: Idealized thoughts and feelings can become too wishful and not based enough on concrete actions. Meditation allows you to identify those ideals that continue to come up in your life.

- Uncover internal resistance: As you meditate, you begin to feel the pull of different feelings. You learn that certain tugs, if resisted even for a moment, lose their attraction, while others become stronger over time. Pay attention to how this feels within your own body.

- Stay in the flow: Allow yourself to drift, seeking the current that pulls you strongly. Your psychic impressions improve as you experiment with following feelings or resisting them.

- Seek your own ideal: Manage your own life and let other people manage their own lives. When you see the ideal in everything, you find that your actions bring greater contentment.

Summary

The concept of self-motivation with the Moon depends on the fact that the easiest way to motive people is to appeal to their most compelling needs. This is true when you want to motivate yourself, too. If you understand what your need or drive is, then you can work toward it consciously, framing all your actions on terms of fulfilling that need, while at the same time helping other people to fulfill theirs.

About the Author

Stephanie Clement, Ph.D. (Colorado) is a professional astrologer certified by the American Federation of Astrologers (AFA). She has been practicing astrology for over thirty years. A board member of the AFA, and member of NCGR, she has served on the faculty of Kepler College and been a speaker at regional conferences. Stephanie has written several books: *Charting Your Spiritual Path with Astrology*, *Power of the Midheaven*, *Mapping Your Birthchart*, and *Mapping Your Family Relationships*.

Choosing Wedding Dates
with Astrology

by April Elliott Kent

Hey, diddle, diddle, the cat and the fiddle, the cow jumped over the Moon.
The little dog laughed to see such sport, and the dish ran away with the spoon.

—Mother Goose

When I returned to school three years ago, I took a sabbatical from astrological counseling, figuring life as a forty-something undergraduate would be demanding enough without the added emotional pressure of advising others about their lives. Gradually, though, I drifted into electional astrology—choosing times for events, usually weddings, based on astrological principles—to pay my tuition. It's satisfying work that suits the Virgo/analytical side of my nature perfectly, an almost purely intellectual exercise as logical and comforting as a crossword puzzle.

Despite my accidental astrological specialty, however, I didn't choose the date of my brother's recent wedding. Rather, the happy couple based their decision purely on practical considerations, the way 99.99 percent of the population chooses wedding dates (albeit with only a 50 percent success rate). And that suited me fine; for although I've found an astrological niche for myself choosing wedding dates for clients, I often worry that in plying this ancient art I may be messing around in matters that would work out just as well, perhaps better, without my interference.

I'm reminded of a bride who, after years in a tortuous relationship, asked me to choose the date for her wedding. I was reluctant, having seen and heard enough about the relationship over the years to doubt that astrology could do much to help this marriage succeed, but I did my best. Finding an astrologically acceptable day and time within the time frame they were willing to consider was difficult, and convincing them to use the time I chose was nearly impossible. But marry they did, at the appointed hour, and managed to stay together several more years, causing each other considerable misery before ultimately divorcing.

I later wondered if the relative harmony of the wedding chart had acted as a kind of cosmic superglue, holding the tenuous union together beyond its natural expiration date. Maybe, had they chosen one of the other astrologically ruinous days they were considering, the whole mess would have been over with a lot more quickly! In cases like this one, good astrology may be employed to ill effect; after all, as any child who has eaten too much candy can tell you, getting what we want is not always what's best for us.

Perhaps, if left to our own devices, we instinctively gravitate to the moments that are right for us to do things—marry, start a business, plant a rose bush—whether or not our efforts lead to the outcome we'd hoped for. In fact, I suspect that using astrology in an attempt to influence the outcome of our actions may be self-defeating. The very human desire to outwit fate may, in fact, deny us our right course of action and neutralize astrology's power to show us both our own motivations and the mysterious workings of spirit.

So maybe my brother and his bride, like the dish and the spoon in the old Mother Goose rhyme, had the right idea: to begin the mad gamble of togetherness by simply running away together, without first asking the astrologer if the time was right!

A Time to Every Purpose

That said, doesn't it stand to reason that if there is indeed "a time to every purpose under heaven," it would make sense to align ourselves and our actions with this purpose? After all, if astrology isn't good for this, what is it good for? I propose that electing wedding dates with astrology be approached as a ritual to bring individual will into alignment with universal wisdom. Employed in this spirit, the electional process can actually yield a better understanding of the forces that significantly impact our lives and decisions.

So the question before us is, once deciding to petition the gods for their blessing on your union, which astrological factors should you look to for verification that you're on the right path or warning that you're on the wrong one? As with all types of predictive astrology, there are numerous rules to follow. Here are just a few important ones to get you started.

Begin with Venus

Venus is the planet most closely associated with weddings and marriage. A wedding chart should feature a strong and happy Venus, as little debilitated by sign, aspect, or retrograde motion as possible. Venus is strongest and happiest in Taurus, Libra, or

Pisces (the signs of her rulership and exaltation), involved in only harmonious aspects with other planets, and placed in an angular house (the first, fourth, seventh, or tenth).

In real life, of course, this dream scenario is rarely achievable, because the ceremony must take place on a Saturday in June when Aunt Ruth is visiting from Portland, when Venus is retrograde in Scorpio and squaring Pluto. So I occasionally find myself recommending dates when Venus is in Aries, Virgo, or Scorpio (the signs of her detriment and fall, where she is least strong). I'll even bend the rules and allow Venus in difficult aspect to Saturn or Pluto if factors in the wedding couple's birth charts support this (such as strong connections at birth between Venus and Saturn or Capricorn, or Venus and Pluto or Scorpio).

On one point, however, I am intractable: Thou shalt not wed when Venus is retrograde. Retrograde periods (represented in an ephemeris by the symbol ℞), when a planet appears to be moving backward in the sky, are times to reflect upon the matters represented by the planet, not to initiate action. Of Venus retrograde, Erin Sullivan writes, "flaws and faults in others can become enhanced, and one might see all the dangers of intimacy, rather than the supportive aspects of it." Hardly sounds like an auspicious moment to begin a marriage!

If you find yourself planning your wedding for a time when Venus is retrograde, heed the wisdom of the retrograde, which urges you to take a second look at your reasons for choosing to marry this person, at this time, and in this way. Venus is retrograde for only forty days every eighteen months; you can almost always wait for it to turn direct.

Mercury

As the planetary ruler of contracts (of which marriage is one example), paperwork, and logistics, Mercury is legendarily problematic when retrograde; items are misplaced, miscommunication is rife, decisions are made based on inadequate information. The message of Mercury retrograde is "redo," "rethink," and even "reconsider"—as entertainers Ben Affleck and Jennifer Lopez apparently did when they postponed their September 2003 wedding during Mercury retrograde!

Mercury is retrograde more often than Venus (about three weeks, four times a year) but it is nonetheless usually possible to avoid scheduling your wedding during these times. Occasionally, though, you're stuck with Mercury retrograde, and in the not uncommon event the bride or groom has been married before the "redoing" symbolism of Mercury retrograde can even be appropriate.

Still, Mercury retrograde has its reputation as a nuisance for a reason, as my brother and his bride found out on their Mercury retrograde wedding day. The wedding was my brother's second—so far, so good. But, despite a very organized bride's best efforts, the wedding was a cornucopia of Mercury retrograde headaches: traffic jams, keys locked in a car, miscued music, a decorative arch that nearly fell on the bride, bad directions, problems with the bridal couple's reservation at the luxury hotel they'd booked for their wedding night—on and on it went. It was a textbook illustration of a vital principle: Weddings are stressful enough without inviting Mercury retrograde to the party!

The Moon

The Moon, ruler of mundane matters and daily routines, looms large in the symbolism of electional astrology. Its position by sign, house, and aspect are seen as a microcosm of how any action initiated under its influence will unfold and ultimately be resolved. In fact, lunar placements that would be perfectly admirable in a birth chart are sometimes considered unacceptable for the purposes of electional astrology. For instance, marrying with the Moon in Scorpio or Capricorn, the signs of its detriment and fall, is to be strenuously avoided. Likewise, a void-of-course Moon (a Moon making no further aspects to other planets before leaving its sign), or the Moon applying to difficult aspects with other planets, is considered tantamount to astrological suicide.

Over the years, though, I've seen enough exceptions to begin to question these rules. Recently I've chosen several wedding dates featuring the Moon in Scorpio or Capricorn, simply because the Moon in those signs harmonized beautifully with other planetary placements on the date. For similar reasons, although traditional rules recommend marrying during the Moon's waxing phases (between the New and Full Moons), this is not always practical, nor in my observation especially important, falling more in the category of "nice if you can get it."

On the other hand, harmony between the Sun and Moon, representing the relationship both between the bride and groom and between the wedding couple and the world at large, is vital. If given a choice between a date with the Moon in Taurus in difficult aspect to the Sun and Uranus, or one with the Moon in Scorpio in good aspect to the Sun, Venus, Mars, and Jupiter, I know which I'd choose! And while I can't always avoid every difficult aspect between the Moon and other planets, I do try to make sure the Moon's last aspect before leaving its sign is a harmonious one (a sextile, trine, or conjunction with Venus or Jupiter). I was taught that the Moon's last aspect in the sign describes the way everything, great or small, will tend to "end up" for the couple. By ensuring that the Moon's last aspect is a happy one, I am hoping the couple will be left feeling that whatever comes their way, "for us, everything seems to always work out okay in the end."

My brother's disastrous Mercury retrograde wedding took place with the Moon in Capricorn, but approaching harmonious aspects to the Sun, Venus, and finally Mercury before leaving its sign. He and his bride accepted the logistical mishaps of their big day with characteristic Capricorn pragmatism. They laughed off the problems, enjoyed their wedding, and radiated love for each other, and their attitudes transformed a feast of problems into a fun and memorable occasion.

Is There a "Right" Day?

Which is more important to your future happiness: a favorable wedding chart, or holding your wedding ceremony when sweet Aunt Ruth can be there to share it with you? Common sense tells us that the best wedding chart in the world will cause more problems than it will solve if you've got to turn your entire life upside down to make it fit! Every wedding chart, like every marriage, has its tough spots, so don't drive yourself (and everybody you know) crazy holding out for a perfect wedding date; it doesn't exist. Work with what you have, and learn what you can from the messages astrology is giving you about the date you've chosen, but understand that much, much more goes into creating a happy marriage than just the wedding date. A strong and happy relationship simply can't be ruined by a wedding chart, even one that breaks every astrological rule in the book!

Conversely, it is a mysterious truth that trying to squeeze an unhappy relationship into a happy marriage chart is nearly always doomed to failure. It is relatively easy to find a good wedding date for a happy, relaxed couple, and almost impossible to do the same for a stressed-out, uncertain couple. Even if I am able to present such a couple with an astrologically fabulous date, something will almost always prevent the marriage from taking place at this favorable moment. Their preferred venue will be unavailable, for instance, or one of them will have an aversion to marrying on a Sunday. So they gradually, unconsciously, negotiate their way back to the date and time that perfectly reveals the most important issues they must face together, then ask for my astrological blessing. Stubbornness? I prefer to think the influence at work is that of the wise Moon, perfect as she is in any sign or aspect, guiding this couple as she has so many others to the starting gate that's exactly right for them—however forbidding it might look to us!

We can approach astrology forcefully and inorganically, as a way of bending life to some abstract ideal. Or we can approach it with the wisdom of the Moon, and the dish and the spoon, respecting its mystery and acknowledging our limited understanding. We can use it to analyze the moments to which we are spontaneously drawn—just as we spontaneously gravitated toward the moment of birth, with all its potential for pain and glory—to see what secrets those moments can reveal to us. And we can use the traditional rules of electional astrology as we might use candles or any other ritual device, not as an inoculation against life but as an invocation to align ourselves with a greater wisdom. And that's not such a bad use for astrology.

Bibliography

Sullivan, Erin. *Retrograde Planets: Traversing the Inner Landscape*. York Beach: Samuel Weiser, Inc., 2000.

March, Marion D., and Joan McEvers. *The Only Way to Learn About Horary and Electional Astrology*. San Diego: ACS Publications, 1994.

About the Author.

April Elliott Kent, a professional astrologer since 1990, is a member of NCGR and ISAR. She has written about the astrology of marriage and the practice of prediction for the *Mountain Astrologer* (USA) and *Wholistic Astrologer* (Australia) magazines and for the online magazine *MoonCircles*. She specializes in the astrology of choosing wedding dates and the study of eclipses, and has authored a self-published report called "Followed by a Moonshadow," based on her work with eclipse cycles. Her Web site is: http://www.bigskyastrology.com.

Moon as Mapmaker: Explore Your Inner World Without Fear

by Lisa Finander

This article explores the process/struggle of moving beyond your mind/ego to discover and enlist the guidance of your inner resources. "Moon as Mapmaker" is the journey/process of exploring your inner landscape by finding your own way and finding your own answers to the questions of: How do you take that first step away from what you have known toward what you want but is still unknown? How do you leave the safety of your everyday life for chaos and nothing to replace it? How can you keep yourself from getting lost in a hopeless spiral of fear? How can you find answers to a life purpose that has yet to be defined? My hope is that at the end of this process, you will realize you are so much more than your conscious mind. Your inner self contains allies, wisdom, vulnerabilities, and talents. Your quest is to go inside and find them.

Learning to navigate your lunar terrain is a choice. The Moon in astrology represents unconscious habits, behaviors, and associations. It describes our dependencies, insecurities, and early experiences. It ascribes emotional responses and values to the experiences of our life through its own unique lens. This emotional lens, created in early childhood, affects how we view the circumstances of our life and how we attach personal significance to them. If we do not explore the contents within this lens, we will continue to view the world as we did when we were children. The challenge of discovering our intrinsic expression of the Moon is to gain emotional maturity and wisdom while preserving the wonder and curiosity of the child. It is my hope that the experiences you gain will expand your sense of self and your possibilities, no matter what house or sign your Moon is in, and no matter how badly afflicted you believe you natal Moon sign to be.

I use the term "map making" in this article to describe the method of creating a visual and intellectual diagram or image of the information gathered from your emotional self. Your emotional self primarily communicates and stores information through symbols so it is important for you to find a comfortable way to record them. Once they are recorded, you can begin to unravel the connection between your thoughts and feelings.

So Let's Begin

Just as light casts a shadow, I believe our conscious dreams, goals, and desires also cast their own shadows. I call them our "shadow dreams." Shadow dreams are the unconscious habits, beliefs, desires, and behaviors we have in relation to our preferred outcome. They are important because they hold energy and operate side by side with our conscious goals. When our dreams are in sync with what we consciously want, we don't notice their existence, but when they are out of alignment, things don't always go as planned. We can feel literally split in two by "thinking" we should want or do something and "feeling" otherwise. Sometimes this split in consciousness creates a pleasant surprise, a chance encounter that changes the focus of our lives and opens us up to new opportunities we previously could not imagine. Other times however, this split is experienced as a sense of loss, leaving us with the feeling we are alienated from our dreams while years of life go by. If you have done your affirmations, written out your goal, and tried to make it happen physically and/or intellectually, but nothing seems to be manifesting, there is a good chance you have a shadow dream operating in another direction. Maybe you have held on to your dream but are afraid or unsure what to do with it, or maybe you do not know what you want, and only that you are dissatisfied with where you are. Either way, displeasure absorbs energy and creates disparaging thoughts that further affect your ability to move in another direction or to move at all. Again, turning inward and looking at the desires of our shadow dream will give us clues.

We live in a culture that can over simplify the process of self-actualization by connecting success to material possessions. Think of all the images we are bombarded with every day in television, movies, music, magazines, and advertising. Our emotional selves absorb these images because images are the language of the emotions. Even if our conscious minds dispel these images as false, we are still affected by them unconsciously. Our shadow dreams contain these artificially created ideals and our presumptions of how we measure up to them.

It started in childhood, when we were influenced by the fairy tales and stories we were told. Our responses to them offer some clues as to what we believe is possible for us in our lives and what we must do to obtain it. In American stories, customarily, a treasure (possessions) is won by the hero/heroine at the end of the story. The wicked are typically punished and/or killed, while the wholesome characters live happily ever after. The story ends at the time the prince and princess characters reach adulthood. They have peaked, no more problems, no more strife. The villains are often old (past eighteen), and not beautiful (other than blonde, fair skinned, and thin) people. Obviously the villains did not get the happily ever after enchantment that the prince and princess did.

Imagine how different our personal stories would be if the characters and media images looked like us and lived in houses like us. In fairy tales, the princess cries until somebody saves her, and the prince obtains victory through persistence and mastery of the emotional world. These are overused models for actualizing our dreams in the world. More importantly, what if you are not our culture's stereotypical prince- or princess-type and/or you have grown beyond past the age and desires of an eighteen-year-old?

Part of the search in discovering who we are and what we want requires us to follow our own path, a path that does not exist in the world yet or at least in its entirety. Consider your life today. What experiences brought you here? All of your experiences are linked together like an intricate maze of stepping stones, some planned, some unplanned. Each destination spurs another journey. When you cannot see the next step and/or do not like the direction your life is going, discovering the contents of your shadow dream is valuable.

Before you can gain access to the contents of your shadow dream, you first need to empty your mind of your conscious desires. Begin by describing in detail what you want to manifest in your life consciously. What are its qualities? How will you recognize it? What will your life be like when you acquire it? When do you want these changes to happen? What do you consciously believe are your obstacles in obtaining it? Do the best you can.

Once you have a pretty good representation of what you consciously want, put it aside, and do not focus on it again until you have finished the next step.

Now it is time to focus on your inner self. This process of unearthing the shadow dream is the domain of the Moon. Information does not surface in an efficient, orderly manner. Remember that you will be collecting irrational, creative, nonlinear, symbolic information. Do not judge, edit, or control the content. Even though you may not understand how they relate to what you want, give yourself freedom to follow the threads. Just meander and enjoy the process of not having to rationalize anything. Here are just a few suggestions of exercises you can try to retrieve information regarding your shadow dream.

- You can create a shadow dream collage by gathering images and phrases you are drawn to intuitively. Then place the collage in an area where it can be viewed frequently and record your impressions.

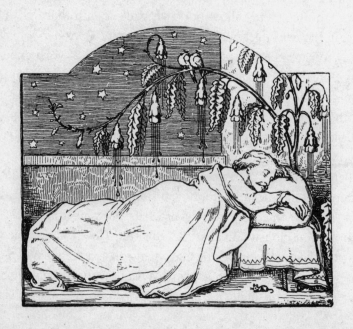

- You can use intuitive tools such as tarot cards, I Ching, etc., and design your own readings that focus on the composition of your shadow dream.
- You can spend time concentrating on your nightly dreams and see what emerges.
- You can create something to represent your shadow dream by either using a skill you already have or learning a new one.
- You can write in a journal, following whatever stream of consciousness appears.

The tools you use are not important, but the atmosphere you use them in is. Pick an activity or process where your conscious mind is not in total control. Do not try to rush the process. Give yourself days/weeks to produce something tangible. Find some time to be alone and tranquil each time you start the process. Begin the process of communicating with your inner self by creating a ritual that can be repeated each time you work on your shadow dream such as; making a special beverage, lighting a candle, holding a special object, invoking guidance, meditating, and/or choosing a special time of day. Once you have generated this information, record any insights. What was your attitude when engaging in this process? Did you look forward to it? Put it off? Note how you felt. Were you: Angry? Resentful? Relaxed? Joyful? Exhausted? Why do you think so? Do you believe the messages of your shadow dream? Are these "truths" still valid?

After completing both steps, compare the two. Which process was easier and most enjoyable? Why? Is one more appealing than the other? Where do your conscious beliefs connect to hidden, unconscious assumptions? Do they support one another positively or negatively? What ideas hold the most energy for you? What thoughts and feelings are connected in such a way that makes it difficult for you to achieve your goal? Which ones make it easier to achieve your goal? Can you reconstruct negative associations between thoughts and feelings into constructive ones? What patterns emerge? What is the intent of each? Can you see the next step in your process? What will help you move forward, backward? Have your desires changed? How? What image best represents your inner self at this time? What about your outer self? Assemble these random parts of information and arrange them on a piece of paper as though you where making a map of where to go from here. Note which items are from your conscious self and which ones from your unconscious self. Did you receive more conscious or unconscious information? What information did you chose to leave off your map? Does your map remind you of or look like anything? What surprised you? Has your sense of self changed? How? Where can you free up some energy to pursuit your dreams?

Here is a brief synopsis of how I experienced the process. You can use my example to clarify parts of the process that seem vague to you and to inspire your imagination. I began my process by focusing on what I wanted to create consciously in the world. I wrote about it as succinctly as I could, but it still seemed unclear to me. I could not picture it in my mind, so I looked for images that matched my goal to create a collage. Finding images was more difficult than I expected, because I could not find ones that accurately showed "me" living my dream. As I continued to collect images, powerful emotions began surfacing. Strong fears and worries raced through my mind as I scanned pictures of women much younger or older than me. Was it too late for me and my dreams? Would I have to wait forever? I decided to set the images I collected aside, since my shadow dream seemed to be calling.

To gain access to the contents of my shadow dream, I also gathered images, but I did so instinctively. I chose things that I was drawn to not worrying if they did not make sense logically. I recorded my dreams. I used tarot cards and other intuitive tools asking for guidance and illumination about what direction I should go. Sometimes I followed an emotion, started reading a book, researched an idea, created something, "did nothing," and recorded the process while observing it. I received a symbol of my lunar map. It looks like the type of sun you would draw in grade school. It is a circle with lines radiating from it. It is a representation of my process. If I choose to use only my mind, I follow only one ray and I do not discover much about myself or about the world. However, if I move organically in a circle around myself and explore all the rays, I can connect the points of the rays and create a bigger circle and bigger sense of self. That bigger circle starts the process over but from an expanded view of life both inside and outside.

Each day as you go about your life, can you stay open to new things, listen to hidden waters, make the "map" of yourself a little bigger by stretching the areas that instinctively want to contract? Some days the voyage is lucid and smooth, other days murky and bumpy. The trick is to learn to float effortlessly on all kinds of waters, observing. Letting things wash in and out and over you. Following the flow for no particular reason, no logical explanation, and moving in directions that appear to be off course. Later when you retrace the steps of your emotional map, you may or may not understand all the pieces of your journey, but you will have a bigger image of who you are. Instead of being a small ego struggling in a big, bad world, you expand your boundaries and give yourself the space and freedom to live in this world. Once people realize they are so much more then their waking consciousness, they experience the whole world differently. Will you make yourself available for the dream to find you?

Every year when I write an article about the Moon for Llewellyn's *Moon Sign Book*, I start on a journey that explores another aspect of the Moon. It is an exciting and fearful process for me. I start out with a loose frame of reference, sometimes only a title, and then submerge myself deeply into the image of the Moon so I can gather the pieces as they float by, waiting to see what unfolds. Usually ideas come quickly enough, and I start exploring. Then the fear sets in and my mind locks in on a certain outcome. The flow stops. I neglect or cannot see the signs that do not support my narrow reasoning. I have made the mistake of deciding too early on what these fragments will become. The battle between my mind and emotions has begun. The increasing fixation upon a predetermined goal increases my fear, and halts the manifestation of my desired outcome. It is difficult at this point to see that I have a choice. Will I allow myself to wander and wonder in this unknown territory or will I impatiently insist that the article follow a certain idea to completion?

About the Author

Lisa Finander is a freelance writer, teacher, and consultant who works with symbolism, including the symbolism of astrology, tarot, and dreams. In her work, Lisa uses symbols practically to bring richness, meaning, and creativity into the lives of others and herself. She loves working with and among nature. She receives much support and inspiration from her husband Brian along with their cats Toby, Jampers, and Yule.

Begin Your Diet and Health Regimen by the Moon

by J. Lee Lehman Ph.D.

For thousands of years, people have used Hippocrates' medical ideas to improve their life experiences. If we are to continue to benefit from his wisdom, and that of his successors like Galen, we have to understand certain precepts of the system. I will begin by outlining certain concepts essential to understanding traditional medical astrology, then I will present and explicate a wonderful technical piece by William Ramesey on how to administer medicines (this includes the timing for beginning a diet!), and finally, for those who are either uninterested in the technical part, or who want a quick reference, I outline all the days in 2005 appropriate to use from Ramesey's model.

Thus, we should probably state from the beginning that Hippocratic medicine as we may choose to incorporate it today can be used and understood as a system which works best for adults, and is strongest at providing us with lifestyle choices that enhance our experience of living.

Before we can discuss diets, we need to understand the humors. "Humors" is the word Hippocrates (born circa 460 BC) applied to the four primary "fluids" of the body: blood, yellow bile, black bile, and phlegm. Each of these four "fluids" is associated with a whole complex of ideas, as shown below.

The Four Humors and their Meaning

- Blood: hot and wet, sanguine temperament, Jupiter-type, the primary humor, enthusiastic, social, ruddy complexion, perspires profusely, tending toward overweight, especially when getting older.
- Yellow bile: hot and dry, choleric temperament, Mars-type, short fuse, bilious, overheated blood, but acts a blood thinner, leaner than sanguine.
- Phlegm: cold and wet, phlegmatic temperament, lunar or Venus-type, couch potato, slow moving, lethargic, keeps the joints and brain functional; produced from immature blood.
- Black bile: cold and dry, melancholic or scholar's temperament, Saturn-type, the sediment or impurities in blood, acrid, Galen (born AD 130) called it the ash of blood.

Health within this system consisted of a proper bodily balance, or eucrasia of fluids, both generally, and by organ. For example, the spleen was considered of the nature of black bile, so an abundance of phlegm in the spleen would be dysfunctional, just as an abundance of phlegm in the brain was considered appropriate.

Wellness consisted of a proper balance of humors; disease occurred when the balance was disrupted, either systemically, or in a particular organ. This disruption could either be as a result of too much of a humor, or too little. (This idea is actually very similar to the Chinese idea that there is both yin excess or yin deficiency; or yang excess or yang deficiency.) When an organ becomes either repleted or depleted of a humor, it aches. The onset of pain is the symptom that tells you that the organ is diseased.

It's worth mentioning that an emphasis on diet represented the upper tier of traditional medicine. As Pomata points out, medieval medicine had arrayed itself into three levels that were also somewhat correlated with social status: herbalism for the poor, barber-surgery for the yeomen and tradesmen, and diet and regimen for the wealthy. And Grant notes that this emphasis on diet and balance fit very well with the Stoicism that had developed under the Roman Empire, and which still held a certain influence over Christianity: controlling one's diet was not merely a marker for civilization and sophistication, it demonstrated one's ability to rise above mere animal desires.

In order for this system to work for you, you have to begin by knowing your own natural balance. You can either learn this experimentally, or you can either do or have an astrologer do the classical temperament calculation. Having determined your temperament, you can then get some ideas about what kinds of foods, drinks, and herbs can either help maintain your balance, or disrupt it.

A simple example: Not all people tolerate "hot" (as in spicy) foods the same way. Hot in this sense is actually hot and dry, as garlic, onions, cayenne, and ginger are all spices classified as hot and dry in the third degree. Degrees of quality are like degrees of burns, with the least extreme being first and the most extreme being third or fourth.

In the opinion of both Hippocrates and Galen, diet and regimen, which includes exercise, sleep, and general lifestyle issues like stress, are the major source of disease, at least apart from pestilence. The reason? Basically, people eat and drink too much, and they eat the wrong sorts of food, and they eat too many different kinds of food at the same time.

Let me try to explain this idea within the humors system, so that you can get to understanding the logic.

The ancients thought of the whole digestive system as a fire, and the acid that we all feel when we regurgitate something is pretty good evidence of this. So a healthy digestion is produced when the stomach and other organs can operate at a consistent flame, so to speak.

Every food has its own unique humoral properties. Let's take a "simple" meal: rosemary chicken, a tossed salad, mashed potatoes, and a glass of wine. The chicken itself would be considered hot and wet, especially if it was basted during the cooking process. The rosemary would be hot and dry. The potatoes would be generically cold and wet as a vegetable, but boiling and then mashing with butter and milk would make them hotter and mainly wet, because the fat of the butter and milk is wet. The use of "dry" for wine also is dry in quality, so if this wine were a sauvignon blanc, then it would probably be considered cold and dry, especially as it would typically be served chilled. In the salad, the different vegetables would all differ in the intensity of their coldness and wetness, and a mustard vinaigrette dressing would be hot, as the mustard is hot and dry, the oil is cool and wet, and the vinegar is hot and dry. Adding salt is a drying agent, while ground pepper is hot and dry.

So all these different qualities get dumped into the stomach in a mix. Having all arrived, it's not that the mixture becomes an average of these qualities, all the original qualities remain. The problem for the stomach is that it now has to "burn" or "concoct" this mixture, and every different component has a different burning signature. So by definition, not all this mixture can burn completely or well. Add to that the possibility that the person has overeaten, and the excess quantity can also overwhelm the digestive fire. Blood is the optimal humoral product of digestion, in part because it is easiest to convert blood into the other three humors. But if everything doesn't burn optimally, humors besides blood are produced. Depending on the extent of deviation from the ideal, these other three humors produced can be either normal or deranged. The deranged humors are effectively toxins that can poison the body unless they are purged.

During the Hellenistic era, the norm was to eat one meal a day. That meant one opportunity per day to produce deranged toxins: We now have three or more opportunities, depending on how many snacks we eat, and whether we tend to mix multiple foods in our snacks. Having accumulated them, how does the body get rid of them? This is where the concept of purging came in.

A purge is a procedure that reduces the quantity of a particular humor. As to how a purge was done depended on what humor was being purged. The most common purge for blood was bloodletting, where anywhere from a couple of teaspoons to a pint or more of blood was taken in order to "refrigerate" (yes, that was really the word used!) the body when it was judged overheated. Purges were meant to dispel matter, but usually not explosively! Any really dramatic effect was to be avoided, because it could put too much of a strain on the body's function, which would be as bad health-wise as the offending humor in the first place.

Feed a Cold, Starve a Fever

Purging can either be for the purpose of removing the deranged humors, or to reduce the total amount of a humor under conditions of surfeit. Purging is generally done with either a procedure or an herb of opposite quality to the humor being purged. You can see this idea commemorated in the old adage "Feed a cold; starve a fever." A cold was considered just that: an excess of cold. When you have a cold, you have a runny nose—which is an excess of phlegm. "Feeding" a cold means that you are heating up your body, because digestion is a hot (and dry) activity. Similarly, "starving" a fever by fasting means you are "cooling" the digestive fires, and hence the body, which is overheated by fever.

To be able to do a proper purge, you have to know which of the four humors you want to purge. William Ramesey's model for purging includes the following ideas for the best purging time:

1. The best Moon is from 15 Libra to 15 Scorpio, although Virgo, Scorpio, and Pisces are generally good.

2. The New Moon up to the Full Moon (waxing) increases moisture (weight); the waning Moon decreases it.

3. Vomiting is likely when the Moon is in Aries, Taurus, Capricorn, or the first 15 degrees of Sagittarius.

4. The Moon should not apply to retrograde planets.

5. The dispositor of the Moon should be strong and oriental (rising before the Sun).

6. The Moon and its dispositor should be free of malefics, and applying to Venus, but not Jupiter. The only purge where it's okay for the Moon to apply to Jupiter is to purge melancholy.

Suppose I notice that I'm getting angry a lot, and I see from my chart (or my astrologer tells me) that my Mars is getting triggered. In this case, I might want to purge choler (yellow bile).

Notice that within this system, purging the humor will then result in a reduction in the emotion associated with the humor. For particular types of purges, there was be special case rules. For choler, in addition to the rules above, I also want the Moon applying to a good aspect to Venus. Thinking of the Venus connection for purging choler, then I might conclude that I really want the Moon in either Libra (Venus' rulership sign) or Pisces (Venus' exaltation sign).

Let's consider this idea by considering how weight loss works according to the humoral system. With the theme of weight loss, my first priority is to look for a waning Moon (decreasing), and my second priority is to minimize the participation of fixed signs in the chart. After I have these conditions met, I will use the considerations given above from Ramesey as a general guide, bearing in mind that another point to consider is that dieting is not supposed to wreak havoc on the person's health.

I have given you a list of days that match Ramesey's criteria. However, please bear in mind that the exact time that you start a diet has bearing, not just the Moon's position, so you may want to consult a qualified electional astrologer to adjust the date to an appropriate starting time.

Purging Moon Dates in 2005
Dates in 2005 that match, or come close to matching, Ramesey's criteria for a good purging Moon:

> January 27 * (dispositor not oriental)
> January 28 * (dispositor not oriental)
> January 29 * (dispositor not oriental)
> February 27* (dispositor combust)
> March 28* (dispositor not oriental)
> April 25* (dispositor not oriental)
> May 2* (dispositor not oriental)
> May 3* (dispositor not oriental)
> May 4* (dispositor not oriental)

May 30* (dispositor not oriental)
May 31* (dispositor not oriental)
June 26* (dispositor not oriental)
June 27* (dispositor not oriental)
July 23* (dispositor not oriental)
July 24* (dispositor not oriental)
August 20* (dispositor not oriental)
August 21* (dispositor not oriental)
September 16* (dispositor not oriental)
September 17* (dispositor not oriental)
October 28
October 29
October 30
October 31
November 27
November 28

While the list isn't that long, every month is represented except December, and who wants to be starting a diet during a holiday season anyway? Also note how few days actually meet the entire model as presented above. And the model I presented is actually a subset of the complete set of rules, since I only considered the Moon!

Now that we have some idea about when it might be a good time to start a diet, a few words are in order about the humoral consequences of diet. In general, both fat and carbohydrates can be considered wet foods. And the process of dieting to lose weight is primarily achieved through drying the body.

Here are some specific ideas for how to dry the body.

- Don't drink with the meal, but only after a delay.
- Hot food (in general) is drying, but only if no drink is taken with the meal.
- Hot foods are drying, and they can also be constipating!

- Sour foods were considered to be drying and hence constipating, causing the body to contract.
- Sharp foods were thought to thin the body through irritation.

Wet foods include:

- Sweet, fat, or rich, which, while moistening, were also considered strengthening.
- It should be noted that "strengthening" is not an automatic, nor an exclusive, quality of wet foods.
- For example, dry wines were believed to be both dry, and to promote strength.

While we're on the topic of wet, it's worth mentioning that many diet types include the recommendation to drink lots of water. One (but not the only) theory for the advantage of drinking water is to put some sort of volume in the stomach, although according to studies reported by Rolls and Barnett, this particular stratagem doesn't work because people differentiate between liquid and solid food, and tend to only feel sated based on the volume of solid food. Apart from its efficacy, the strategy of drinking lots of water has certain humoral considerations attached to it.

- Drinking a lot of water should increase the wetness of the body.
- This may still allow you to dry the body. Why? If the extra water is being used to flush metabolites from the body, this can have the net effect of drying, because the water then acts as a diuretic.
- Note above that you may more easily attain dryness by not drinking at meals, but concentrating your water consumption between meals.
- But if you are naturally wet to begin with, then fluid retention could consume the greater amount of extra water, thereby increasing instead of decreasing weight.

To give you an idea of how the diet works for each constitution type, I've summarized the four main humoral diets, as derived from Galen.

The Hot & Dry Diet
- Alcohol and any liquids neat, not diluted: no mixed drinks nor wine coolers.
- Hot liquids, but not in large amounts. Bread and only roasted meats, few vegetables, copious quantities.
- Vegetables served should be broiled or braised. Foods highly seasoned, as with pepper, cayenne, basil, bay leaves, garlic, mustard, rosemary, saffron, sage, tarragon, or ginger.
- Fruits baked, and preferably dried out.
- Radishes, onions, rhubarb, rice, grapes, walnuts. All foods to be served hot.

The Hot & Wet Diet
- Copious drink, but diluted and in small quantities: a good time for hot teas and other warm drinks.
- Meats or vegetables boiled or stewed, or prepared in sauces.
- Asparagus, chestnuts, endive, figs, pasta.
- Baked fruits in their own juices.
- Gruel, oatmeal or other cooked cereals.

The Cold & Wet Diet
- Copious drink, but diluted and cold, such as wine coolers or diluted fruit juice, such as flavored sparkling water.
- Raw fruits and vegetables, cooked beans or lentils, raw cucumber, lettuce, mint, peaches, pumpkins and other gourds, raspberries, strawberries, thyme, little grain.
- If you must cook something, boil it, but consider serving it cool.
- Smaller quantities of food.

The Cold & Dry Diet

- Alcohol and any liquids neat, not diluted: no mixed drinks or wine coolers.

- Cold liquids, but not in large amounts.

- Bread and only roasted meats, few vegetables in small quantities.

- Vegetables served should be broiled or braised.

- Fennel, quinces, dried fruits.

- All foods to be served cold or at room temperature where feasible.

The idea would be that each of these dietary types spells out what we might call a baseline diet for that constitutional type, or else a general plan for a shift in direction if one wants to trend toward a different temperament type. The caution is that one can only stray so far from one's native type without possibly injuring one's health. (The question of whether the diet would be a success in any case is yet one more consideration!)

Since the usual ideal in weight loss is to attempt to dry the body, it's worth mentioning some of the characteristics that Galen gave to diseases of a dry nature. The appearance of these symptoms would suggest that you may have pushed your body further than it's willing to go, and that you should cut back on the severity of your diet:

- Pleurisy

- Lung inflammation

- Lung affectations without expectoration

- Constipation

- Dry sores

Hopefully, these precepts will give you some ideas about when and how a dietary plan should be devised. It's important to remember that one of the most fundamental tenets of Hippocratic medicine is that each person has his or her own unique balance point. We must respect these individual differences even as we use the humoral classification system to design an appropriate approach.

Bibliography

Grant, Mark. *Galen on Food and Diet*. Routledge: New York, 2000.

Jones, W. H. S., translator. *Hippocrates II*. Loeb Classical Library: Harvard University Press: Cambridge, 1923, 1981.

Pomata, Gianna. *Contracting a Cure. Patients, Healers and the Law in Early Modern Bologna*. The Johns Hopkins Press: Baltimore, 1994, 1998.

Potter, Paul, translator. *Hippocrates V*. Loeb Classical Library: Harvard University Press: Cambridge, 1988.

Ramesey, William. 1653. *Astrologia Restaurata; or Astrology Restored: Being an Introduction to the General and Chief Part of the Language of the Stars*. Printed for Robert White: London.

Rolls, Barbara, and Robert A. Barnett. *The Volumetrics Weight Control Plan*. HarperTorch: New York, 2002.

About the Author

J. Lee Lehman has a Ph.D. in botany from Rutgers University. She is author of *The Ultimate Asteroid Book*, *Essential Dignities*, *The Book of Rulerships*, *Classical Astrology for Modern Living*, *The Martial Art of Horary Astrology*, and a translation from the French of *Papus' Astrology for Initiates*. She originated the Classical Studies course curriculum, which includes horary, natal, electional, medical, gaming, mundane, and advanced horary. She teaches classes in Amsterdam, and she is a professor and academic dean at Kepler College. In her spare time, she studies herbalism and Chang-Hon-style tae kwon do. Lee was the recipient of the 1995 Marc Edmund Jones Award.

Harness the Energy of the Lunar Phases

by June Crane

The best time to start a project is when the Moon is waxing or increasing from new to full. This lunar cycle occurs each month, twelve or thirteen times a year, and consists of an ebb and flow of energy that's observed in all of nature. Nature wakes up in spring, grows in summer, harvests in fall, and retreats for renewal in winter. Then the wheel turns and the year begins again. This growth, peak, climax, and descent of energy can be observed in all cycles and harnessed once a month to accomplish your goals. All you'll need is a calendar of the New and Full Moons.

Within the lunar cycle there are eight phases that each carry their own distinct energy. Each phase has been found to result in manifesting a specific type of result when activities are started in them. They are as follows: new, crescent, first quarter, gibbous, full, disseminating, last quarter, and balsamic. The planning dates below represent these eight powerful cycles.

Imagine manifesting thirteen goals a year! When you consistently follow the guidelines below you can't help but experience an increased sense of self-mastery as you achieve your hearts desire. Here are a few suggestions for increasing your success.

- Keep a journal to track activities and record your progress
- Ritual reinforces intention and will be a tremendous aid in reaching your goal. It need not be esoteric; a special dinner can commemorate the inception of your idea.
- Keep your intention focused.
- Match the sign of the New Moon to the nature of your goal as follows.

New Moon in Capricorn on January 10
Exercise discipline in your life for personal goals or financial planning.

New Moon in Aquarius on February 8
Join new groups and increase your social activities. Learn new computer skills.

New Moon in Pisces on March 10
Launch new creative and spiritual activities. Remember to be specific.

New Moon in Aries on April 8
Initiate enterprising activities and encourage your competitive side.

New Moon in Taurus on May 8

Develop new financial and professional tools and start savings plan. Acquire home furnishing, redecorate, add to wardrobe.

New Moon in Gemini on June 6

Start a journal, attend classes, plan travel, increase social activities.

New Moon in Cancer on July 6

Plan domestic and family activities, spend time nurturing self and loved ones. Start cooking class.

New Moon in Leo on August 5

Have some fun, entertain, take up a new sport. Put the spotlight on romance and creativity.

New Moon in Virgo on September 3

Establish new regimes for diet and fitness, create healthy lifestyle. Clear up clutter. Add new look to wardrobe.

New Moon in Libra on October 3

Focus on increasing communication and cooperation in all partnerships. Start an artistic or musical project.

New Moon in Scorpio on November 2

Let go of past issues that have you feeling stuck. Clean house physically, mentally, emotionally, and financially. Establish new values that support your growth in the now.

New Moon in Sagittarius on December 1

Plan journeys, participate in spiritual, learning, and social activities. Cultivate friendships.

New Moon in Capricorn on December 31

Take an honest assessment of your progress in the past year. Honor and acknowledge your accomplishments.

Let's begin at the New Moon and start an activity schedule. Each day is counted from the day of the New Moon.

Day 1–3 (New Moon)

Start with a desire, meditate. Make a keyword list of different projects you're interested in accomplishing. Start your journal.

Day 4–6 (Crescent)

Pick one specific goal and write it down. At this point, keep it secret to avoid negativity and potential interference from outside sources. Gather tools, information, and a picture that represents the desired result. Do something special to celebrate the new beginning!

Day 8–9 (First Quarter)

Take action. Pretend you've already reached your goal and build activities that support it's growth. Examine what isn't working. What roadblocks and obstacles are you encountering? Change your plans to navigate those issues. Are you supporting your own idea? Nurture yourself and your project.

Day 11–12 (Gibbous)

Feed the goal by doing related activities. Visualize the results and get ready for them.

Day 13–15 (Full Moon)

The Full Moon will shine her light on what is and isn't working. If you have neglected supporting your goal, it will start to show now. Ask yourself if your input has been positive or negative, and renew effort.

Day 18–19 (Disseminating)

Make adjustments based on what was revealed at the Full Moon, and share your results. Be positive and stand up for your idea.

Day 22–23 (Last Quarter)

Make decisions, evaluate what is and isn't working. If you haven't achieved your desired results, look back in your journal and determine if there's anything you could have done differently. Make note of this so as to avoid that pitfall next time. Don't be negative do symbolic cleansing to neutralize the project. Positive results can be celebrated and taken to a new level (if you desire) in next cycle.

Day 26–28 (Balsamic)

Time of completion and release. Detach and let go. Open yourself up to art, music, or aromatherapy to create a peaceful and receptive state and prepare for the new cycle. Be aware of where you are sending your energy. What you think about multiplies!

Working in concert with the lunar phases can be an amazing and productive process. Each goal you work on will be a learning experience supplying insight into your personal growth. With focus and intention you'll be rewarded with an increased sense of self-worth as you accomplish your goals. Lots of good luck to you!

About the Author

June Crane is a professional consulting astrologer, intuitive consultant, lecturer, and teacher with over twenty-five years experience. Specializing in personal, electional, and relocation astrology, she is a certified Astro*Carto*Graphy interpreter. Her teaching philosophy focuses on presenting knowledge in a warm and direct manner, which makes learning accessible to all. In addition to her private consultations, she travels and lectures nationally on astrology and the tarot as well as facilitating sacred tours. June is active in the astrological community as a regional coordinator for NCGR and publicity director for the New Jersey chapter. She can be contacted through her Web site: www.starpathz.com.

Business
and
Legal
Section

CONTRACT

INVOICES

2005 Economic Forecast

by Dorothy J. Kovach

What is above does influence what is below, and there is no place where we can see celestial magnetism with more crystal clarity than when we observe the fluctuating dance that Wall Street does. I believe astrology will make its breakthrough toward acceptance with the general public through its financial wing. Even the most astrologically skeptical traders know the market is cyclical, because there is no place where the movements of the planets is more apparent than in the market. Wise business people now turn to astrology to give them the edge that their flowcharts overlook. Business astrologers are careful to take note of all the planets, but especially the slowest moving of the visible planets, Jupiter and Saturn, because they are what make a market "bullish" or "bearish."

Jupiter in 2005

When astrologers talk about the "good life," we are referring to the big daddy of them all—Jupiter. We could say that he is the Santa Claus of the planets. If he were a person on Wall Street, he would be the "fat cat," the CEO, the guy with lots of bucks to spend on a big car, the mansion, the chauffeur and all the trimmings. Jupiter brings us the bull market, where everything we touch goes up and our portfolios earn double-digit returns.

Jupiter stays approximately one year in each of the signs, and whatever sign Jupiter is in will point out sectors of growth in the year ahead. In 2005, Jupiter will continue his sojourn through the sign of partnership, Libra. A thing of beauty is a joy to behold, and those companies in the business of making us beautiful will see expansion for at least the first two quarters of the year. Beauty can be in the form of cosmetics or companies that nip and tuck an aging baby-boomer population. From fashion to plastic surgery, Jupiter in Libra will bring bounty.

Jupiter is also the planet of partnership, and businesses that traditionally bring people together, from negotiators to caterers, will do well. The Internet shines on dating, which has become the mainstream way of meeting one another, and venture capitalists are taking note.

Jupiter in Libra

Libra is an intellectual sign. We can expect to see growth in tech stocks. Jupiter will be in the fifth house of the national chart if we use the traditional Gemini rising chart. The fifth house represents speculation. This will bring profits to the gaming industry in the first half of the year.

Knowing when to hold and when to fold is key if we want to take advantage of the times. Therefore, we need to be very mindful to take some of our money out of speculation by summer. The ability to win may be greatly overshadowed by other factors. Believe it or not, there are those who do yet not realize that markets are not the modern equivalent of a bank in terms of safety. Luck can turn sour if we keep it all on the table, when Jupiter collides with the South Node in the third quarter. The wise will make the necessary adjustments. Fools rush in, and so be advised to hold back from investing in stocks in August and early September. Jupiter will be opposite 19 Aries, the degree darkened by an eclipse in early September. The ancients associated this degree with the founding chart of England, therefore, I suggest to those of you with investments in Great Britain to keep a very close eye.

Jupiter in Scorpio

Scorpio is a dark sign. Fall fashions might lean toward the macabre, with black prevailing, but look for purple and navy, too. The morbid business of "death" will see profits rise in 2005. And people are more on edge and less likely to negotiate, especially once Jupiter enters Scorpio. We may see the war on terrorism take a bloody turn. It is not all dark somber news, though. Jupiter in Scorpio may well bring great breakthroughs in surgery, and the restoration of the body. While cloning is somewhat limited, we may see the beginnings of body limb and organ regeneration.

Scorpio rules all that is private and taboo. Among the oldest taboos is sex. With Jupiter in the sign of the "privates," we may see even more money to be made in the

$8 million skin biz. This includes everything from x-rated videos to lingerie. Double-digit earnings will continue in the porn business as it goes legitimate. Jupiter will smile on quiet behind the scenes businesses that conduct their operations behind closed doors, too. This includes all forms of surveillance businesses, including private investigators. The "behind closed doors" aspect of Jupiter in Scorpio may also result in a rise in illegal syndicates, from the mob to secret societies.

Saturn in 2005

Saturn in Cancer

What goes up must come down, and this is where Saturn comes in. Whatever goes too high too fast is brought back down to Earth by the ringed planet. Saturn continues through Cancer until summer. When interest rates were low and the stock market dropped, the real estate market boomed. Saturn's placement in Cancer is a sign to take some profits in real estate before it comes back down to reality. Business does not do well in sentimental Cancer because investors value security and are less likely to take on risk.

Saturn's transit in the monetary segment of the U.S. chart will leave people with less money, and with less discretionary income at their disposal, people are less likely to invest in business ideas, so business sags. Wise investors should try to emulate surfers and know how to take the wave when it is low enough to get a good ride (always getting ready to get off when the wave has peaked), and not even bother to go out when there is no surf. Stock prices tend to stall as security issues gain precedence. Saturn's placement in Cancer is a warning to those who have been playing the "borrow up" debt game—don't be caught like road kill as interest rates begin to rise.

Saturn in Cancer, the sign of oceans, can cause trouble in shipping, too. Regulations and various troubles at sea will be problematic in the first half of the year. People can be touchy, as they feel the financial pinch. Labor is restless, and we may see more striking for better wages, especially in the custodial positions.

Even as the pundits laud a recovery, it occurs without job creation. Many who lost their jobs in the technology and manufacturing shake out, are still jobless. Those who have found jobs are working in the lesser paying service sector. Cancer rules the stomach, and so the food industry may see trouble as people are more sensitive to the foot they eat. This might imply trouble for the food supply, or outbreaks of food poisoning. Expect to see household name brands suffer when Saturn is in Cancer. But on the bright side, medicine will continue to make great strides in its battle against the disease cancer.

Saturn in Leo

Saturn enters Leo in mid-July. As noted, wherever Saturn goes things will wither. Leo rules royalty, and when Saturn is in Leo, the rich and famous lose their luster. (Incumbents beware!) When people don't trust their leaders, rebellion is in the air. Leo sits on the cusp of the third house of the Gemini rising chart of the U.S. There may be a slowdown in businesses that move goods and ideas from one place to the other. With this in mind, we can expect trouble on the highways.

Technology suffers. Those who have gotten "tech heavy" might consider taking some profits. Saturn here often points to an insecure economy. Leo is synonymous with gold, and one would think Saturn here would bring prices down, but historically, Saturn in Leo has made gold more valuable. People do not trust the "powers that be" and seek that which has intrinsic value.

Jupiter and Saturn

Jupiter brings us an expanding economy. If Jupiter had its way, the economy would expand and expand. When Jupiter is in charge, we wind up with our stocks at record highs, but the price per earnings are off the roof. In other words, the real profits of the companies we invest in are overpriced. When this happens, Saturn enters with a heavy hand, bringing reality back to the market. The dance these two planets do tells us much about the state of the economy at any given time.

There has been a massive amount of money pumped into the economy in the past few years in the form of both low interest rates and tax refunds. Money was made readily available in the form of low interest loans to both private individuals and business. This "stimulus" greatly helped an economy still reeling from the dot-com busts, 9/11, and corporate scandals. As this money worked into the system, the business climate thrived because companies were both able to cut business expenses and borrow cheaply. This is a perfect example of Jupiter and Saturn in harmony in the heavens (as it was in 2003). Saturn provided low interest rates and Jupiter brought a certain amount of optimism back to business. The result was expanded profits. With this came exuberant growth. However, some might argue that this was synthetic growth. It takes two to three years for money to work its way into the system, which is about the amount of needed for Jupiter and Saturn to move into inharmonious position and—you guessed it—record growth comes back down to Earth. Even though we watched the stock market recover somewhat in the last few years, the fact is, old jobs did not come back. Regardless of what the stock market does, or what the pundits tell you, there can be no real recovery without some sort of real job growth to accompany it. Without job growth, the economy is in recovery in name only. This would be an economy where only Jupiter reigned supreme, but we know now that no economy is independent of reality and that is where Saturn comes in.

The market is a capitalistic entity and one that is based purely on the bottom line—profit and loss. With a record deficit created by the government in recent years, we are going to see Saturn and Jupiter at odds as an indication that the "jobless" recovery is stagnate. We can expect to see more layoffs, and fewer jobs created when production returns and more businesses export their operations abroad.

The key phrase for the square aspect is: "Any growth is checked." This is a time to consolidate debts, and to rein in unnecessary spending. This will not be a year of double-digit earnings, so we will want to have our stocks and holdings very diversified. Don't blindly trust the words of others—ever.

North Node (Dragon's Head) in Aries

Not surprisingly, the North Node is bullish. The sign it traverses through indicates which sector will drive the market during the next eighteen months. The location of the North Node shows what will drive the tastes and desires of the buying public. The North Node is in the "me" sign of Aries in 2005. Those things connected to movement are likely to be places of growth. This includes everything from machinery to martial arts movies. The sword is mightier than the pen during these times, so the peaceful will suffer. Though war is not good for living beings, it can be a speculator's heaven. Markets are not living breathing entities. They are a place of speculation, and war producers thrive during war. Red is the color of Aries. The press adage, "If it bleeds it leads," becomes reality as the War on Terrorism becomes more visceral. While there is always hope for peace, it is less likely to really happen when the North Node is in Aries because people want what they want and they and they want it "now." Aries is a sign of action that hates waiting. Therefore, if a war is in progress when the North Node enters, the odds favor said war turning far bloodier. The North Node was in Aries in 1968, the year marked by the assassinations of Reverend Martin Luther King, Jr. and Robert F. Kennedy, as well as the rise in bloody casualties in both Vietnam and abroad, and riots in the streets domestically.

Dragon's are very connected to the lore of China, and when the North Node goes into Aries we will probably also see so called, "Sleeping Giant" sleep no more. The North Node in Aries has been particularly influential to the development of the People's Republic of China. Already the supplier to the world, there is no doubt that Chinese products and listed stocks will continue to be "hot" in 2005. The North Node in Aries has always been associated with great conquests, but it is especially true for the people of China. The North Node was stationed in Aries when Japan began its invasion of the mainland and surrounding area in 1931. The next time the North Node was here, in 1949, the People's Republic of China was born. When the North Node entered Aries in 1968, the United States became embroiled indirectly with China over Vietnam.

As the power of China grows, it becomes more likely this sleeping giant will awake and be more than willing and able to flex its muscles in the year ahead. This means the price of Chinese goods will likely go up in 2005. With most of our goods now imported, and the dollar at extremely weak levels, it will be harder to afford even the most basic of goods.

Another byproduct of the North Node in Aries is that markets tend to heat up. When the market heats up too quickly, the result is often the dirty word of economists everywhere, "inflation." When this happens, the "powers that be" in this case, the Federal Reserve Board of Banks will raise interest rates a notch. The reason that they do this is because the health of our economy is based upon the strength or weakness of our currency. When the North Node is in Aries, there is a natural tendency for it to undermine the value of our hard-earned money. When interest rates go up, then the market tends to lag.

Rams are not noted for their patience, but are known to butt heads and be pushy. This is because Aries above all is a hot and jumpy sign. It acts first, and talks about it later. Therefore when the Moon's shadow passes through this sign, all things military are greatly expanded. From a political standpoint, it is not the year that will see peace on Earth and goodwill toward man. We should keep an eye on those businesses that provide the government with weaponry and all those that supply the Pentagon, as war seems to be eminent once again in the coming months.

On the body, Aries rules the head (the mother of invention is necessity) and we can expect a myriad of new ideas springing forth from the head while the North Node is in Aries. Markets are driven by desire, and there is no sign, except maybe Scorpio, that is so full of wants. Therefore, an Aries North Node is a very positive thing for military producers. Look for technological suppliers to the Pentagon, and surveillance manufacturers like TRW, and other war contractors.

Aries is associated with young men and those things that move fast. We can expect to see American car and motorcycle manufactures starting to get ahead from something other than their real estate holdings. Companies like General Motors are expected to start seeing some better days, thanks chiefly to their factories overseas. Even long-ailing automaker Ford can look for a boost after years in the doldrums.

South Node (Dragon's Tail) in Libra

Conversely, the sign where the Dragon's Tail is located will tell us what products and sectors will go sour in 2005. The South Node will be moving through the sign of Libra. Libra is a Venus-ruled sign that loves above all peace, harmony, and all that is nice. Since sectors where the South Node moves lag and dwindle, some dichotomy takes place because Libra is also the sign that Jupiter will be in. This creates a bit of conflict because Jupiter tends to smile on sectors and make them go up. When these two celestial idioms combine, it is more likely that those with a soft and generous heart will become easy prey for the wolves out to

get their money. The wise will be very careful before committing their hard-earned cash to any expensive project.

Libra is an air sign, and air signs have to do with ideas and intellectual properties when applied to the market place. With Jupiter also in Libra, it has to do specifically with "hot air." This could be a sign of a very hot market the first half of the year, especially in intellectual companies, like software and networking, but it also can bring the market down very quickly. It is therefore of utmost importance that those who are considering investing in the stock market or any expensive item to make certain that they know the full value of the item. Read the fine print. We look for the intellectual sector to heat up and then cool down as imported goods become more expensive and money becomes tighter in the second half of the year.

It is important for investors not to be lulled into complacency, by recent gains. No matter how many people invest in the market, it is still and always will be a place of risk, and those who want to make money are warned not to procrastinate about learning the basics about financial investments. When the South Node is in Libra, there are confidence people afloat whose sole purpose in life is to separate the unwary from their hard-earned assets. Part of the problem is that people spend more time learning about the car they buy than the mutual fund they invest in. This is not a year to trust anybody with your future. Rule of thumb is: If it sounds too good to be true, it probably is. It is important that you make certain you are investing in the stock, and not taken in by the charismatic person selling it. Advisors can give flawed examples of return. The fact is that people are just more inclined to be gullible than they normally are at times like these. If a broker tries to tout the things like "information ratios" or purchases based upon "beta" stock performances, get a second or even a third opinion. Remember that it's your money.

Invest only after doing your homework. When Jupiter is with the South Node, people tend to hear only what they want to hear. When these two are together, charities are to be particularly investigated before randomly giving your money. South Node in Libra can lull investors into thinking that they do not have to work for money. People are more susceptible to falling into confidence scams. We need to remember that good intentions alone cannot make money grow. In this climate, we can expect the gaming industry to do well. Since this combination falls in the national sector of the chart that has to do with speculation, the market, itself may see a bit of a slowdown the second quarter.

The South Node in Libra spells trouble for all those who hope for peace. Peaceful protesters, and otherwise quiet demonstrators be advised: The police are less patient than they have been in recent years. This is a recipe for trouble; it may even be deadly. Look for more protest in 2005. Extremist fervor is greatly enhanced when idiom of asceticism and denial meet the planet of religion. When the South Node meets Jupiter some become willing to risk even their life for a cause.

A thing of beauty may be a joy to behold, but if the signature is a fraud, the owner may cry. The South Node in Libra can bring to light forgeries in art pieces. Art dealers and auction houses are warned that ancient art masterpiece may not be what it appears. Beauty sells in the first half but not the second. This is a warning: If you're involved in this field, save your profits in fat times because meager times may be in store the second half of the year. This includes beauticians, hair stylists, and cosmetics manufactures.

People are less patient, and negotiations tend to break off at these times. We may see the counseling businesses not do as well as they have in the past few years because fewer people are willing to spend money to talk about their problems when they can get a prescription for medication that will make them "feel fine" for a lot less financial and emotional investment. Diplomacy always suffers under this influence, and organizations dedicated to peace like the United Nations will see its power further eroded.

The Outer Planetary Influence

Financial astrologers are very keen to keep an eye on the outer planets. The signs that they are in and their slow movement influence major economic desires and shifts in the national desires, thereby affecting their purchasing direction.

Uranus

One of the most important outer planets in the markets is Uranus because it rules invention and is directly linked to the computer industry. Since the technology sector basically moves ahead of the rest of the market, it is considered something of a celestial bell weather of the economy. Because Uranus is the planet of "shock," knowing its movements in advance gives us the edge on when the market is going to abruptly turn from bull to bear. It is also one of the leading indicators to watch for market recovery.

Uranus continues in one sign for approximately eight years. When Uranus was in Aquarius in the 1990s, it brought us the technology boom. In 2005, Uranus will continue its sojourn through the sign Pisces—the sign directly linked to the drug sector. As Uranus is the sign of invention, when this planet makes its way through Pisces, it heralds many new and remarkable medical cures and innovations making their way to market. Especially marked for growth during this time will be the biotechnology sector. We will also see some very revolutionary things done with body parts and cloning. Biotech and genetic engineering firms will do quite well in 2005. Not only will biotechnology do well, but all pharmaceuticals will do well, especially those companies ready to try new and innovative techniques. The drug sector will do especially well in the last quarter, when Jupiter enters Scorpio and shines his bounty in the drug sector.

Neptune in Aquarius

Neptune will be in Aquarius the entire year. Neptune is symbolic of those things with fuzzy edges that are hard to grasp. It is liquid in nature, and is said to represent those ethereal things like fantasies and dreams. Therefore, in business, Neptune has a special affinity for the movie, drug, and gas industries. We call the glamorous actors and actresses in the movies "stars" and some have been compared to American royalty. Therefore, we might suspect that Neptune has an affinity with the sign Leo. Since Aquarius is opposite Leo, when Neptune is in Aquarius, the movie industry experiences woes. Aquarius is a sign linked with freedom and innovation. Companies like Disney and Sony have their work cut out for them, with competition coming not only from digital piracy. The drug industry, another Neptune-ruled industry, will do extremely well in 2005, with certain key bills that have passed favoring the industry, as a whole as well as many new and miracle drugs coming down the pipeline. The government climate for allowing these new drugs to the market quickly also helps these companies profit. Another industry slated to do well will be the energy companies. Energy deregulation will make great changes in the way energy comes to homes. More and more of the nation relies on natural gas to heat their homes, and because many of the nation's electrical generating facilities are run by natural gas we will see it become more and more a major player in the coming year ahead.

Pluto in Sagittarius

Pluto is the modern ruler of death and regeneration. Pluto has to do with all the grim and ugly things we don't like to look at or talk about in polite conversation. Among the industries Pluto rules are the nuclear industry, wastewater management, and prostitution. Wherever Pluto is placed will stir up a great passion that can become so strong as to be come obsessive. When obsessive, Pluto will do whatever it takes to get its way. Sagittarius is the domain of all that is religious. When Pluto is in Sagittarius, extreme religious beliefs often drive people to take up drastic measures in the name of the god that they believe in. As we saw from 9/11, this can include death. Historically, holy wars have been fought when Pluto went through this most religious of all the signs. The Crusades for example were fought when Pluto was in Sagittarius.

Pluto in Sagittarius has made doing business abroad much more difficult. This will continue to have a depreciating effect on the airline industry and the travel business as a whole. Pluto here is not completely a sad story. Sagittarius is a lucky sign, and Pluto has to do with those things that are underground. Mining companies here and abroad, like 3M, have seen their profits rise. Pluto entered Sagittarius back in 1995, and since that time we have witnessed many business move their operations abroad. This outsourcing contributes to our present jobless recovery. Fewer companies are willing to pay the cost of American labor when they can pay a fraction by hiring firms abroad. Since 1980, technology has led the way in recovery by providing highly paid jobs, but when those jobs are relocated offshore, any recovery is in name only. Consider investing in the very offshore companies that are taking the work, like India's Infosys.

2005 Market Watch

January

Merchants rejoice after a good holiday season, but the economy is showing signs of heating up. Take some chips off the table especially in communications sector, around the 9th. Foreign holdings peak around the 18th—consider taking some profits. Expect some bump-up for mining stocks and minerals the last week of January, and some good short-term investment opportunities at the end of the month. The key word here is "short."

February

This may not be the month to let the good times just roll along. Many stocks will be seeing peaks as the gods smile on the tech, communications, and banking sectors. These three lead the way as Jupiter heads away from square to Saturn. We'll see some nice trading around the 9th and after the 16th, when good news from the tech industry helps bring markets up. Interest rates could be on the rise. Consider taking profits on fast tracks around the 22nd. Be on your toes.

March

Prices may go up, and not just at the gas pump. Tensions mount toward the 9th, and again after the equinox. Military contractors and pharmaceuticals will profit. The New Moon on March 10 implies there is still money to be made in foreign stocks. Take care to have all important documents signed by the 18th, the last business day before Mercury turns retrograde, when bad news may signal a sell-off. Clean your financial house of nonproducers.

April

Look for a pickup in tech stocks after the 12th, when business plans finally come together as Mercury turns out of retrograde and combustion. We get good tech news, but rumors are rampant. Look for a bump-up in biotech midmonth as Mars conjoins Neptune. If it sounds too good to be true, it probably is. Watch for banking stocks to move up midmonth, too. Rates may rise. Take some chips off the table the last week of April, when the market cools.

May

Gold is looking good the first week, but the market may stumble this month with Uranus and Mars near the antiscion of the South Node. Look for market optimism to sink as surprise forces the market to accept reality. It is a good time to be conservative with investments. Review all mutually held assets and funds. Be prepared to make some informed decisions regarding any unproductive sectors.

June

This is a worrisome month. Take extra precautions to know your portfolio, especially in the tech stocks and communication sector, which could have some air taken out of it around this time. Take profits as the trend turns downward in the equities markets. The wise will turn to more conservative and value-oriented investments. Military supplier stocks and treasuries are looking good.

July

Take some profits on gold before Saturn enters Leo in the second week. Over all, stocks continue to stumble in July. Check the fine print in any and all agreements. Know what the other hand is doing as Jupiter heads toward the Dragon's Tail. Religious fervor is at a high. It could spook the market even further as war jitters come home. Bears out in force drag the NASDAQ down until at least third week. Bad tech news spurs sell-off that threatens to bring down entertainment stocks with it. Best stocks are in mining, energy, and the banking sectors.

August

You may want to take some chips off the table this month as troubles in the War on Terrorism dog the market. A cloud hangs over mutually held assets. Defer signing important agreements until after the 21st while Jupiter moves past the South Node. Sign then only if you have vetted the fine print. All partnerships have a cloud over them at this time. Divorce is on the rise; counselors and divorce lawyers will see brisk business this month. Pay extra attention to financial matters. The war on terrorism spooks the market near the end of the month.

September

Investigate but do not buy in September. Recovery continues to lag as Saturn in Leo keeps the investment climate chilly. Silver linings come from biotech and technology a brighten market doldrums around the 6th and again around the 15th. All told, this is a good month to keep resources in safe places. War jitters rankle investors around the 19th. There may be some bad banking news at the end of the month.

October

Have some assets in cash at the beginning of month, when Mars turns retrograde and stumps the market. Gold loses some luster around the 6th, while some positive numbers bring smiles back to investors. There is not enough good news now, though, as war worries dominate the market.

November

The South Node seems to have extracted enough blood from tech, communications, and networking related sectors for now. Sign all important business transactions before Mercury goes retrograde on the 13th. Jupiter's entry into Scorpio suggests wise investors should consider shifting some nonperforming telecom and communications assets into biotech. Watch for a rise in surveillance stocks.

December

Business gets a boost at the start of the month. Close business deals and sign important papers on the 3rd and 4th, when Mercury is direct. The talk is about construction. Medical devices will be seeing a boost, and some breakthroughs in those in the business of creating body parts can be expected. Watch for a rise in surveillance stocks. Choose pharmaceuticals with care.

About the Author

Dorothy J. Kovach is a full-time astrologer, trends and timing expert based in northern California. She consults with businesses and individuals interested in finding the best time to start projects for successful outcomes. Her specialty is horary astrology—answering direct questions using astrology. She has successfully applied the ancient methods to predict the financial markets, and is best known for having called the end of the bull market to the month, some five years in advance. She was a regular contributor to the *Horary Practitioner*. Her articles have appeared the *Journal of the British Astrological Association*, *The Traditional Astrologer*, and www.stariq.com. She has been the author of the economic forecasts in the Llewellyn *Moon Sign Book* since 2003. You may reach her by email at dorothy@worldastrology.net, or through her Web site: www.worldastrology.net.

How the Moon Will Work For You Is Your Business

by Maggie Anderson

Almanacs were first designed to benefit a largely rural population. Farmers needed information about Moon cycles in order to know when to plant and harvest, pluck chickens, and make moonshine. This was long before the universe dreamed up the Small Business Administration, cafeteria-style benefit packages, or the IRS. Fortunately, today's almanac readers have as many opportunities to work with Moon phases as great-great-grandpa did. It's just a matter of knowing how and when.

Many modern laborers have exchanged a simple outdoor life of physically demanding labor for sedentary indoor work. Because we spend our days and nights in dry, temperature-controlled buildings, it's sometimes hard to imagine that the cycles of nature still apply to us. Most of us do notice that the people we work with are occasionally overcome by Full Moon madness (while we remain immune). Even in an office full of state-of-the-art technology, we must interact with other humans who are definitely affected by the man in the Moon.

If you haven't had time to candle eggs or make cheese lately, perhaps it's because you're too busy with your working life. Luna would love to help. You can be more effective if you coordinate your actions with one of nature's primary cycles, those of the Moon. For your part, all you need do is follow the Moon phases and signs in this almanac, then plan ahead. Pick and choose the correct days to perform those modern, business-related tasks that are every bit as challenging as making hay while the Sun shines.

Why Do It?

Our goal in studying Moon phases is to act in harmony with nature. The underlying belief in this process is that it's better to conform our activities to the cycles of nature than to go against them. Humans that live in northern climates are already attuned to the phases of the Sun as it travels north and south of the equator. We wouldn't plant an outdoor flower garden in Minneapolis in December, or take a ski trip to Wisconsin in July because the Sun's cycles have become general knowledge that we unconsciously incorporate into our everyday lives.

In cultures that are closer to the equator, where warm temperatures are constant, people are more aware of the Moon's cycles. Some of these countries use calendars based on the Moon rather than Old Sol. Moon phases are fast moving and subtle. They affect all biological life on earth, including reproduction. As humans, we are part of a cyclical life process, whether we're country folks or city dwellers. Because the Moon affects us at very basic levels, acting in accordance with Moon cycles will give us an edge as we go about our daily business.

New Moon/Full Moon?

The lunar cycle begins when the Moon is in the same degree of the zodiac as the Sun. It's seen as a small sliver of light in the night sky. Because the Moon is the fastest moving heavenly body, it passes the Sun's position quickly, at approximately twelve and a half degrees per day. As it separates from the Sun, the reflected light on the Moon increases until it is filled out with light. This New to Full Moon period lasts approximately fourteen days.

While the light of the Moon is "growing" is a good time to begin activities you would like to be increased. Ask yourself: "Do I want to experience more or less of this?" If the answer is, "more," then make your first best efforts when the Moon is new.

The Full Moon back to New Moon phase begins immediately after the Moon is full. The light of the Moon will decrease each night until it once again becomes a small crescent. This phase also lasts approximately fourteen days.

During a Full Moon, you'll notice that there will be a culmination of events set in progress at the New Moon. The decreasing Moon phase is the best time to start events that you would like to have diminished. This is the best time to implement programs to eliminate unwanted behaviors: employees taking personal phone calls, communication glitches, and expense report abuses, for example. It's also said to be an excellent time to do things that are necessary but tedious activities that you do not want to ever enlarge, such as restocking the supply shelves or cleaning the office refrigerator.

Cardinal, Fixed, or Mutable?

After you've decided which Moon phase best suits your needs, it's time to consider the signs of the zodiac. This will provide a further refinement of your universal purpose, for the Moon behaves differently depending both on the phase and sign she is in. The triplicities (cardinal, fixed, and mutable signs) help us sort it all out.

Having the Moon in one of the cardinal signs (Aries, Cancer, Libra, or Capricorn) is like putting your personal advance team on the ground, ready to run with your special assignment. These are the start-up signs and excellent for launching any new project. Naturally, they are superior signs to have in combination with New Moons.

Once headed in a particular direction, the fixed signs (Taurus, Leo, Scorpio, and Aquarius) are hard to move off course. Make sure the New Moon is in one of these when initiating any long-term business plans, such as capital improvements, expansions, and all others involving financial growth.

The mutable signs (Gemini, Virgo, Sagittarius, and Pisces) are the multitaskers of the zodiac. Choose the Moon in a mutable sign when you want to accomplish two or more things at the same time. Note that, because these signs are changeable, the law of unintended consequences can come into play. You may sometimes even change your mind about your goals before your plans are realized.

The Man in the Moon Meets the Zodiac Signs

Aries the Ram

He's a bold risk-taker, one of the very best start-up signs, especially for any enterprise that requires motivating people to act in their own best interests. Aries is Mars ruled and connected with physical activity.

New Moon: Launch any venture that can be labeled "self-improvement," whether on a physical, emotional, intellectual, or spiritual level. Aries is a great motivator and will help you give super pep talks to your team. These talks are most effective when you want to help others reach their personal goals and full potential.

Full Moon: Begin programs designed to decrease self-defeating behaviors. This is a great time to stop smoking, go on weight loss program, or kick other bad habits. Many successful businesses have been built on these themes.

Taurus the Bull

Be careful what you work for when the Moon is in Taurus: the results will be long lasting. Venus, the planet of money, governs this sign, so it's a natural for taking care of your organization's finances.

New Moon: Begin arrangements with banks and other financial groups that will handle your investments. This is an earthy sign with an affinity for plants and music. Sign contracts for landscaping, lawn maintenance, indoor plant care, and piped-in music while the New Moon is in Taurus.

Full Moon: Review your financial investments and make necessary adjustments. Fill out your expense reports. Organize documents you will need later for tax purposes. Send yourself a big bouquet of flowers for a job well done.

Gemini the Twins

This chatty sign is ruled by Mercury, and good communications are their specialty. Choose this sign for your dealings with telephone and cell phone representatives, auto and computer sales people, delivery and messenger services, and technicians who keep your office equipment running smoothly.

New Moon: Sign contracts with representatives of companies mentioned above. Begin a local advertising campaign in the print media or on the radio. Write and send important letters. Install new software on your computer. Purchase or lease a company car. Accept and make important deliveries.

Full Moon: Arrange for routine maintenance on all office equipment and automobiles. Troubleshoot computer problems. Look into miscommunications and take steps to prevent them from occurring in the future. Write important company memos.

Cancer the Crab

The Moon is happiest when she's in her home territory of Cancer. Here, she loves to initiate activities that nurture others on an emotional and physical level. There's no better sign to choose for dealing with food and drink, antiques, daycare, and nursing.

New Moon: Sign contracts for food service and bottled water. Plan your organization's holiday party or an awards dinner for retired employees. Arrange fund raising dinners while the Moon is in Cancer. Take a prospective client out for lunch. Begin onsite daycare for children of employees.

Full Moon: Initiate new rules that might apply to food, drink, children, or other family involvement in the workplace. Hold meetings about pension plans and other retirement-related issues.

Leo the Lion

When the Moon is in this sign, it helps facilitate the arts and all forms of pleasure, including gaming, golfing, and other kinds of individual sports. Leo is competitive but fair and has a taste for luxury.

New Moon: Launch sales contests between employees and give generous prizes for the winners. Purchase fine art to decorate the corporate headquarters. Plan a banquet for board members or visiting dignitaries. Purchase a corporate membership at a country club. The employee summer family picnic will be memorable if held while the Moon is in Leo.

Full Moon: Discontinue making risky investments. Adopt personnel policies that are aimed at cutting excess socialization in the workplace. Launch family leave and adoption programs for employees and their families.

Virgo the Virgin

This Mercurial sign is at it's finest when overseeing the smooth functioning of your office. The Moon in Virgo is connected with accounting, and other detail work, employee health matters, and all labor conditions.

New Moon: Sign contracts with a new accounting firm while the Moon is in this sign. Update your facilities to meet OSHA requirements. When changing employee insurance companies or benefits, do it with the New Moon in Virgo. Hold meetings with labor representatives or quality control consultants.

Full Moon: Review all employee benefits and make sure your records are up to date. Analyze expenditures for insurance and pension benefits. Complete all paperwork necessary to put your organization in compliance with local, county, state, and federal codes.

Libra the Scales

Ruled by sociable Venus, the Moon in Libra just wants everyone to get along—and be beautiful! Any business or activity that involves bringing people together socially has an affinity with Libra. It is connected with the fashion, jewelry, and design industries.

New Moon: Begin mediation that will assist your organization to work cooperatively with other people. This could involve your competitors, lawyers representing them, your suppliers, or trade groups. Launch any business that helps people or their immediate surroundings look and feel better. Meet your competitors in a social setting.

Full Moon: Consult with crisis counselors to alleviate stress in the workplace. Initiate yoga or other programs for employees that are conducive to maintaining physical and spiritual balance.

Scorpio the Scorpion

Mars, one of the cosmic troublemakers, governs this sign. It's associated with wills, estates, trusts, taxes, debt, loans and other financial obligations, insurance, financial losses, and money owed to others. Deal with these critical issues while the Moon is in Scorpio.

New Moon: Best for making any sort of legal arrangements that involves money and other assets. Of course, you must read the fine print before signing any documents on the dotted line. Once signed, these may not be altered. Apply for commercial loans, mortgages, life insurance, and insurance benefits while the Moon is in Scorpio.

Full Moon: Review and update your financial documents. Pay taxes and bills. Talk with your banker, tax accountant, or insurance representative about extending or altering their services.

Sagittarius the Archer

Wise old Jupiter is the ruler of Sagittarius and there are many arenas under his domain. The Moon here will help you connect in a positive manner with lawyers, politicians, religious leaders, foreigners, travel agents, colleges and universities, and anyone that represents the popular culture.

New Moon: Consult with your company lawyer or plan a court date while the Moon is in this sign. Connect with politicians or hire a lobbyist. Have an office blessing or make long-distance travel arrangements. Hold university-level continuing education classes at your workplace. Sign a contract with a popular Hollywood star to represent your product.

Full Moon: Take any certification tests that are necessary for you to maintain your business. Check the academic credentials of applicants. Review travel-related expense reports. Collect and study academic research related to your business.

Capricorn the Goat

Saturn rules this sign and helps to bring order and discipline to most enterprises begun while the Moon is transiting. Cappy has connections with government and big business, as well as the members of your board of directors, if you have one. It's associated with all Very Important People.

New Moon: Meet with representatives of any government agencies that have oversight responsibilities for your organization. Plan meetings for your board of directors. Get together with the top management of corporations. If you are top management, meet with your employees.

Full Moon: Arrange for audits to be performed. Develop your organization's annual report. Incorporate new management directives into your daily policies and procedures. Make a new organization chart and distribute it.

Aquarius the Water Bearer

Traditional astrologers assign Saturn to this sign also but the energies manifest a bit differently than in Capricorn. Good teamwork and humanitarian concerns are facilitated while the Moon is in Aquarius. Modern technology is highlighted here also, especially the airlines.

New Moon: Launch activities that require the cooperation of groups of workers. Assign team leaders. Employee training programs are best begun with the New Moon in this sign. Begin United Way campaigns or any other efforts to raise funds for charitable organizations.

Full Moon: Review and update personnel files. Interview potential employees for job openings. (Those hired should begin work during a New Moon.) Attend technology shows and exhibitions. Purchase items that will increase your organizations productivity.

Pisces the Fish

Generous Jupiter rules this compassionate sign. The Fish are connected with organizations that serve the infirm, poor, or downtrodden—not necessarily a prime demographic target of the for-profit sector. However, many readers may work in non-profit organizations or provide them with products and services.

New Moon: Launch sales campaigns for items to be marketed to hospitals, clinics, nursing homes, prisons, or any other end-of-life institution and their employees. Hire a company nurse or contract for employee assistance programs. Arrange for a blood drive at the office. Recruit volunteers.

Full Moon: Review your companies pension program, its obligations, and funding. Begin an alcohol and drug awareness program for employees. Make a corporate donation to a charity or non-profit group.

About the Author

Maggie Anderson is an astrologer, writer, and gardener. She makes her home in the heartland (Mount Vernon, Iowa), where she maintains a full-time astrological practice and teaches classes in astrology. Maggie second specialty involves "all affairs of the heart," which allows her to utilize her experience as a family therapist when counseling astrology clients. Her interest in world affairs is evident in the mundane astrology writings on her Web site, www.astromaggi.com.

The Entrepreneurial Moon

by Leeda Alleyn Pacotti

When faced with employment or financial loss, most people consider going into business for themselves. It seems feasible. Where else can you get the kind of income that supports your debt obligations and lifestyle expenditures? Unemployment compensation covers only the barest of living expenses for one person, without regard for familial responsibilities underwritten by the earnings of a primary or secondary breadwinner.

Entrepreneurship or self-employment offers other attractive possibilities for the person who must replace lost or future income. You can command your own hours, work at what you like, and people or other businesses will recognize the value of what you offer and pay you for it! You can start with next to nothing and skyrocket into financial bliss. While these are the hopeful attitudes of most people grasping for financial solvency in the midst of crisis, they bear little resemblance to the sound, and sometimes skeptical, perspective necessary to uphold you through the stress of starting business.

What are the likely situations you'll encounter? Fortunately, the placement of the Moon in your horoscope suggests a wealth of personal information to help you make strategic decisions and sustain you through some tough moments.

The Moon and the Flow of Money

The Moon, like the Sun, is a light in the horoscope, with movement that is always forward or progressive. Considered the lesser light, the Moon reflects the Sun's steady rays and is, like the Sun, an enduring and hopeful blessing. When putting your reliance on the Moon, you can have faith in its promises.

Unlike the Sun, however, the Moon goes through phases in its orbit, as viewed from Earth. While the Moon has wonderful effects, its changeful character alters or extends the time to manifest its sure promises. In your horoscope, the influence of the lunar orb suggests fluctuations and obvious rhythms of activity. Its placement by zodiacal sign and mundane house can explain whether you'll see success slowly or quickly, suffer protracted lean times, or prolong your business as a financial mainstay.

As a beneficent influence, the Moon becomes an important indicator of the process and eventuality of success, vibrating sympathetically with Saturn, the ruler of the tenth house of career, public image, and prestige. As the ruler of the opposing fourth house of foundation, the Moon projects a psychological impetus to be recognized by others for our inner worth. Although this impetus is directed toward Saturn's house for manifestation, the Moon always indicates our inner motivation to seek this recognition in a productive and satisfying way. Because of this underlying need for recognition by the world at-large, the Moon can be viewed as a "lower octave" vibration of Saturn. Tapping into the source of our desires for success creates a shortcut through Saturn's conservative developments.

Making a Go of It

As a foreshadow of Saturn's pronounced and careful growth, the Moon is a decidedly practical influence. When you first become aware that you may suffer a serious financial shortfall or lose your employment, begin planning immediately, starting with a realistic appraisal of what funds and energies you can expend toward entrepreneurship. Utilize relationships you've accumulated during your work years; talk forthrightly with bankers, lawyers, and other consultants about your situation and prospects.

The Moon rules commonplace items, everyday habitual uses, and ordinary needs, all the products, objects, and services we rely on to make good use of the day's remainder. Often, these

things are unobtrusive, overlooked, disregarded, or taken for granted. They can include menial or distasteful products and services. However, if any of these are out of place or missing, a person feels a definite loss of structure in performing other activities. For example, a commuter who habitually purchases a morning paper can feel confused and out-of-sorts for the rest of the day if all papers were sold out before his ride.

The promise of the Moon in entrepreneurship is for you to make excellent profits by attending to the basic needs of other people and businesses. The commonplace is not glamorous, but it is bountiful. You can start small and aim high, when you understand that others desire fulfillment of their needs. A steady business product or service, with built-in demand, keeps you busy and gives you satisfaction, possibilities for expansion, and potential for long-term financial support.

How Fast Can You Progress?

The placement of the Moon by sign signifies your basic attitudes and energies toward starting, building, and staying in business. Although anyone can find a business pursuit, the astrological quality of the Moon's sign shows your likely approach to stabilize the endeavor and create a viable income.

When the Moon is in the cardinal signs of Aries, Cancer, Libra, or Capricorn, you prefer to go alone, moving forward quickly and taking the lead in the field you choose. The cardinal signs often stun observers with how quickly they size up resources and events to create an advantage or capture a section of the market. Over the long run, business will fluctuate, usually due to an innate or identifiable seasonality. Initially, though, some excellent people will step forward as business allies, because they recognize a winner.

The fixed signs of Taurus, Leo, Scorpio, and Aquarius establish a firm, secure foundation. In these signs, the Moon appraises resources and opportunities carefully, making sure they will develop into sound prospects. The fixed signs do best by researching the entrepreneurial field for at least six months and investigating the likely client base. While there may be some early delays on the overall direction or approach of business, the fixed signs will not be stopped and persist to success.

The placement of the Moon in the mutable signs of Gemini, Virgo, Sagittarius, or Pisces usually shows a sense of urgency. Because these signs experience a marked volume of changes in life, they are likely to be the ones least prepared financially to underwrite a business. Often, they will rely on or defer to the advice, and sometimes the decisions, of others to create an immediate success. However, if they can forego pie-in-the-sky expectations and honor the Moon's promise of the commonplace, they can cultivate simple businesses and high client volumes.

Where to Do Business

The Moon's residence by house in your natal horoscope indicates the best base of operations for your success. If the Moon is in your third or fourth house, you'll do best by limiting operations and clients to your hometown or home county. For statewide or territorial operations, the Moon gives success when in the fifth house. To create a strong client base or operations on a national level, the Moon must be in the second or sixth houses.

For international concerns, the placement of the Moon suggests three possibilities. Operations and clientele in adjoining countries to your home country come with the Moon in the first and seventh houses. Distant countries, usually in overseas concerns, can be successfully undertaken when the Moon is in the twelfth and eighth houses. For those who desire clients anywhere in the world, without restraint of trade or limitation of clientele, the Moon in the ninth, tenth, or eleventh houses gives the strongest success.

Keep in mind that your immediate needs are to replace your current income and create secure returns in the future. Remember to start small, and delay development or expansion for later years. Following the Moon's indications can save you some costly drains on your time, energy, and limited funds.

Enhancing Entrepreneurial Success

The following lunar placements give a more personal description of your demeanor as an entrepreneur and some general considerations to create an initial success. Although some suggestions are offered about potential businesses, observe your environment and the business climate. A good and continuous income or profit is always made by doing what others consider thankless, lowly, or lacking in prestige. With some careful scrutiny, you'll find a wonderful opportunity to meet your individual needs and provide lucrative benefits.

Moon in Aries or First House

The influence of Aries manifests as freedom of movement. You like to be seen as in charge and an expert in your field, with original ideas. Your best clients will be executives and managers, who appreciate your outgoing style. Consider consultation for business start-ups and writing or assessing business plans. Because Aries rules motor vehicles, offer services to renew auto registrations or provide personalized advice and assessment, when others purchase vehicles.

Start your business with no employees, and use temporary services. Consider a home office, mobile office, or small furnished incubator with clerical services. Delay equipment purchases for as long as possible. You need to watch your expenditures, both business and personal, because you can easily outspend your cash flow. In advertising, spread the money where it draws customers or clients, rather than just creating name recognition. Be sure to get good tax advice, although keeping your own books gives you insight on your progress.

Moon in Taurus or Second House

The Taurus Moon prefers calculated, limited movement. You want to project a sense of establishment. Carefulness and certainty are the criteria for your timing to initiate or sustain business efforts. You know to wait out fluctuations, and expect gradual improvements in business and personal finances. Your natural inclination toward finance prepares you as a consultant in loan origination, mortgage brokering, and negotiations in any field. Consider representing artists or craftsmen, whose works exemplify beauty and value. Purely mundane businesses include gardening and landscaping.

You naturally keep your expenditures low and limit large costs. Travel is not a high demand, because you are more hospitable on your own turf. A small suite suits your presentation and must have a meeting room. As needed, acquire basic office equipment, although you will purchase used but very good furnishings. Sweets will probably be on every table and desk top, so keep to less costly hard candies.

Moon in Gemini or Third House

Your Gemini Moon makes you on the go, talkative, and congenial. You prefer a changing pace and environment, which stimulate your many bright ideas. The spoken or written word is your stock in trade; you'll feel more comfortable with report writing or preparing bid solicitations. If you need more movement, consider local delivery and courier services, especially in congested areas. As a manufacturer's representative, you stay fast on your feet, by introducing new products to market. Being personable, expect and cultivate referrals from friends, family, and previous employments.

You find management of an office bothersome, which translates as no employees. Because you are easily distracted from chores, consider subleasing an office with secretarial services thrown in. If such an arrangement is too great a responsibility, try a home office or mobile office. Your high-end expenditures will be mobile electronics; just be sure these are instrumental to your business operations. As a must, faithfully use a bookkeeper.

Moon in Cancer or Fourth House

The Cancer Moon likes to stay put and is very interested in monetary acquisition. Be careful with a home business, which can disrupt your privacy. Expect a broad, diverse clientele, which regards you as an authority. For you, home is where the money is, and you can consider home repairs, renovations, and household janitorial. Catering and lunch sales to offices satisfy your interests in food. If you like open space, consider farm clean-ups and renovations.

You prefer trusted employees, but you may have to begin with temporary services. When you do hire, create a core of good people and augment them with project employees. Because most of your service work will be on-site, consider low-end office or retail space, with lease provisions for expansion. Durable expenditures will be for well-maintained furniture, vehicles, tools, and equipment. Liability can seriously undermine your efforts; be sure to carry excellent insurances.

Moon in Leo or Fifth House

The Leo Moon has probably caused you some losses from speculation, with business as the next logical way for you to obtain serious money. Your style is up-front, flamboyant, intelligent, and above the crowd. Not one to be cramped, you shine at meetings, preferring to be seen and known. Consider brokering for marriage or high-ticket items, such as antiques. You enjoy creating an excellent presentation, which works in your favor as an agent, manager, or publicist.

You've probably started your business with some personal funds to project just the right image. Begin with an executive incubator suite and up-scale home furnishings. Windows and sunshine are a must. All other expenditures can be kept low, except personnel. As your business develops, you will hire very reliable people. However, you will probably never need more than three and will compensate them much higher than the market suggests. You are well qualified to keep your own books, which strengthens your acumen for self-compensation and bonuses.

Moon in Virgo or Sixth House

Quiet and careful, the influence of the Virgo Moon gives a considered approach and awareness of rules and regulations impinging on any business operations. Expect to travel throughout your locality. You are very familiar with fluctuations in employment matters and may have entered business, due to a recent employment separation. Undaunted and focused, you move forward with poise and rightfully deserve adulation from the rest of the zodiac for your perseverance. Attention to detail serves best in bookkeeping or tax consultation. With a natural understanding of health, consider commercial janitorial or health and medical refuse collection. Governmental contracting with such agencies as the EPA and FEMA is immensely lucrative. As with employment matters, sales drift up and down; be sure to watch your expenditure flow.

Hire employees on a temporary or subcontractual basis. Lease a no-frills small warehouse or industrial space for adequate accommodation and expansion. Although most of your furnishings are used, be sure electronic equipment and tools are state-of-the-art. In all business matters and contracts, carry high coverage for liability and disability insurances.

Moon in Libra or Seventh House

Your Libra Moon needs a relaxed, measured pace, inducing calm and quiet. You focus on the intellectual and theoretical, enjoying a graceful beauty within the mind as well as the body. Usually educated, but always thoughtful, you are sought for an intelligent appraisal of knotty problems. Using your mind is the mainstay of any business venture. Consider writing contracts and grants, preparing regulatory or legislative reviews, or offering paralegal services. Your hallmark is objectivity, which is best utilized for arbitration. Always congenial with large groups, consider event or wedding planning.

Over time, you will acquire no more than one or two employees, but start first with a skilled administrative assistant. A small office in an inconspicuous location will keep your rent low. Understated furnishings and hideaway equipment eliminate distractions and noise, which intrude on your thoughts. Surround yourself with soft colors and floral displays. In any form of legal services, acquire protective bond insurance.

Moon in Scorpio or Eighth House

The Scorpio Moon is elusive, reserved, and mysterious. Although you will make no open admission, you seek power, status, and wealth, which puts others in awe of you. Your closed-mouth approach is perfect for nondisclosure. In running a business, you are cautioned against monetary fluctuations, when you rely too heavily on the cash flow of others. The Plutonic influence from Scorpio makes you pre-eminently qualified to tackle extreme businesses, such as hazardous waste clean-ups, surveillance, and corporate spying. Perceiving gold in a mud heap, you can amass wealth from garbage and refuse removal or pollutant mop-ups.

Hiring employees requires a long-term commitment, which you can delay until business stabilizes. In the meantime, acquire services through a payroll contractor or other subcontractors. You can start in an incubator office and move quickly to a small industrial space. If you are on the go more than you expected, purchase mobile electronics or use an answering service to connect with your cell phone.

Moon in Sagittarius or Ninth House

The influence of Sagittarius on your Moon makes you open, gregarious, expansive, and expressive. You are on the move in speech and action, with high expectations for success. However, your impressions of the business environment often don't match the realities, so seek some good advice from a quieter member of the zodiac, such as a Libra or Aquarian. Serving as an agent or representative for authors or sports figures satisfies your sense of excitement. If you have a good focus of mind, consider travel writing or other freelance pursuits, where you can travel for research. If you need to limit your movements, consider writing advertising copy on a contractual basis.

You tend to be extravagant with employees, leaving little profit for yourself. Consequently, hire no one. A furnished incubator or mobile office suits your limited needs; consider a laptop computer and peripherals with satellite capabilities. Taxes will be your biggest concern. Put a tax consultant on retainer, and watch your meal and travel receipts.

Moon in Capricorn or Tenth House

Capricorn is the sign of business, causing your lunar expression to be practical and conservative. You are the most likely to start business on a shoestring. Even if you've never been in business before, you know the field and have unconsciously been sizing it up. You are intimately familiar with changes or fluctuations in career, but you have strong and serious expectations for improvement. On a business-to-business basis, you are an excellent consultant for sales, bookkeeping, or any services relating to business development.

You need an older, experienced receptionist, who knows how to be a strong gatekeeper and helps you gauge incoming clientele. At most, have only one or two employees. Take a small office, with an open-ended lease, in case you have to expand or minimize operations in a hurry. The established look suits your tastes. Acquire standard equipment and high-quality used furnishings.

Moon in Aquarius or Eleventh House

Unconventional and unpredictable, the business approach of the Aquarian Moon leaves others scratching their heads. No one understands how you succeed with your outlandish methods. You are reserved and private, finding the comments of others destructive toward your careful, intricate thought processes. Consequently, you prefer to be alone. Put your brilliant mind to work in data services or as a computer broker on a consultant basis. If you are highly trained in a scientific field, consider research and development contracts or experimental projects.

Employees only get in your way; do not hire any. For immediate business start-up, use a home office, but be sure to put in separate phone lines to avoid interference with family calls. Eventually, you will need either a tool or lab area. Lease a small industrial space. If expenditures must be kept low, consider renovating a garage or out-building on your property to accommodate the physical demands of your business.

Moon in Pisces or Twelfth House

Pisces has the most sympathetic and considerate business approach of all signs. Your Moon makes you withdrawn, quiet, slow-paced, and amiable. It's easy for others to steamroll you with incessant neediness. Of all signs, you must to be very careful with your pocketbook. Otherwise, you erode your profits by acting as a private charity. To put some space between you and the personal needs of others, consider grant and fund development for nonprofit organizations, hospitals, and other social service organizations. If you have talents with animals, consider training dogs or horses. The charitable approach to other life forms appeals to you and works well for teaching continuing education classes on animal husbandry and gardening. To satisfy your enjoyment of the group, try convention coordination.

Keep your needs simple with no employees. A home office also keeps expenditures down, but obtain separate phone and fax lines. You tend to be secretive and benefit from using "front" services, such as an answering service and post office box to conceal your identity or scope of business.

Hunting the Moon

Although, as pointed out earlier, there are affinities between Saturn and the Moon, they are opposites by house rulership. In business matters, Saturn can have a continuously depressing effect on business efforts and results, if it is natally within the twenty degrees preceding the Moon's birth placement. Because the Moon progresses through the zodiac in approximately twenty-eight years and Saturn emulates this movement by transit in about the same period, Saturn can trail the Moon in a close or wide conjunction throughout the entire life. This astrological phenomenon is known as "hunting the Moon."

In this case, Saturn makes the Moon overly cautious and fearful of risk. While you might be able to start a business, it will likely have a short duration or reach a pinnacle of success in a short time. Thereafter, the business may suddenly or gradually drain resources and time, showing little return.

If you have these natal placements at birth and decide to go into business, consider doing so as a stop-gap measure for income. Take advantage of this momentary reprieve, and choose a business avenue that enhances your resume, as you continue to search for a position in your chosen career or profession.

Suggested Reading

"Sepharial." *The Manual of Astrology*. London: W. Foulsham & Co., Ltd., 1962.

About the Author

Leeda Alleyn Pacotti practices as a naturopathic physician, nutritional counselor, and master herbalist, specializing in dream language, health astrology, and mind-body communication.

Farm, Garden, and Weather Section

Gardening by the Moon

Today, people often reject the notion of gardening according to the Moon's phase and sign. The usual nonbeliever is not a scientist but the city dweller who has never had any real contact with nature and little experience of natural rhythms.

Camille Flammarian, the French astronomer, testifies to the success of Moon planting, though:

"Cucumbers increase at Full Moon, as well as radishes, turnips, leeks, lilies, horseradish, and saffron; onions, on the contrary, are much larger and better nourished during the decline and old age of the Moon than at its increase, during its youth and fullness, which is the reason the Egyptians abstained from onions, on account of their antipathy to the Moon. Herbs gathered while the Moon increases are of great efficiency. If the vines are trimmed at night when the Moon is in the sign of the Lion, Sagittarius, the Scorpion, or the Bull, it will save them from field rats, moles, snails, flies, and other animals."

Dr. Clark Timmins is one of the few modern scientists to have conducted tests in Moon planting. Following is a summary of his experiments:

Beets: When sown with the Moon in Scorpio, the germination rate was 71 percent; when sown in Sagittarius, the germination rate was 58 percent.

Scotch marigold: When sown with the Moon in Cancer, the germination rate was 90 percent; when sown in Leo, the rate was 32 percent.

Carrots: When sown with the Moon in Scorpio, the germination rate was 64 percent; when sown in Sagittarius, the germination rate was 47 percent.

Tomatoes: When sown with the Moon in Cancer, the germination rate was 90 percent; but when sown with the Moon in Leo, the germination rate was 58 percent.

Two things should be emphasized. First, remember that this is only a summary of the results of the experiments; the experiments themselves were conducted in a scientific manner to eliminate any variation in soil, temperature, moisture, and so on, so that only the Moon sign is varied. Second, note that these astonishing results were obtained without regard to the phase of the Moon—the other factor we use in Moon planting, and which presumably would have increased the differential in germination rates.

Dr. Timmins also tried transplanting Cancer- and Leo-planted tomato seedlings while the Cancer Moon was waxing. The result was 100 percent survival. When transplanting was done with the waning Sagittarius Moon, there was 0 percent survival. Dr. Timmins' tests show that the Cancer-planted tomatoes had blossoms twelve days earlier than those planted under Leo; the Cancer-planted tomatoes had an average height of twenty inches at that time compared to fifteen inches for the Leo-planted; the first ripe tomatoes were gathered from the Cancer plantings eleven days ahead of the Leo plantings; and a count of the hanging fruit and its size and weight shows an advantage to the Cancer plants over the Leo plants of 45 percent.

Dr. Timmins also observed that there have been similar tests that did not indicate results favorable to the Moon planting theory. As a scientist, he asked why one set of experiments indicated a positive verification of Moon planting, and others did not. He checked these other tests and found that the experimenters had not followed the geocentric system for determining the Moon sign positions, but the heliocentric. When the times used in these other tests were converted to the geocentric system, the dates chosen often were found to be in barren, rather than fertile, signs. Without going into a technical explanation, it is sufficient to point out that geocentric and heliocentric positions often vary by as much as four days. This is a large enough differential to place the Moon in Cancer, for example, in the heliocentric system, and at the same time in Leo by the geocentric system.

Most almanacs and calendars show the Moon's signs heliocentrically—and thus incorrectly for Moon planting—while the Moon Sign Book is calculated correctly for planting purposes, using the geocentric system. Some readers are confused because the Moon Sign Book talks about first, second, third, and fourth quarters, while other almanacs refer to these same divisions as New Moon, first quarter, Full Moon, and fourth quarter. Thus the almanacs say first quarter when the Moon Sign Book says second quarter.

There is nothing complicated about using astrology in agriculture and horticulture in order to increase both pleasure and profit, but there is one very important rule that is often neglected—use common sense! Of course this is one rule that should be remembered in every activity we undertake, but in the case of gardening and farming by the Moon if it is not possible to use the best dates for planting or harvesting, we must select the next best and just try to do the best we can.

This brings up the matter of the other factors to consider in your gardening work. The dates we give as best for a certain activity apply to the entire country (with slight time correction), but in your section of the country you may be buried under three feet of snow on a date we say is good to plant your flowers. So we have factors of weather, season, temperature and moisture variations, soil conditions, your own available time and opportunity, and so forth. Some astrologers like to think it is all a matter of science, but gardening is also an art. In art, you develop an instinctive identification with your work and influence it with your feelings and wishes.

The *Moon Sign Book* gives you the place of the Moon for every day of the year so that you can select the best times once you have become familiar with the rules and practices of lunar agriculture. We give you specific, easy-to-follow directions so that you can get right down to work.

We give you the best dates for planting, and also for various related activities, including cultivation, fertilizing, harvesting, irrigation, and getting rid of weeds and pests. But we cannot tell you exactly when it's good to plant. Many of these rules were learned by observation and experience; as the body of experience grew we could see various patterns emerging that allowed us to make judgments about new things. That's what you should do, too. After you have worked with lunar agriculture for a while and have gained a working knowledge, you will probably begin to try new things—and we hope you will share your experiments and findings with us. That's how the science grows.

Here's an example of what we mean. Years ago, Llewellyn George suggested that we try to combine our bits of knowledge about what to expect in planting under each of the Moon signs in order to gain benefit from several lunar factors in one plant. From this came our rule for developing "thoroughbred seed." To develop thoroughbred seed, save the seed for three successive years from plants grown by the correct Moon sign and phase. You can plant in the first quarter phase and in the sign of Cancer for fruitfulness; the second year, plant seeds from the first year plants in Libra for beauty; and in the third year, plant the seeds from the second year plants in Taurus to produce hardiness. In a similar manner you can combine the fruitfulness of Cancer, the good root growth of Pisces, and the sturdiness and good vine growth of Scorpio. And don't forget the characteristics of Capricorn: hardy like Taurus, but drier and perhaps more resistant to drought and disease.

Unlike common almanacs, we consider both the Moon's phase and the Moon's sign in making our calculations for the proper timing of our work. It is perhaps a little easier to understand this if we remind you that we are all living in the center of a vast electromagnetic field that is the Earth and its environment in space. Everything that occurs within this electromagnetic field has an effect on everything else within the field. The Moon and the Sun are the most important of the factors affecting the life of the Earth, and it is their relative positions to the Earth that we project for each day of the year.

Many people claim that not only do they achieve larger crops gardening by the Moon, but that their fruits and vegetables are much tastier. A number of organic gardeners have also become lunar gardeners using the natural rhythm of life forces that we experience through the relative movements of the Sun and Moon. We provide a few basic rules and then give you day-by-day guidance for your gardening work. You will be able to choose the best dates to meet your own needs and opportunities.

Planting by the Moon's Phases

During the increasing or waxing light—from New Moon to Full Moon—plant annuals that produce their yield above the ground. An annual is a plant that completes its entire life cycle within one growing season and has to be seeded each year. During the decreasing or waning light—from Full Moon to New Moon—plant biennials, perennials, and bulb and root plants. Biennials include crops that are planted one season to winter over and produce crops the next, such as winter wheat. Perennials and bulb and root plants include all plants that grow from the same root each year.

A simpler, less-accurate rule is to plant crops that produce above the ground during the waxing Moon, and to plant crops that produce below the ground during the waning Moon. Thus the old adage, "Plant potatoes during the dark of the Moon." Llewellyn George's system divided the lunar month into quarters. The first two from New Moon to Full Moon are the first and second quarters, and the last two from Full Moon to New Moon the third and fourth quarters. Using these divisions, we can increase our accuracy in timing our efforts to coincide with natural forces.

First Quarter

Plant annuals producing their yield above the ground, which are generally of the leafy kind that produce their seed outside the fruit. Some examples are asparagus, broccoli, Brussels sprouts, cabbage, cauliflower, celery, cress, endive, kohlrabi, lettuce, parsley, and spinach. Cucumbers are an exception, as they do best in the first quarter rather than the second, even though the seeds are inside the fruit. Also plant cereals and grains.

Second Quarter

Plant annuals producing their yield above the ground, which are generally of the viney kind that produce their seed inside the fruit. Some examples include beans, eggplant, melons, peas, peppers, pumpkins, squash, tomatoes, etc. These are not hard-and-fast divisions. If you can't plant during the first quarter, plant during the second, and vice versa. There are many plants that seem to do equally well planted in either quarter, such as watermelon, hay, and cereals and grains.

Third Quarter

Plant biennials, perennials, bulbs, root plants, trees, shrubs, berries, grapes, strawberries, beets, carrots, onions, parsnips, rutabagas, potatoes, radishes, peanuts, rhubarb, turnips, winter wheat, etc.

Fourth Quarter

This is the best time to cultivate, turn sod, pull weeds, and destroy pests of all kinds, especially when the Moon is in the barren signs of Aries, Leo, Virgo, Gemini, Aquarius, and Sagittarius.

Moon in Aries
Barren, dry, fiery, and masculine sign used for destroying noxious weeds.

Moon in Taurus

Productive, moist, earthy, and feminine sign used for planting many crops when hardiness is important, particularly root crops. Also used for lettuce, cabbage, and similar leafy vegetables.

Moon in Gemini

Barren and dry, airy and masculine sign used for destroying noxious growths, weeds, and pests, and for cultivation.

Moon in Cancer

Fruitful, moist, feminine sign used extensively for planting and irrigation.

Moon in Leo

Barren, dry, fiery, masculine sign used only for killing weeds or cultivation.

Moon in Virgo

Barren, moist, earthy, and feminine sign used for cultivation and destroying weeds and pests.

Moon in Libra

Semi-fruitful, moist, and airy, this sign is used for planting many crops, and producing good pulp growth and roots. A very good sign for flowers and vines. Also used for seeding hay, corn fodder, and the like.

Moon in Scorpio

Very fruitful and moist, watery and feminine. Nearly as productive as Cancer; used for the same purposes. Especially good for vine growth and sturdiness.

Moon in Sagittarius

Barren and dry, fiery and masculine. Used for planting onions, seeding hay, and for cultivation.

Moon in Capricorn

Productive and dry, earthy and feminine. Used for planting potatoes and other tubers.

Moon in Aquarius

Barren, dry, airy, and masculine sign used for cultivation and destroying noxious growths and pests.

Moon in Pisces

Very fruitful, moist, watery, and feminine sign especially good for root growth.

A Guide to Planting

Using Phase & Sign Rulerships

Plant	Phase/Quarter	Sign
Annuals	1st or 2nd	
Apple tree	2nd or 3rd	Cancer, Pisces, Taurus, Virgo
Artichoke	1st	Cancer, Pisces
Asparagus	1st	Cancer, Scorpio, Pisces
Aster	1st or 2nd	Virgo, Libra
Barley	1st or 2nd	Cancer, Pisces, Libra, Capricorn, Virgo
Beans (bush & pole)	2nd	Cancer, Taurus, Pisces, Libra
Beans (kidney, white, & navy)	1st or 2nd	Cancer, Pisces
Beech tree	2nd or 3rd	Virgo, Taurus
Beet	3rd	Cancer, Capricorn, Pisces, Libra
Biennials	3rd or 4th	
Broccoli	1st	Cancer, Pisces, Libra, Scorpio
Brussels sprout	1st	Cancer, Scorpio, Pisces, Libra
Buckwheat	1st or 2nd	Capricorn
Bulbs	3rd	Cancer, Scorpio, Pisces
Bulbs for seed	2nd or 3rd	
Cabbage	1st	Cancer, Scorpio, Pisces, Libra, Taurus

Plant	Phase/Quarter	Sign
Cactus		Taurus, Capricorn
Canes (raspberry, blackberry, and gooseberry)	2nd	Cancer, Scorpio, Pisces
Cantaloupe	1st or 2nd	Cancer, Scorpio, Pisces, Libra, Taurus
Carrot	3rd	Taurus, Cancer, Scorpio, Pisces, Libra
Cauliflower	1st	Cancer, Scorpio, Pisces, Libra
Celeriac	3rd	Cancer, Scorpio, Pisces
Celery	1st	Cancer, Scorpio, Pisces
Cereals	1st or 2nd	Cancer, Scorpio, Pisces, Libra
Chard	1st or 2nd	Cancer, Scorpio, Pisces
Chicory	2nd, 3rd	Cancer, Scorpio, Pisces
Chrysanthemum	1st or 2nd	Virgo
Clover	1st or 2nd	Cancer, Scorpio, Pisces
Corn	1st	Cancer, Scorpio, Pisces
Corn for fodder	1st or 2nd	Libra
Coryopsis	2nd or 3rd	Libra
Cosmo	2nd or 3rd	Libra
Cress	1st	Cancer, Scorpio, Pisces
Crocus	1st or 2nd	Virgo
Cucumber	1st	Cancer, Scorpio, Pisces

Plant	Phase/Quarter	Sign
Daffodil	1st or 2nd	Libra, Virgo
Dahlia	1st or 2nd	Libra, Virgo
Deciduous trees	2nd or 3rd	Cancer, Scorpio, Pisces, Virgo, Taurus
Eggplant	2nd	Cancer, Scorpio, Pisces, Libra
Endive	1st	Cancer, Scorpio, Pisces, Libra
Flowers	1st	Libra, Cancer, Pisces, Virgo, Scorpio, Taurus
Garlic	3rd	Libra, Taurus, Pisces
Gladiola	1st or 2nd	Libra, Virgo
Gourd	1st or 2nd	Cancer, Scorpio, Pisces, Libra
Grape	2nd or 3rd	Cancer, Scorpio, Pisces, Virgo
Hay	1st or 2nd	Cancer, Scorpio, Pisces, Libra, Taurus
Herbs	1st or 2nd	Cancer, Scorpio, Pisces
Honeysuckle	1st or 2nd	Scorpio, Virgo
Hops	1st or 2nd	Scorpio, Libra
Horseradish	1st or 2nd	Cancer, Scorpio, Pisces
Houseplants	1st	Libra, Cancer, Scorpio, Pisces
Hyacinth	3rd	Cancer, Scorpio, Pisces
Iris	1st or 2nd	Cancer, Virgo
Kohlrabi	1st or 2nd	Cancer, Scorpio, Pisces, Libra

Plant	Phase/Quarter	Sign
Leek	1st or 2nd	Cancer, Pisces
Lettuce	1st	Cancer, Scorpio, Pisces, Libra, Taurus
Lily	1st or 2nd	Cancer, Scorpio, Pisces
Maple tree	2nd or 3rd	Virgo, Taurus, Cancer, Pisces
Melon	2nd	Cancer, Scorpio, Pisces
Moon vine	1st or 2nd	Virgo
Morning glory	1st or 2nd	Cancer, Scorpio, Pisces, Virgo
Oak tree	2nd or 3rd	Virgo, Taurus, Cancer, Pisces
Oats	1st or 2nd	Cancer, Scorpio, Pisces, Libra
Okra	1st	Cancer, Scorpio, Pisces, Libra
Onion seed	2nd	Scorpio, Cancer, Sagittarius
Onion set	3rd or 4th	Libra, Taurus, Pisces, Cancer
Pansy	1st or 2nd	Cancer, Scorpio, Pisces
Parsley	1st	Cancer, Scorpio, Pisces, Libra
Parsnip	3rd	Taurus, Capricorn, Cancer, Scorpio, Capricorn
Peach tree	2nd or 3rd	Taurus, Libra, Virgo, Cancer
Peanut	3rd	Cancer, Scorpio, Pisces
Pear tree	2nd or 3rd	Taurus, Libra, Virgo, Cancer
Pea	2nd	Cancer, Scorpio, Pisces, Libra

Plant	Phase/Quarter	Sign
Peony	1st or 2nd	Virgo
Pepper	2nd	Cancer, Pisces, Scorpio
Perennials	3rd	
Petunia	1st or 2nd	Libra, Virgo
Plum tree	2nd or 3rd	Taurus, Virgo, Cancer, Pisces
Poppy	1st or 2nd	Virgo
Portulaca	1st or 2nd	Virgo
Potato	3rd	Cancer, Scorpio, Taurus, Libra, Capricorn
Privet	1st or 2nd	Taurus, Libra
Pumpkin	2nd	Cancer, Scorpio, Pisces, Libra
Quince	1st or 2nd	Capricorn
Radish	3rd	Cancer, Libra, Taurus, Pisces, Capricorn
Rhubarb	3rd	Cancer, Pisces
Rice	1st or 2nd	Scorpio
Rose	1st or 2nd	Cancer, Virgo
Rutabaga	3rd	Cancer, Scorpio, Pisces, Taurus
Saffron	1st or 2nd	Cancer, Scorpio, Pisces
Sage	3rd	Cancer, Scorpio, Pisces
Salsify	1st or 2nd	Cancer, Scorpio, Pisces

Plant	Phase/Quarter	Sign
Shallot	2nd	Scorpio
Spinach	1st	Cancer, Scorpio, Pisces
Squash	2nd	Cancer, Scorpio, Pisces, Libra
Strawberry	3rd	Cancer, Scorpio, Pisces
String bean	1st or 2nd	Taurus
Sunflower	1st or 2nd	Libra, Cancer
Sweet pea	1st or 2nd	
Tomato	2nd	Cancer, Scorpio, Pisces, Capricorn
Shade trees	3rd	Taurus, Capricorn
Ornamental trees	2nd	Libra, Taurus
Trumpet vine	1st or 2nd	Cancer, Scorpio, Pisces
Tubers for seed	3rd	Cancer, Scorpio, Pisces, Libra
Tulip	1st or 2nd	Libra, Virgo
Turnip	3rd	Cancer, Scorpio, Pisces, Taurus, Capricorn, Libra
Valerian	1st or 2nd	Virgo, Gemini
Watermelon	1st or 2nd	Cancer, Scorpio, Pisces, Libra
Wheat	1st or 2nd	Cancer, Scorpio, Pisces, Libra

Easy on the Knees Gardens

by Maggie Anderson

Humans and vegetables have a lot in common: Once past their prime, both plump up, develop spots, and become all wrinkly. Perhaps it's because older gardeners can identify with every point on the growing cycle of life that we excel at gardening. For the under-fifty crowd, deadheading spent flower blooms is a chore. For seniors, it's an act of love for other living entities.

As we age, however, our bodies will sometimes resist the gardening experience. Arthritic hands stiffen up after an afternoon of pulling weeds. Achy limbs won't stretch and bend when hoeing as they did years ago. As much as we'd love to continue doing everything the same way we've always done it, adjustments must be made. We're older and wiser now and have gathered lots of tips that make our time in the flower beds and vegetables patches more enjoyable. Here are a few pointers that have helped me continue gardening in retirement.

In Gardening, Size Does Matter

By the time we're offered our first senior discount, most gardeners realize that small really is beautiful. Lifting tiny flowerpots does not result in back strain. A simple, sharp spade is adequate to dig into the earth at a slower pace, and we won't need to put on a truss before getting behind one—unlike when we use big gas-powered tillers. Huge, motorized gardening equipment that shakes its operator up, down, and sideways is to be avoided by seniors at all costs.

If you have downsized to a smaller home and yard, you may no longer have a good spot to plant huge canna bulbs. If not, consider planting a small patch of brilliant purple Japanese irises. The effect will be just as dramatic. You can try growing cucumber varieties like Salad Bush and Patio Pickles instead of the standard sprawling vine varieties. The smaller plants will produce as many fruits as their cousins, and taste just as good, too. Growing some things on your patio or deck is another option. Cucumbers, peppers, tomatoes, and herbs will all grow happily in containers.

Many gardening catalogs now cater to individuals with smaller appetites by offering seed varieties for produce that is just the right size for one or two meals. If you've ever tried to eat a ten-pound cabbage before it goes bad, you'll really appreciate the new Gonzales mini-cabbages, and Sugar Baby watermelons and Delicata squash are a more reasonable size than their hefty twenty-pound open-pollinated relatives.

Condo-dwellers, you might find your green thumbs limited by the association rules. If you find it limiting to confine your gardening talents to a few square yards of dirt, perhaps your city has space in a community garden patch you can get. Call Parks and Recreation for more information, but avoid signing up for more space than you can reasonably manage.

Ah! Those Grandiose Gardening Fantasies

Physical fitness experts tell us that gardening is great exercise and that we should continue doing it in order to stay fit. While it's true that digging a big hole for a new shrub may make grandpa break into an aerobic sweat, many gardening benefits come from simply being out of doors and in touch with the elements. Fresh air and sunshine are as important for the well-being of humans as they are for a beautiful rose bush. We can moderate our exercise levels a bit and still reap the benefits of being in our gardens.

As we approach retirement age, our goals in all areas of life are better realized if we aim for quality instead of quantity. Like gardeners of any age, senior's hopes for bigger and better gardens may be revived each spring with the arrival of seed and nursery catalogs. Try to resist the temptation. You'll be happy you did by midsummer. If you can't bear the thought of scaling back, at least do not enlarge your garden past the point of your strength and endurance.

Most of us older tillers of the soil are in tune with our bodies and aspirations, but just in case you're still dreaming of growing a 650-pound pumpkin to enter into a giant pumpkin contest next October, consider the following: How many trips to your pumpkin patch with the water tank will it take to make your orange beauty a prize winner? Can you rent a team of high-school football players to hoist it onto a flatbed truck and deliver it to the autumn fair? Who in your family will offer to help you transform your prizewinner into 1,000 pies and 3,000 pints of pumpkin butter?

As in other times of life, it pays to plan ahead. Large gardens need huge investments of time and labor. They can result in enormous amounts of flowers, produce, and more than a few trips to the chiropractor. A bumper crop of sweet corn alone can keep a granny shucking for days, when she'd much rather be out line dancing with her friends. Before planting, remember how prolific your seeds, plants, and shrubs have been in the past. Make a dozen "Everything in Moderation" bookmarks for your seed catalogs and let this saying become your gardening mantra.

Never Plant Anything That Says "Wild" on the Seed Package

Perennial plants are one thing, but plants that indiscriminately sow themselves from seed heads are quite another. If you're looking for ways to cut back on planting chores, the "wild" option will be self-defeating. This is as true of beautiful wild flowers as it is of wild garlic chives and angelica or wild roses. It may seem that sowing an empty flower bed with a small packet of wild flowers is an intelligent shortcut to repetitious planting, but the law of unintended consequences applies here.

Wild plants refuse to be contained after the second year of planting. Without constant vigilance, the winds will blow those little wild seed heads into every open crack and crevasse of the garden and yard and sidewalk! Wild rose hedges will expand exponentially and in directions that are positively unnatural. "Naturalize" only if you have acres and acres to fill in and have the option to burn it off when needed, with the help of your local volunteer fire department.

Green Is Mean: Bright Is Better

As a youthful gardener with 20/20 vision, I often missed seeing ripe green vegetables because they got lost in the camouflage of green foliage backgrounds. The number of "past their prime" produce in my garden mysteriously multiplied as I aged. Finally, the year I fed more super-sized peas to the compost bin than to my family, I realized it was time to plant varieties that would accommodate my failing vision. Now, whenever possible, I grow light-colored vegetables that are easy to spot among the green leaves and vines.

If you've ever ended a gardening season with vines full of lumpy-bumpy, dried-up green beans, you know all about the kind of gardener's remorse generated by over-ripe vegetables. Next season, why not plant yellow wax beans or a magical purple-pod variety that becomes green when cooked? They'll dangle like bright Christmas ornaments on your bean vines and you can see them get ripe.

Harvesting should not turn into a guessing game. Green zucchini, if overlooked, will silently develop into oversized, inedible, yellow submarines. Light-skinned zucchini varieties like Papaya pear, however, are every bit as wonderful as their green cousins. When they reach peak perfection, they're as bright as sunshine and cannot be ignored.

Globe-shaped lemon cucumbers are a delicate pale yellow when just the right size of maturity—and they're delicious—while their green cousins provide less subtle hints of ripeness. Try the pale yellow colored varieties for both fresh use and pickling making. When sowing lettuce, make it a Mesclun mix that includes many different shades of green, along with a few red varieties. Bright Lights chard adds cheery color to a garden or to your flower beds. And red and yellow peppers cry out to be picked while their shy green look-alikes disappear in the foliage.

Aim toward bright colors in perennial plantings also. Red currants are easier to spot when ripe than are black ones. Red raspberries demand to be noticed, while berries of darker shades can ripen and fall off the vine or be eaten by the birds before they're spotted. What is most important here is the contrast. Your garden will be more interesting and easy to harvest if it includes specimens of varying shades.

Never Bend Over

Stoop labor is neither comfortable nor becoming for seniors. There are already too many wooden cutouts of the backsides of gray-haired gardeners decorating flower beds in suburban America. Refuse to show the world your derriere as you weed and seed. Invest instead in the ultimate gardening luxury: raised beds. These should not be the kind with sleep-number mattresses. Rather, they are wooden boxes built to a height that allows you to sit or stand while you garden.

There are many variations on the raised bed theme but the higher you build them the more they cost. They can be constructed from many materials, including treated wood, old railroad ties, stone, bricks, or concrete blocks. I have even seen with my own eyes a curious raised bed made of four used tractor tires with potatoes growing happily in the center. (Men: Do not try this at home without the permission of your loved one.)

If for some reason you can't raise your dirt containers up to a height that is just right for you, plant flowers and vegetables varieties that grow on vines and up trellises and poles. It requires little effort to tend to eye-level purple clematis or beans. Your eyeglasses are less likely to slide off your nose when standing as when you're bending over to garden.

Protect those Limbs

Are your knees as tender and knobby as freshly dug Jerusalem artichokes? Avoid planting them directly on God's green earth. Instead, arrange to insert something soft between your lower limbs and the hard ground. Kneepads are the best intervention and have an added advantage of making you look sporty. If you don a pair of these beauties, your neighbor may mistake you for a hockey fan and ask you to predict the next Stanley Cup winner.

Flexible rubbery mats also provide good knee protection. They have one big disadvantage: Very unattractive leap-frog-like movements are required to repeatedly place the pad under your knees as you move along the garden path. I recommend these only to kneelers that have very private gardening spots. Knee hopping is right up there with scooting as an undesirable option for sophisticated, older gardeners.

Good Tools Can Be Your Best Friends

Most seniors have already learned one of the most important lessons in life: Always work with the right equipment! Nowhere is good equipment more important than when gardening. Many of us have recently learned how much easier it is to haul forty-pound bags of top soil to their destinations with a helpful dolly. Wheelbarrows still play an important role in any sort of yard work and you should have a good one that is easy to roll.

Ladders are easy to fall off of. As a rule, anyone with old and brittle bones should avoid climbing on them whenever possible. There are times when reaching the apples and peaches at the top of the tree is necessary, but a well-designed fruit picker does the job best. Small hand tools should be ergonomically correct and fit the user perfectly.

Continue to look for tools that will make your gardening life easier. Our "golden years" is the time in life to downsize from a heavyweight tiller to the small but efficient pony-sized model. New tools and gadgets are introduced each year and some will be just the thing you've been searching for!

A general rule is to purchase tools of superior quality whenever possible. With loving care, they will last for many years. This includes cleaning, sharpening, oiling, and proper storage at the end of each season. It may not be possible to find the best tools at all hardware or discount stores. Search your seed and nursery catalogs or locate a specialty store that offers well made tools for gardeners. Good tools can sometimes be found at Spring Flower and Garden Shows, too. If they're out of your price range, add several to your Christmas wish list and offer these as ideas to your children and other relatives as a gift option.

A Virgo Harvest Moon

by Janice Sharkey

*". . . and the corn turn to gold
at harvest-time, and the Moon
in her ordered wanderings
change from shield to sickle,
and from sickle to shield."*
—Oscar Wilde

What springs to mind when you think of a Harvest Moon? A glowing full-bodied Moon bursting with light, magnetic energy pushing the Earth's water table up to overflowing? Or does it conjure up a reflective good night on a summer past? To some it is the reaping of the seeds we have sown, the rewards of honest toil and our partnership with nature. That season of "mists and mellow fruitfulness," when Mother Nature bears her best fruits at and around a Harvest Moon, usually falling in mid-September with the Full Moon nearest the Autumnal Equinox, rising nearly at the same hour for several days.

August and September are traditional months associated with harvest-time due to the Autumnal Equinox around September 24, which signals the beginning of autumn and the gathering of crops. Virgo is symbolic of this period not only because the Sun is in this sign until September 24, but also because a harvest Full Moon is likely to occur in Virgo. In autumn, Virgo is always a waning Moon (after Full Moon). The virgin symbolizes practical service linked to Mother Earth whether for healing or feeding. Although we tend to think of Virgo being a barren sign, which is true, she also generates growth.

Under a Virgo Moon, we would ideally turn over the soil, weed, prune, and generally tidy up our gardens. It is also an opportunity to focus on plants that are problematic and possibly transplant them to a better site. Certainly a Virgo Moon is a time to reorganize your garden, being practical about what should really go where and making gardening less work in the future and possibly earning you more time to relax. Repair work should go on at this time to be ready for the winter weather. But what about that other hidden side to a Virgo Moon, when sowing or planting would positively encourage better gardening?

Well, planting under a Virgo Moon has been known as a "root day" because it actively enhances root growth. What could be better for a plant's development than a strong root system—the foundation for healthy growth. Virgo is good for growing vines if blooms are wanted rather than fruit.

Certainly, the whole scale of vertical gardening would do well planted under a Virgo Moon. Climbers are tall plants that are not only attractive in themselves but do an invaluable service in covering unsightly walls, or just adding that extra dimension of height to a garden design. Tall plants can act as a shield against blistering hot sun, aiding shade and moisture retention. When the autumnal winds get going, this tall leafy growth will also be a windbreak to protect less hardy plants.

A Virgo Moon is considered to be a barren time. If we think of a plant like a human body, then Virgo rules the digestion. When we consume vegetables, we are eating the "stored food" in the part of the plant that is edible. Digestion of this stored food within the plant will produce energy during the growing season, but at the end of the year there will be no food stored up, which is why plants take on a tough vine-like appearance when planted under a Virgo Moon. A Virgo Moon is a good time to plant an apple or pear tree. During this time, Virgo is a positive force to grow for abundance.

Mercury rules Virgo. Hermes, the winged messenger to the ancient gods and symbol of Mercury, typifies speedy restlessness, sending messages and swift action to heal the mind and digestion. Culpepper ascribed the virtues of Mercury as attending to the ills of the stomach and of the mind or respiratory system.

A Selection of Herbs Ruled by Mercury

Plant	How to Use	Therapeutic Value	Harvest
Lavender	Aromatherapy	Mood enhancer, burns and bruises	Flower
Parsley	Culinary	Vitamins, minerals	Leaves
Fennel stalks	Culinary/tea	Digestion, stomach	Seeds
Valarian	Herbal	Nervous system	Roots
Dill leaves	Herbal/tea	Digestion, stomach	Seeds

Harvesting Seeds and Herbs

Natural herbs are harvested fresh. They can be more advantageous to our body than modern drugs because they are organic and contain a combination of natural forces that are released into the body in the proportion needed. The body easily converts them into healing action, so herbs can and should be used as a prevention as well as a cure where possible to many everyday ailments.

We can use herbs as infusions, decoctions, formentations, salves, and poultices. It is best to gather herbs under the Virgo Moon for disorders of the digestive organs, pancreas, or nervous complaints.

So the position of the Moon in the zodiac has a crucial bearing on gathering and using medicinal herbs. A herb that is gathered for the healing or strengthening of those parts of the body that are governed by that zodiac sign of the gathering day is especially effective. For instance, if you have a sore throat you would gather some thyme and infuse this in a tea (add honey) under the sign of Taurus Moon, which relates to healing the throat.

Preserving Herbs

The correct time for storing and filling jars or cardboard boxes is always when the Moon is on the wane, regardless of the date the herbs were gathered. Putting herbs into containers during a waxing Moon could cause them to rot. Paper bags or dark jars are ideal for storing herbs because they keep the sunlight and moisture from them.

Plants have varying drying times. Ensure that herbs gathered when the Moon is waxing undergo some of their drying process during the waning Moon.

Hang a selection of plants, such as marjoram, thyme, and parsley, upside-down like a bunch of flowers. Hanging it this way not only ensures they will dry efficiently, but they give the surrounding area a wonderful bouquet to cleanse your spirit.

Fresh Harvest

Usually herbs and vegetables such as spinach, cress, and salad greens eaten fresh and raw from the garden have the greatest value.

Harvesting Parts of the Plant

Roots should be collected when the sap has decreased and the Moon is in Virgo or waning during spring or autumn; harvest in late evening if possible.

Leaves can be harvested almost throughout the year provided plants are young. Late morning, when the Moon is waxing, between a New and Full Moon is the best, or on leaf days under a Cancer, Scorpio, or Pisces Moon. Herbs gathered under a Scorpio Moon possess special curative power and are better for storing.

Leaves harvested under Cancer or Pisces should be used right away.

Flowers are best gathered in spring and summer around mid-day, and ideally when the Sun is shining or the weather is warm and dry, during a waxing or Full Moon. Fruit and seeds should be ripe and picked or collected during summer or autumn in dry weather. Fruits and seeds harvested when the Moon is waxing must be used immediately. Choose gathering days in fruit/seed under a fire sign Moon.

Harvesting

Harvest root crops for food during the Third or Fourth Quarter, and in a dry sign such as Aries, Leo, Sagittarius, Gemini, or Aquarius. Harvesting root crops intended for seed, such as sweet potatoes, should be done at the Full Moon. Whereas, grain that is to be stored or used for seed should be collected first after the Full Moon, but avoid gathering under a watery sign. Pick fruit in the decrease of the Moon and in fire signs.

Power of the Full Moon

The day of the Full Moon is an outstanding collecting time for almost all herbs and parts of herbs. Roots in particular, when gathered at the Full Moon, or when the Moon is on the wane, have greater curative powers than at other times. Moreover, roots, especially those which could heal a serious complaint, should not be exposed to the Sun and preferably be harvested around the evening light and ideally near an actual Full Moon.

Harvesting By Moonlight

The poet Wordsworth worshiped nocturnal nature, too, when he wrote:

> "In common things that round us lie/some random truths he can import/the harvest of a quiet eye that broods/and sleeps on his own heart."

Moonlight gardening may seem mad. Just when you are ready to put your feet up and close the door on the garden, why bother to venture out into a nocturnal world to pick a lettuce or two? Yet the optimum time for harvesting salad is between 8 am and 1 pm. If the salad greens are refrigerated promptly, they will stay fresh for three or four days longer than those picked at other times. Why? One reason is a build-up of sugars and salts in the leaves during daytime. Sweet basil has been shown to last up to 170 percent longer when collected at night. How does this happen? Is it by magic or is there a deeper, logical answer lurking in the atmosphere? Mother Moon holds the secret. It is not mere wishful thinking but rather the Moon's gravitational pull on the Earth's moisture. This assertion is now being backed up by scientific evidence. So if, as we know, every organism on this planet is largely made up of water, it makes sense to work in harmony with the ebb and flow of the Moon's energy.

With the Sun we can see its effect on plant life as even the sunflower turns to face the rays from the solar planet. Yet the Moon's magnetic energy has always remained more mysterious. There are two effects at work: moonlight, plus the Moon's gravitational pull on the Earth's water, both of which increase and decrease with the waxing and waning of the Moon. Moonlight leads to better top growth, while root growth is stimulated when the water table drops as a result of reduced gravitational pull. Seeds are best planted at a New Moon or just after while crops harvested at night, around Full Moon are particularly moist. Full Moon is also the time to transplant but pruning should be left until levels of sap in the plant have fallen which is during the last quarter prior to a New Moon.

Why does the Moon have this effect on the tides? The Moon orbits the Earth as the Earth orbits the Sun. The Moon is so close to the Earth that its gravitational influence is greater than that of the Sun. Tides can be high or low. The highest tides occur when the Sun, Earth, and Moon align at New or Full Moon. At the half-Moon stage, the Moon's gravitational pull on the Earth is at right angles to that of the Sun, which counteracts it, resulting in the lowest high tides of the lunar month. It is best to plant biennials, perennials, shrubs, bulbs, and those plants that need a firm hold on the Earth at a Full Moon or during the third quarter. The fourth phase just prior to a New Moon is a barren phase. The water is drawn deep into the earth and is not available to plants. Therefore it is a good opportunity to undertake various garden maintenance jobs and weeding, mowing, etc. Trees and shrubs are pruned at this quarter and are less likely to bleed as profusely as at a Full Moon.

A waxing Moon, which is increasing in light from new to full, east of the Sun, is prominent in the sky during the afternoon, evening or early part of the night. When it is full, the Moon must be opposite to the Sun, so it rises at sunset, sets at sunrise, and shines all night.

A waning Moon (decreasing from full to new), being to the west of the Sun, is likely to be seen later in the night or in early morning.

Design with a Virgo Theme

Who is Virgo? The virgin (we see her as a mother/daughter figure providing dutiful service to those in need) is synonymous with the sign Virgo. She is characteristically modest, yet meticulous in everything she pursues. There is a practical, earthy responsibility about her, which she bears well. We see this especially in her instinctive need to heal with herbs ruled by her sign such as lavender, valarian, and the humble buttercup.

The planet Mercury rules her, which reflects her capacity for analytical thought and her intelligence but also the power to be too critical of herself and others. Those plants related to healing the nervous system, stomach, and intestines come under Virgo's rulership. In the medieval *French Book Of Hours,* published in 1423, she is shown working at the harvest, a Mother Earth figure reaping the corn and using the land to replenish the body. Mercury symbolizes the great communicator, but unlike when it is in Gemini (which it co-rules), Mercury in Virgo is expressed through teaching, healing, and critical analysis in order to reach a better understanding of the world and her place in it.

Virgo comes under the element of earth, so practicalities, such as where to situate that compost bin or herb wheel so it can be reached easily, should be the basic starting point to any garden design. "Reality" is another watch-word when dealing with the earth element. For instance, there is no point in desiring an abundant floral Eden if you have children and pets who want to run wild within it and use it as a play park.

To a certain extent formal structure does appeal to a person with a strong Virgo signature in their birth chart. Designing a knot garden or having evergreen box topiary can be appealing for its shape and symbolic structure. Medicinal herbs are a favorite not just because they are practical as healing plants but also for their beauty. So a place should be made for herbs—if only tucked away into a miniature window box or given space to flourish in a herb wheel.

Stepping into a medieval garden has a strong Virgo symbolism because there the choices are reduced to plants that heal or are of service to daily life, such as ridding the air of obnoxious odors or scenting a carpet. You would find sprigs of lavender, thyme, or similar herbs there to discourage insects with in the medieval garden. Plants were part of virtually every facet of life in the fourteenth century. They symbolized our relationship with the cosmos as well as our aspirations in love and death. What could be more apt than to recreate a medieval garden to represent the true characteristics of Virgo—the woman ready to heal our wounds with lavender or win our hearts with a forget-me-not.

Psychologically, blue is a calming, therapeutic color. Navy blue, a Virgo color, gives strength and confidence, while an earthy dark brown suggests practical reality rooted in the earth, with green acting as a balancing color that energizes growth. Yellow, which is traditionally associated with Mercury, can be used to contrast with the blues and browns. Color has a crucial role to play in good garden design. Blue helps to create space and widen up vistas as well as giving a peaceful mood. Color can be seen in everything and painted with good effect from a tint onto a fence just as much as from the tint of a flower.

Earthenware is an ideal material to use in a Virgo garden. The fact that it is made from the earth itself is symbolic. Crank clay is excellent to use in pottery for outside, and it can be sculptured before being fired in a kiln. Its appearance is that of light sandstone and can be aged easily by painting on yogurt or letting nature take her course. I sculptured a Virgo gardener harvesting herbs, which sits nestled among the lavender and thyme within a herb wheel during summer. When winter approaches, I move her to a sheltered spot away from the extreme elements of rain, frost, and snow. Virgo symbolism can be used in all sorts of materials such as in glass made into stained glass windows or ornaments. Motifs of the virgin/daughter or Earth Mother can all be easily crafted to shine through glass and awaken our perception of her throughout the year when autumn has fallen and another season unfolds.

Plants were part of virtually every facet of life in the fourteenth century. They symbolized our relationship with the cosmos as well as our aspirations in love and death. What could be more apt than to recreate a medieval garden to represent the true characteristics of Virgo the woman ready to heal our wounds with lavender or win our hearts with a forget-me-not.

About the Author

Janice Sharkey is a dedicated astrological gardener. She studied and gained the certificate from the London Faculty of Astrological Studies and practices lunar and organic gardening. She designs gardens to reflect an individual's birth chart and has clients from as near and far as the United Kingdom and the U.S. Her hobbies include pottery and making astrological themes in stained glass. When she is not stargazing or planting, she's enjoying time with her husband William and two kids, David and Rose. For information on Moon gardens and design, email: astrologygarden@aol.com.

Kitchen Concoctions for Pest Control

by Louise Riotte

When we start talking about garden pests most of us relate our thinking to those insects and beasties detrimental to fruits and vegetables. But there are pests which we humans are often confronted with and it is often beneficial to know how to deal with them on an emergency basis. While most insects' bites and stings are relatively harmless, they can result in considerable discomfort and often simple kitchen remedies can alleviate the pain.

According to *The Rulership Book* by Rex Bills, Pluto and Scorpio rule insects in general. Helen and John Philbrick, in *The Bud Book*, give further detail: "The male is indicated by the planetary symbol for Mars and the female by the symbol for the planet Venus." Bites and stings are also ruled by Mars.

Mosquitoes (ruled by Pluto)

Mosquitoes, according to Dr. Ralph Murphy, a pediatrician, are most active during early morning and early evening hours when the Sun is less intense. In warm climates these are the hours when many gardeners choose to work, making them a prime target from mosquitoes. Dr. Murphy suggests that if bites have already occurred, soaking washcloths in hot water, wringing them nearly dry, and applying them to mosquito bites for two seconds will relieve discomfort for two hours.

Ticks (ruled by Saturn)

Tick bites are of great concern due to the risk of disease. Ticks are worse some years than in others, even infesting flower and vegetable gardens, and grass and trees in residential areas.

If you discover a tick on your skin, it's best to remove it with a sharp pair of tweezers. Place one tong between the tick and the skin and ease the insect off sideways. Credit cards or anything with a flat surface can be used. If these are unavailable a thick dollop of petroleum jelly over the tick, which suffocates it, will be helpful. Be sure to wash your hands and the bite area thoroughly with soap and water following tick removal.

Ticks are notorious for carrying a disease called Rocky Mountain spotted fever. Symptoms of this illness appear three to fourteen days after the bite occurs. Warning signs include sudden onset of bodily aches, chills, headache, malaise, and high fever. A rash usually appears five to eight days after the onset of other symptoms. This rash is red, not itchy, and either pinhead size or slightly stringy in appearance. It starts at the wrists and ankles and moves toward the center of the body. If any or all of these symptoms occur, see a physician.

Bees and Wasps
(ruled by Mercury and Virgo)

People who are allergic to insect venom may have serious reactions from honeybee stings, as well as those of hornets, yellow jackets, and paper wasps. Wasps, I have observed, are the main pollinators of cream and black-eyed peas, therefore, I usually harvest these early in the morning when wasps are less active. Either bumblebees or honeybees can pollinate squash. Most of these insect stings are momentarily painful and are followed by swelling and discomfort. Only the honeybee leaves its stinger in the skin. The stinger can be removed by carefully lifting it out with the edge of a knife or nail file. Do not squeeze the stinger as this will inject more venom under the skin. After removing the stinger, wash the area with soap and water, and apply a paste of baking soda and water to alleviate the itching and pain. Wrapping the area in ice-cold compresses also relieves discomfort, but don't place ice directly on the skin. I have also found that if I take two aspirin tablets the swelling will be held down, but they must be taken immediately after the sting occurs.

Fiddleback Spiders (ruled by Saturn)

Black widow spiders are seldom encountered in gardens, but the fiddleback spider may be present almost anywhere. Also called the brown recluse, its bite can be very serious and require treatment by a physician, and possibly even hospitalization. While it's commonly identified by a violin-shaped pattern on its back, the markings can vary. For this reason, a bite from any brown spider should be watched carefully for signs of blistering or ulceration.

Most spider bites produce a stinging sensation, redness, and swelling. These symptoms soon disappear. But the fiddleback causes a chronic effect to the skin. Redness and swelling are followed by a "bubble" over the bite and the appearance of a red ring resembling a bull's-eye. The bubble then ruptures and forms a crust, and the skin sloughs off, leaving an ulcer. This process continues to repeat itself, eventually wearing away the tissue below the skin. If you suspect you've been bitten, watch the area carefully and call your physician at the first sign of the bite doing more than forming a simple red bump.

Wooly Gray Caterpillars (ruled by Venus and the Moon)

The harmless looking wooly gray caterpillars, which are fairly common in gardens, can cause intense pain if picked up or touched because its hairs embed in the skin. The hairs are difficult to see, but the affected area may become reddened. Try covering the area with Scotch tape and pulling the hairs out as the tape is peeled away.

Fleas (ruled by Pluto)

Household pests can also be a big problem to the homeowner. In the spring of 1991, I saw a big upsurge in the flea population due to a combination of heavy rains and humid weather, the likes of which had not been seen for many years. Strangely, the infestations were rather spotty, affecting certain areas worse than others—even in the same town some areas had more fleas than others. The pet population did not seem to be a factor, for many households that had not pets were affected. Things got so bad that the problem was frequently aired on radio and television broadcasts, with new remedies suggested almost daily. It was also suggested that several controls be tried, as what would work in one area helped not at all in another.

In past years, I had always been able to control fleas in the spring flea season by sprinkling chlordane over my carpets with a duster, leaving it down for a few days and then vacuuming it up. After several applications to catch the hatch-out of any eggs, the flea problem disappeared. Last spring it simply didn't work. Then my daughter-in-law told me about a family with pets who had cleared their household by sprinkling common salt on their carpets, leaving it down and then vacuuming. In desperation I tried it, and it worked! I don't know how or why, but I theorize that it works somewhat on the same principle as diatomaceous earth, which cuts the insects' bodies. Used in the garden, diatomaceous earth kills insects with hard-shelled bodies but it will not injure soft-bodied earthworms.

Ants (ruled by Mercury and Pluto)

Ants, black or red, large or small, can be a real problem in the household, particularly if they come up, as mine did, in the bathroom and around the stone fireplace. After buying several highly recommended sprays and powders at the supermarket and using them with no appreciable results, I remembered an old remedy my mother had used. I cut up a cucumber (Moon in Cancer) and placed strips and chunks of it by the cracks where ants were coming through. It seemed like a minor miracle—in just a few hours the ants were gone.

Another old-time repellent that is helpful is to plant tansy (Venus, Jupiter, and Gemini) by the front and back doors. Ants definitely don't like tansy, sometimes called "bitter buttons." Crush a few springs occasionally and lay them by the door if the ants are entering your house.

Roaches (ruled by Pluto)

The same muggy weather that caused the explosion in the flea population also seemed to affect those other little horrors—roaches. I tried a number of remedies, but, to my surprise, the cucumber strips also worked on the roaches. When I began laying them around to foil the ants, the roaches disappeared, too. I also followed the advice of my neighbor and plugged up the spaces where the pipes entered under the kitchen sink with steel wool.

Of course cleanliness and careful storage of food are all helpful, but re-infestation can occur if roaches are under the house and come up through walls and cracks, or they may be accidentally brought in in bags and boxes from the grocery store.

According to the book *Common Sense Pest Control*, other effective remedies include boric acid diatomaceous earth, and silica gel. Boric acid is one of very few materials that does not repel cockroaches, so they are not able to avoid it as they do other compounds. It acts like a stomach poison and they have not developed resistance to it. It is also the safest roach control product to use around humans and pets. It has a slow killing action, though, taking five to ten days. Diatomaceous earth and silica gel are non-toxic to humans and pets, and are effective against roaches when used as dusts. Both of these products kill roaches by abrading their outer coverings, allowing metabolic sap to leak out, causing them to dehydrate and die.

Mice (ruled by Pluto)

The old-time mousetrap is still one of our best bets. The use of traps alone or in conjunction with baits, with increased emphasis on habitat alterations, will help extend the useful life of baits. One of the biggest problems with mice is that they seem to develop a resistance to baits quickly.

There are herbal repellents as well. The leaves of the dwarf elder (*Sambucus ebulus*) will drive mice away from stored grain, and, presumably, from the house. The vetchling or everlasting pea (*Lathyrus latifolius*, L.) repels mice and other small rodents. Legumes are Venus-ruled. The presence of spearmint (ruled by Jupiter and Venus) growing near a house is reported to repel various rodents. The spurges (*Euphorbia lathyrus* and *E. lactea*) have the reputation of repelling moles and mice.

Clothes Moths (ruled by Gemini, Mercury, and Neptune)

Camphor is a natural product distilled from the camphor tree (*Cinnamomum camphora*) and has been known as an insect repellent since ancient times, and it is still sold as a moth repellent. Synthetic camphor, available in some drugstores, has properties identical to those of the natural product. It is produced from pine turpentine. Do not treat camphor lightly, for it is a poison. It can be purchased in ball, flake, or cake form, from a pharmacy or hardware store. It is also a fumigant.

Lavender herb will repel moths that attack woolen clothes and carpets. Used indoors, mint will repel clothes moths. Moths may also be repelled by sprinkling dried leaves of wormwood, southernwood, rosemary, sage, santonica, and tansy.

Moth Pests of Stored Food and Other Products

Prevention is the simplest and best way to deal with stored-product pests. Since most problems begin when the insects are transported into the house with the product, it is wise to inspect all food before purchase. The use of poisons should not be necessary in the management of stored-food pests. Destroy noxious growths, and this includes animal pests, when both Sun and Moon are in barren signs and the Moon is decreasing—fourth quarter is preferred. Barren signs are Leo, Aries, Virgo, Aquarius, Gemini, and Sagittarius—listed according to the degree of their non-productive or barren qualities.

If prevention and cleanliness do not solve your stored-food problem, remove the contents from cupboards and drawers and apply an insecticidal dust, such as silica aerogel or diatomaceous earth to cracks where pests congregate. Cover the bottoms of drawers and shelves with shelf paper to keep the chemical dust off dishes and utensils. Where this does not provide adequate control, spray empty cupboards with an insecticide. When the insecticide has dried, cover surfaces with shelf paper, and replace food, dishes, and utensils. Do not apply insecticides to any surface that comes into contact with food, dishes, or utensils.

Protective Possibilities

Wearing protective clothing can reduce the risk of insect bites and other health hazards. Children hiking or playing in wooded areas should always wear shoes and socks. For garden wear, long-sleeved shirts, long pants, and hats cut down exposure areas.

The Sun is the cause of at least 90 percent of skin cancer cases and about 80 percent of this damage occurs in the first twenty years of life.

Angelica essential oil combined with St. Johnswort flower oil is known as an outstanding wound remedy and nervine. It is rapidly gaining attention as a strengthener of the immune system, too. It also makes an excellent sunscreen, shielding overly intense light.

Insects seem to be attracted to brightly colored, dark, and rough fabrics, but not as much to white clothing with a hard finish. Bees are attracted to highly scented colognes, perfumes, suntan lotions, and powders.

Wearing lightweight clothing, which covers the body, also protects against poison oak and poison ivy.

Bathe before opening a bee hive or in any way working with bees, as they are sensitive to sweat and body odors.

This article originally appeared in Llewellyn's 1993 Moon Sign Book. It is reprinted with permission.

Night Gardens

by Janice Sharkey

"What has the night to do with sleep?"
—Keats

There is something almost hypnotic about a clear night's sky. It's possible that the glimpse into the infinite star studded cosmos wakes up our inner sense of oneness. This link with the universe can also remind us of our unique infinitesimal contribution as just one being, one grain of sand on our earthly seabed not to mention life on any other planet. This cosmic energy swilling all around us is more evident when the night has a starry face, but whatever the time, day or night, those everchanging forces have an effect on what is generated on and within our Earth.

Under the cover of darkness, lunar gardening becomes an adventure. For centuries many farmers and gardeners have carried on the long tradition of harvesting by moonlight for they know that this is actually the best time to gather crops. (The hour of moonrise is an important time in gardening and harvesting on hour either before or after moonrise is the ideal period to obtain maximum yield.) Try to sow and plant as close to the hour on each day (with adjustments to your longitude and latitude) wherever possible. In the United Kingdom, moonrise happens in the daytime during the waxing phase. Once into a waning phase, the Moon rises during night time. For any other longitude, obtain the time of Moon rising (GMT) by adding one hour per fifteen degrees of longitude due west.

Many jobs in the garden, such as sowing or planting root vegetables, planting biennials, perennials and bulbs, can be undertaken during the third and fourth quarter. Trees, shrubs, berried plants, onion sets, potatoes, grapes, and winter wheat are best planted at this time during the decrease of the light from a Full to New Moon. When harvesting fruits that are to be preserved, they are best picked at a New Moon since they will store better, whereas fruits to be eaten fresh are best picked at a Full Moon for their succulence. Crops should be harvested in the same Moon sign element in which they were sown if the requirement is to obtain seeds for next year's crop.

Night Gardening Activities

Venturing out into the garden during evening as night falls is an excellent time to catch garden pests. Slugs and snails come out and are more readily seen in the evening and can be rounded up. Vine weevil and similar beetles snack on foliage, not to mention that they leave their eggs to later hatch out and devour the roots of potted plants. Taking a tour of the garden as the light decreases using torch light can alert you to those nasty pests. It can allow you to take action such as setting an insect trap with something as simple as wax around the rim of a pot.

Certain traps within the greenhouse can be put in place specifically for night time. Humane traps, such as a miniwire cage with a cube of cheese, will enable you to trap mice and evict them without injury later. Setting saucers of water inside the leg of benches and tables can prevent insects from crawling up the legs to get at plants. Beneficial creatures such as frogs and toads, which are insectivorous, should be welcomed into the greenhouse. Putting sticky traps to hang from the roof help keep down aphids and alert you to take further action. It is important to encourage, through diverse planting, beneficial creatures such as naturally occurring pest predators and parasites.

Birds are useful in the garden, too. Other pest-eating mammals, such as bats, shrews, and hedgehogs, will dine on slugs and reduce your workload. Installing a pond will encourage a breeding site for amphibian toads and frogs as well as give you an added world of plant life in water.

You maybe fortunate to have hedgehogs visiting and dining on a pest while you catch the last of the evening light. The fourth quarter—the dark Moon prior to a New Moon—is ideal for not only pest control but weeding and turning over the soil to allow birds to peck at any unwanted insects which could otherwise remain and later eat your future crops.

Nocturnal gardening awakens your senses. During that time, birds singing to reassert their territorial rights are a gardener's delight and confirmation that your garden is worthy as one of nature's bird-tables. As the light recedes, other life comes into its own, such as the midge or the firefly, as it swarms around in search of its prey.

Just as the firefly has developed its light to glow in the dark, so, too, some plants, predominantly of certain colors such as yellow, white, or gray, are able to "glow" and become luminous when the rest of the garden border has gone to sleep.

Yellow is a powerful color and acts to increase space. Since the golden foliage of many plants will scorch in full sunshine, such an area will do well in light shade and come into its own during evening time. Yellow can bring a sense of well being to a garden even in a dull day. Floral white comes a close second in bringing a late burst of color to a garden at dusk. Think of the

swaying of ox-eye daisies or margurites as a blackbird bids good night, it conjures up a summer's night to remember.

After the summer has past, the fall can bring many shades of yellow, but in the form of berries and bark for autumn and winter color.

As the light recedes within a garden, other forms take shape. The textural, foliar shapes of leaves appear almost as silhouettes, for example. Sitting out on a veranda watching the Sun shed its last light on the day can be both tranquil and uplifting, making us aware of a deeper often hidden side to the garden—form. The outline of trees and shrubs take on a mysterious look; the breeze may make the foliage dance as night steps in to walk with the Moon.

As the day reaches its close, there is nothing better than relaxing and listening to the garden coming alive. One crucial sense that is often forgotten is scent and its role in the nocturnal garden.

It isn't just for our benefit that some plants perfume the night air, they do so for very practical reasons. Protection and fertilization. Certain plants come under attack at night, so to combat this some emit a scented chemical that attracts other insects that will eat the predator. Some, like pelargoniums, have scented oils which deter pests. Some plants are fertilized by night larvae insects and their scent is strongest in the dark because they have to attract insects like moths via their scent rather than sight and usually over a longer distance.

Several plants only open their flowers or release their scent in the evening. The moonflower (*Ipomoea alba*) is one example of a night flower. It gives a rich perfume and its saucer-like white flowers are luminous. Other well-known scented plants actually intensify their aroma considerably at night. Even more reason to choose a sheltered seat and create a tranquil place to chill out and inhale the sweet scented air after a day's work.

You must provide shelter if you want to capture aroma, though. If gardens are too exposed, all aroma is blown away. Create screening from walls, hedges, bamboo, or willow. Travel around your garden at night and follow your nose. Certain plants growing in their natural state have an active and relevant healing role, capable of inducing a beneficial reaction simply through the release of minute quantities of essential oils through their leaves, flowers, or fruits. So for those insomniacs restless in the night, try a little spot of night gardening and let the scent of lavender or chamomile induce relaxation and send messages to your stressed being to switch off.

Night-scented Plants

Plant	Rulership	Color
Datura	Jupiter	White or yellow
Lily regale	Venus	White/pink
Iris pallida	Jupiter	Purple
Night phlox	Saturn	White to pink
Honeysuckle	Mars/Mercury	Yellow or red
Evening Primrose	Mercury	Buttercup yellow
Moonflower	Moon	White
Nicotiana	Mars	Purple/white

Pathways should have some aromatic "brush me" plants like lavender or "crush me" herbs such as thyme, which can be made into a carpet with gravel or paving to allow footsteps to release its refreshing scent. If your space is limited and you cannot stretch to a bench and arbor, a scented window box will work wonders as the perfume wafts into your home. Remember that scent can be portable by creating scented containers that can be moved to where you are. Try elevating scent nearer to your nose by placing pots on raised walls or adjustable tiered hanging baskets. The choice is limitless.

With the night, we associate the Moon. Cancer is ruled by the Moon and we can easily link Moon ruled plants and their symbolism with Cancer. Evening is often associated as a reflective, dreamy time. In the garden it is then that many plants come alive not only in flower but in scent. Moonflower is one such Cancer plant, named as it opens its blossoms in the evening and releases its fragrance as a natural defense against pests, either to attract insects that will eat predators or ward them off.

Germination is a critical time in plant formation, which is a nurturing role of Cancer. Many plants under this sign also exude milky sap such as the moonstone, succulents, and moonflower. Even the moonseed plant *Menispermum* produces a crescent-shaped seed in a shape of a waxing Moon. The moonflower if placed near to a melon plant is said to help germinate it.

Although water is nourishing, it can also be a destructive force as most coastlines will show. Planting grasses helps to anchor the soil and stop erosion. As well as this there is a wealth of interesting grasses to choose to suit every soil and garden. Culpeper assigns the Moon as ruling grass due to its often diuretic ability. Nowadays we can just admire its beauty and sound as it rustles in the breeze whether it be the sacred bamboo to the bountiful miscanthus. Many, like bamboo, are evergreen and lots have wonderful variegated leaves.

As the song goes "By the light, of the silvery Moon," this hue typifies the color of Cancer. All tints of white to gray, silver, and green are symbolic of this sign. The white rose in its simplistic cool beauty is extremely fragrant at night. *Papaver orientalis*, with its luscious flowers and maroon-colored centers, belongs in the summer border. Palm trees come under the auspices of Cancer possibly because of the coconut milk, or due to its sheltering habit of fan-shaped leaves and their production of white flowers (as in the washintonias thread palm). As a protection from the rigors of salt, many coastal plants have silvery foliage due to the small thin hairs that give the leaf its silvery shade. Plants like senecio or lamb's lugs with their silvery gray foliage make excellent border dividers. The Cancer crab is symbolic of where living organisms began—in the water. That journey of evolution as life stepped from the water's edge symbolized by crustacean life guided by the Moon's gravitational pull, allowed life to venture onto land. The Moon not only acts as a light to nocturnal life but also a barometer to the water table and plays a crucial role in all manner of life.

2005 Gardening Dates

Dates	Qtr.	Sign	Activity
Jan. 4, 7:00 pm-Jan. 6, 10:44 pm	4th	Scorpio	Plant biennials, perennials, bulbs and roots. Prune. Irrigate. Fertilize (organic).
Jan. 6, 10:44 pm-Jan. 8, 11:11 pm	4th	Sagittarius	Cultivate. Destroy weeds and pests. Harvest fruits and root crops for food. Trim to retard growth.
Jan. 8, 11:11 pm-Jan. 10, 7:03 am	4th	Capricorn	Plant potatoes and tubers. Trim to retard growth.
Jan. 10, 7:03 am-Jan. 10, 10:07 pm	1st	Capricorn	Graft or bud plants. Trim to increase growth.
Jan. 12, 9:50 pm-Jan. 15, 12:27 am	1st	Pisces	Plant grains, leafy annuals. Fertilize (chemical). Graft or bud plants. Irrigate. Trim to increase growth.
Jan. 17, 7:06 am-Jan. 19, 5:24 pm	2nd	Taurus	Plant annuals for hardiness. Trim to increase growth.
Jan. 22, 5:42 am-Jan. 24, 6:21 pm	2nd	Cancer	Plant grains, leafy annuals. Fertilize (chemical). Graft or bud plants. Irrigate. Trim to increase growth.
Jan. 25, 5:32 am-Jan. 27, 6:24 am	3rd	Leo	Cultivate. Destroy weeds and pests. Harvest fruits and root crops for food. Trim to retard growth.
Jan. 27, 6:24 am-Jan. 29, 5:13 pm	3rd	Virgo	Cultivate, especially medicinal plants. Destroy weeds and pests. Trim to retard growth.
Feb. 1, 1:51 am-Feb. 2, 2:27 am	3rd	Scorpio	Plant biennials, perennials, bulbs and roots. Prune. Irrigate. Fertilize (organic).
Feb. 2, 2:27 am-Feb. 3, 7:21 am	4th	Scorpio	Plant biennials, perennials, bulbs and roots. Prune. Irrigate. Fertilize (organic).
Feb. 3, 7:21 am-Feb. 5, 9:32 am	4th	Sagittarius	Cultivate. Destroy weeds and pests. Harvest fruits and root crops for food. Trim to retard growth.
Feb. 5, 9:32 am-Feb. 7, 9:26 am	4th	Capricorn	Plant potatoes and tubers. Trim to retard growth.
Feb. 7, 9:26 am-Feb. 8, 5:28 pm	4th	Aquarius	Cultivate. Destroy weeds and pests. Harvest fruits and root crops for food. Trim to retard growth.
Feb. 9, 8:59 am-Feb. 11, 10:21 am	1st	Pisces	Plant grains, leafy annuals. Fertilize (chemical). Graft or bud plants. Irrigate. Trim to increase growth.
Feb. 13, 3:18 pm-Feb. 15, 7:16 pm	1st	Taurus	Plant annuals for hardiness. Trim to increase growth.
Feb. 15, 7:16 pm-Feb. 16, 12:18 am	2nd	Taurus	Plant annuals for hardiness. Trim to increase growth.
Feb. 18, 12:13 pm-Feb. 21, 12:54 am	2nd	Cancer	Plant grains, leafy annuals. Fertilize (chemical). Graft or bud plants. Irrigate. Trim to increase growth.
Feb. 23, 11:54 pm-Feb. 25, 10:59 pm	3rd	Virgo	Cultivate, especially medicinal plants. Destroy weeds and pests. Trim to retard growth.
Feb. 28, 7:21 am-Mar. 2, 1:29 pm	3rd	Scorpio	Plant biennials, perennials, bulbs and roots. Prune. Irrigate. Fertilize (organic).

Dates	Qtr.	Sign	Activity
Mar. 2, 1:29 pm- Mar. 3, 12:36 pm	3rd	Sagittarius	Cultivate. Destroy weeds and pests. Harvest fruits and root crops for food. Trim to retard growth.
Mar. 3, 12:36 pm- Mar. 4, 5:12 pm	4th	Sagittarius	Cultivate. Destroy weeds and pests. Harvest fruits and root crops for food. Trim to retard growth.
Mar. 4, 5:12 pm- Mar. 6, 6:49 pm	4th	Capricorn	Plant potatoes and tubers. Trim to retard growth.
Mar. 6, 6:49 pm- Mar. 8, 7:32 pm	4th	Aquarius	Cultivate. Destroy weeds and pests. Harvest fruits and root crops for food. Trim to retard growth.
Mar. 8, 7:32 pm- Mar. 10, 4:10 am	4th	Pisces	Plant biennials, perennials, bulbs and roots. Prune. Irrigate. Fertilize (organic).
Mar. 10, 4:10 am- Mar. 10, 9:03 pm	1st	Pisces	Plant grains, leafy annuals. Fertilize (chemical). Graft or bud plants. Irrigate. Trim to increase growth.
Mar. 13, 1:05 am- Mar. 15, 8:44 am	1st	Taurus	Plant annuals for hardiness. Trim to increase growth.
Mar. 17, 7:44 pm- Mar. 20, 8:17 am	2nd	Cancer	Plant grains, leafy annuals. Fertilize (chemical). Graft or bud plants. Irrigate. Trim to increase growth.
Mar. 25, 6:00 am- Mar. 25, 3:58 pm	2nd	Libra	Plant annuals for fragrance and beauty. Trim to increase growth.
Mar. 27, 1:29 pm- Mar. 29, 6:56 pm	3rd	Scorpio	Plant biennials, perennials, bulbs and roots. Prune. Irrigate. Fertilize (organic).
Mar. 29, 6:56 pm- Mar. 31, 10:48 pm	3rd	Sagittarius	Cultivate. Destroy weeds and pests. Harvest fruits and root crops for food. Trim to retard growth.
Mar. 31, 10:48 pm- Apr. 1, 7:50 pm	3rd	Capricorn	Plant potatoes and tubers. Trim to retard growth.
Apr. 1, 7:50 pm- Apr. 3, 1:31 am	4th	Capricorn	Plant potatoes and tubers. Trim to retard growth.
Apr. 3, 1:31 am- Apr. 5, 4:45 am	4th	Aquarius	Cultivate. Destroy weeds and pests. Harvest fruits and root crops for food. Trim to retard growth.
Apr. 5, 4:45 am- Apr. 7, 7:28 am	4th	Pisces	Plant biennials, perennials, bulbs and roots. Prune. Irrigate. Fertilize (organic).
Apr. 7, 7:28 am- Apr. 8, 4:32 pm	4th	Aries	Cultivate. Destroy weeds and pests. Harvest fruits and root crops for food. Trim to retard growth.
Apr. 9, 11:50 am- Apr. 11, 6:55 pm	1st	Taurus	Plant annuals for hardiness. Trim to increase growth.
Apr. 14, 5:03 am- Apr. 16, 10:37 am	1st	Cancer	Plant grains, leafy annuals. Fertilize (chemical). Graft or bud plants. Irrigate. Trim to increase growth.
Apr. 16, 10:37 am- Apr. 16, 5:17 pm	2nd	Cancer	Plant grains, leafy annuals. Fertilize (chemical). Graft or bud plants. Irrigate. Trim to increase growth.
Apr. 21, 3:27 pm- Apr. 23, 10:25 pm	2nd	Libra	Plant annuals for fragrance and beauty. Trim to increase growth.

Dates	Qtr.	Sign	Activity
Apr. 23, 10:25 pm- Apr. 24, 6:06 am	2nd	Scorpio	Plant grains, leafy annuals. Fertilize (chemical). Graft or bud plants. Irrigate. Trim to increase growth.
Apr. 24, 6:06 am- Apr. 26, 2:46 am	3rd	Scorpio	Plant biennials, perennials, bulbs and roots. Prune. Irrigate. Fertilize (organic).
Apr. 26, 2:46 am- Apr. 28, 5:33 am	3rd	Sagittarius	Cultivate. Destroy weeds and pests. Harvest fruits and root crops for food. Trim to retard growth.
Apr. 28, 5:33 am- Apr. 30, 7:54 am	3rd	Capricorn	Plant potatoes and tubers. Trim to retard growth.
Apr. 30, 7:54 am- May 1, 2:24 am	3rd	Aquarius	Cultivate. Destroy weeds and pests. Harvest fruits and root crops for food. Trim to retard growth.
May 1, 2:24 am- May 2, 10:43 am	4th	Aquarius	Cultivate. Destroy weeds and pests. Harvest fruits and root crops for food. Trim to retard growth.
May 2, 10:43 am- May 4, 2:36 pm	4th	Pisces	Plant biennials, perennials, bulbs and roots. Prune. Irrigate. Fertilize (organic).
May 4, 2:36 pm- May 6, 8:01 pm	4th	Aries	Cultivate. Destroy weeds and pests. Harvest fruits and root crops for food. Trim to retard growth.
May 6, 8:01 pm- May 8, 4:45 am	4th	Taurus	Plant potatoes and tubers. Trim to retard growth.
May 8, 4:45 am- May 9, 3:29 am	1st	Taurus	Plant annuals for hardiness. Trim to increase growth.
May 11, 1:20 pm- May 14, 1:17 am	1st	Cancer	Plant grains, leafy annuals. Fertilize (chemical). Graft or bud plants. Irrigate. Trim to increase growth.
May 19, 11:30 am- May 21, 7:49 am	2nd	Libra	Plant annuals for fragrance and beauty. Trim to increase growth.
May 21, 7:49 am- May 23, 11:38 am	2nd	Scorpio	Plant grains, leafy annuals. Fertilize (chemical). Graft or bud plants. Irrigate. Trim to increase growth.
May 23, 4:18 pm- May 25, 1:11 pm	3rd	Sagittarius	Cultivate. Destroy weeds and pests. Harvest fruits and root crops for food. Trim to retard growth.
May 25, 1:11 pm- May 27, 2:10 pm	3rd	Capricorn	Plant potatoes and tubers. Trim to retard growth.
May 27, 2:10 pm- May 29, 4:09 pm	3rd	Aquarius	Cultivate. Destroy weeds and pests. Harvest fruits and root crops for food. Trim to retard growth.
May 29, 4:09 pm- May 30, 7:47 am	3rd	Pisces	Plant biennials, perennials, bulbs and roots. Prune. Irrigate. Fertilize (organic).
May 30, 7:47 am- May 31, 8:07 am	4th	Pisces	Plant biennials, perennials, bulbs and roots. Prune. Irrigate. Fertilize (organic).
May 31, 8:07 pm- Jun. 3, 2:20 am	4th	Aries	Cultivate. Destroy weeds and pests. Harvest fruits and root crops for food. Trim to retard growth.
Jun. 3, 2:20 am- Jun. 5, 10:36 am	4th	Taurus	Plant potatoes and tubers. Trim to retard growth.

Dates	Qtr.	Sign	Activity
Jun. 5, 10:36 am– Jun. 6, 5:55 pm	4th	Gemini	Cultivate. Destroy weeds and pests. Harvest fruits and root crops for food. Trim to retard growth.
Jun. 7, 8:46 pm–Jun. 10, 8:39 am	1st	Cancer	Plant grains, leafy annuals. Fertilize (chemical). Graft or bud plants. Irrigate. Trim to increase growth.
Jun. 15, 8:59 am– Jun. 17, 5:23 pm	2nd	Libra	Plant annuals for fragrance and beauty. Trim to increase growth.
Jun. 17, 5:23 pm– Jun. 19, 9:45 pm	2nd	Scorpio	Plant grains, leafy annuals. Fertilize (chemical). Graft or bud plants. Irrigate. Trim to increase growth.
Jun. 21, 10:52 pm– Jun. 22, 12:14 am	2nd	Capricorn	Graft or bud plants. Trim to increase growth.
Jun. 22, 12:14 am– Jun. 23, 10:36 pm	3rd	Capricorn	Plant potatoes and tubers. Trim to retard growth.
Jun. 23, 10:36 pm– Jun. 25, 11:03 pm	3rd	Aquarius	Cultivate. Destroy weeds and pests. Harvest fruits and root crops for food. Trim to retard growth.
Jun. 25, 11:03 pm– Jun. 28, 1:51 am	3rd	Pisces	Plant biennials, perennials, bulbs and roots. Prune. Irrigate. Fertilize (organic).
Jun. 28, 1:51 am– Jun. 28, 2:23 pm	3rd	Aries	Cultivate. Destroy weeds and pests. Harvest fruits and root crops for food. Trim to retard growth.
Jun. 28, 2:23 pm– Jun. 30, 7:45 am	4th	Aries	Cultivate. Destroy weeds and pests. Harvest fruits and root crops for food. Trim to retard growth.
Jun. 30, 7:45 am– Jul. 2, 4:26 pm	4th	Taurus	Plant potatoes and tubers. Trim to retard growth.
Jul. 2, 4:26 pm– Jul. 5, 3:07 am	4th	Gemini	Cultivate. Destroy weeds and pests. Harvest fruits and root crops for food. Trim to retard growth.
Jul. 5, 3:07 am– Jul. 6, 8:02 am	4th	Cancer	Plant biennials, perennials, bulbs and roots. Prune. Irrigate. Fertilize (organic).
Jul. 6, 8:02 am– Jul. 7, 3:11 pm	1st	Cancer	Plant grains, leafy annuals. Fertilize (chemical). Graft or bud plants. Irrigate. Trim to increase growth.
Jul. 12, 4:09 pm– Jul. 14, 11:20 am	1st	Libra	Plant annuals for fragrance and beauty. Trim to increase growth.
Jul. 14, 11:20 am– Jul. 15, 1:51 am	2nd	Libra	Plant annuals for fragrance and beauty. Trim to increase growth.
Jul. 15, 1:51 am– Jul. 17, 7:35 am	2nd	Scorpio	Plant grains, leafy annuals. Fertilize (chemical). Graft or bud plants. Irrigate. Trim to increase growth.
Jul. 19, 9:26 am– Jul. 21, 7:00 am	2nd	Capricorn	Graft or bud plants. Trim to increase growth.
Jul. 21, 7:00 am– Jul. 21, 8:55 am	3rd	Capricorn	Plant potatoes and tubers. Trim to retard growth.
Jul. 21, 8:55 am– Jul. 23, 8:12 am	3rd	Aquarius	Cultivate. Destroy weeds and pests. Harvest fruits and root crops for food. Trim to retard growth.

Dates	Qtr.	Sign	Activity
Jul. 23, 8:12 am-Jul. 25, 9:23 am	3rd	Pisces	Plant biennials, perennials, bulbs and roots. Prune. Irrigate. Fertilize (organic).
Jul. 25, 9:23 am-Jul. 27, 1:54 pm	3rd	Aries	Cultivate. Destroy weeds and pests. Harvest fruits and root crops for food. Trim to retard growth.
Jul. 27, 1:54 pm-Jul. 27, 11:19 pm	3rd	Taurus	Plant potatoes and tubers. Trim to retard growth.
Jul. 27, 11:19 pm-Jul. 29, 10:02 pm	4th	Taurus	Plant potatoes and tubers. Trim to retard growth.
Jul. 29, 10:02 pm-Aug. 1, 8:52 am	4th	Gemini	Cultivate. Destroy weeds and pests. Harvest fruits and root crops for food. Trim to retard growth.
Aug. 1, 8:52 am-Aug. 3, 9:10 pm	4th	Cancer	Plant biennials, perennials, bulbs and roots. Prune. Irrigate. Fertilize (organic).
Aug. 3, 9:10 pm-Aug. 4, 11:05 pm	4th	Leo	Cultivate. Destroy weeds and pests. Harvest fruits and root crops for food. Trim to retard growth.
Aug. 8, 10:08 pm-Aug. 11, 8:35 am	1st	Libra	Plant annuals for fragrance and beauty. Trim to increase growth.
Aug. 11, 8:35 am-Aug. 12, 10:38 pm	1st	Scorpio	Plant grains, leafy annuals. Fertilize (chemical). Graft or bud plants. Irrigate. Trim to increase growth.
Aug. 12, 10:38 pm-Aug. 13, 3:47 pm	2nd	Scorpio	Plant grains, leafy annuals. Fertilize (chemical). Graft or bud plants. Irrigate. Trim to increase growth.
Aug. 15, 7:13 pm-Aug. 17, 7:39 pm	2nd	Capricorn	Graft or bud plants. Trim to increase growth.
Aug. 19, 1:53 pm-Aug. 19, 6:52 pm	3rd	Aquarius	Cultivate. Destroy weeds and pests. Harvest fruits and root crops for food. Trim to retard growth.
Aug. 19, 6:52 pm-Aug. 21, 7:01 pm	3rd	Pisces	Plant biennials, perennials, bulbs and roots. Prune. Irrigate. Fertilize (organic).
Aug. 21, 7:01 pm-Aug. 23, 9:58 pm	3rd	Aries	Cultivate. Destroy weeds and pests. Harvest fruits and root crops for food. Trim to retard growth.
Aug. 23, 9:58 pm-Aug. 26, 4:43 am	3rd	Taurus	Plant potatoes and tubers. Trim to retard growth.
Aug. 26, 4:43 am-Aug. 26, 11:18 am	3rd	Gemini	Cultivate. Destroy weeds and pests. Harvest fruits and root crops for food. Trim to retard growth.
Aug. 26, 11:18 am-Aug. 28, 2:57 pm	4th	Gemini	Cultivate. Destroy weeds and pests. Harvest fruits and root crops for food. Trim to retard growth.
Aug. 28, 2:57 pm-Aug. 31, 3:14 am	4th	Cancer	Plant biennials, perennials, bulbs and roots. Prune. Irrigate. Fertilize (organic).
Sep. 31, 3:14 am-Sep. 2, 3:56 pm	4th	Leo	Cultivate. Destroy weeds and pests. Harvest fruits and root crops for food. Trim to retard growth.
Sep. 2, 3:56 pm-Sep. 3, 2:45 pm	4th	Virgo	Cultivate, especially medicinal plants. Destroy weeds and pests. Trim to retard growth.

Dates	Qtr.	Sign	Activity
Sep. 5, 3:52 am- Sep. 7, 2:10 pm	1st	Libra	Plant annuals for fragrance and beauty. Trim to increase growth.
Sep. 7, 2:10 pm- Sep. 9, 10:03 pm	1st	Scorpio	Plant grains, leafy annuals. Fertilize (chemical). Graft or bud plants. Irrigate. Trim to increase growth.
Sep. 12, 2:56 am- Sep. 14, 5:02 am	2nd	Capricorn	Graft or bud plants. Trim to increase growth.
Sep. 16, 5:24 am- Sep. 17, 10:01 pm	2nd	Pisces	Plant grains, leafy annuals. Fertilize (chemical). Graft or bud plants. Irrigate. Trim to increase growth.
Sep. 17, 10:01pm- Sep. 18, 5:43 am	3rd	Pisces	Plant biennials, perennials, bulbs and roots. Prune. Irrigate. Fertilize (organic).
Sep. 18, 5:43 am- Sep. 20, 7:47 am	3rd	Aries	Cultivate. Destroy weeds and pests. Harvest fruits and root crops for food. Trim to retard growth.
Sep. 20, 7:47 am- Sep. 22, 1:07 pm	3rd	Taurus	Plant potatoes and tubers. Trim to retard growth.
Sep. 22, 1:07 pm- Sep. 24, 10:10 pm	3rd	Gemini	Cultivate. Destroy weeds and pests. Harvest fruits and root crops for food. Trim to retard growth.
Sep. 24, 10:10pm- Sep.25, 2:41 am	3rd	Cancer	Plant biennials, perennials, bulbs and roots. Prune. Irrigate. Fertilize (organic).
Sep. 25, 2:41 am- Sep. 27, 10:03 am	4th	Cancer	Plant biennials, perennials, bulbs and roots. Prune. Irrigate. Fertilize (organic).
Sep. 27, 10:03 am- Sep. 29, 10:44 pm	4th	Leo	Cultivate. Destroy weeds and pests. Harvest fruits and root crops for food. Trim to retard growth.
Sep. 29, 10:44 pm- Oct. 2, 10:24 am	4th	Virgo	Cultivate, especially medicinal plants. Destroy weeds and pests. Trim to retard growth.
Oct. 3, 6:28 am- Oct. 4, 8:03 pm	1st	Libra	Plant annuals for fragrance and beauty. Trim to increase growth.
Oct. 4, 8:03 pm- Oct. 7, 3:28 am	1st	Scorpio	Plant grains, leafy annuals. Fertilize (chemical). Graft or bud plants. Irrigate. Trim to increase growth.
Oct. 9, 8:43 am-Oct. 10, 3:01 pm	1st	Capricorn	Graft or bud plants. Trim to increase growth.
Oct. 10, 3:01 pm- Oct. 12, 12:05 pm	2nd	Capricorn	Graft or bud plants. Trim to increase growth.
Oct. 13, 2:05 pm- Oct. 15, 3:39 pm	2nd	Pisces	Plant grains, leafy annuals. Fertilize (chemical). Graft or bud plants. Irrigate. Trim to increase growth.
Oct. 17, 8:14 am- Oct. 17, 6:04 pm	3rd	Aries	Cultivate. Destroy weeds and pests. Harvest fruits and root crops for food. Trim to retard growth.
Oct. 17, 6:04 pm- Oct. 19, 10:44 pm	3rd	Taurus	Plant potatoes and tubers. Trim to retard growth.
Oct. 19, 10:44 pm- Oct. 22, 6:41 am	3rd	Gemini	Cultivate. Destroy weeds and pests. Harvest fruits and root crops for food. Trim to retard growth.

Dates	Qtr.	Sign	Activity
Oct. 22, 6:41 am- Oct. 24, 5:48 pm	3rd	Cancer	Plant biennials, perennials, bulbs and roots. Prune. Irrigate. Fertilize (organic).
Oct. 24, 5:48 pm- Oct. 24, 9:17 pm	3rd	Leo	Cultivate. Destroy weeds and pests. Harvest fruits and root crops for food. Trim to retard growth.
Oct. 24, 9:17 pm- Oct. 27, 6:28 am	4th	Leo	Cultivate. Destroy weeds and pests. Harvest fruits and root crops for food. Trim to retard growth.
Oct. 27, 6:28 am- Oct. 29, 6:15 pm	4th	Virgo	Cultivate, especially medicinal plants. Destroy weeds and pests. Trim to retard growth.
Nov. 1, 2:29 am- Nov. 1, 8:25 pm	4th	Scorpio	Plant biennials, perennials, bulbs and roots. Prune. Irrigate. Fertilize (organic).
Nov. 1, 8:25 pm- Nov. 3, 8:55 am	1st	Scorpio	Plant grains, leafy annuals. Fertilize (chemical). Graft or bud plants. Irrigate. Trim to increase growth.
Nov. 5, 1:17 pm- Nov. 7, 4:31 pm	1st	Capricorn	Graft or bud plants. Trim to increase growth.
Nov. 9, 7:22 pm- Nov. 11, 10:22 pm	2nd	Pisces	Plant grains, leafy annuals. Fertilize (chemical). Graft or bud plants. Irrigate. Trim to increase growth.
Nov. 14, 2:02 am- Nov. 15, 7:58 pm	2nd	Taurus	Plant annuals for hardiness. Trim to increase growth.
Nov. 15, 7:58 pm- Nov. 16, 7:10 am	3rd	Taurus	Plant potatoes and tubers. Trim to retard growth.
Nov. 16, 7:10 am- Nov. 18, 2:42 pm	3rd	Gemini	Cultivate. Destroy weeds and pests. Harvest fruits and root crops for food. Trim to retard growth.
Nov. 18, 2:42 pm- Nov. 21, 1:10 am	3rd	Cancer	Plant biennials, perennials, bulbs and roots. Prune. Irrigate. Fertilize (organic).
Nov. 21, 1:10 am- Nov. 23, 1:41 pm	3rd	Leo	Cultivate. Destroy weeds and pests. Harvest fruits and root crops for food. Trim to retard growth.
Nov. 23, 1:41pm- Nov. 23, 5:11 pm	3rd	Virgo	Cultivate, especially medicinal plants. Destroy weeds and pests. Trim to retard growth.
Nov. 23, 5:11 pm- Nov. 26, 1:58 am	4th	Virgo	Cultivate, especially medicinal plants. Destroy weeds and pests. Trim to retard growth.
Nov. 28, 11:33 am- Nov. 30, 5:32 pm	4th	Scorpio	Plant biennials, perennials, bulbs and roots. Prune. Irrigate. Fertilize (organic).
Nov. 30, 5:32 pm- Dec. 1, 10:01 am	4th	Sagittarius	Cultivate. Destroy weeds and pests. Harvest fruits and root crops for food. Trim to retard growth.
Dec. 2, 8:42 pm- Dec. 4, 10:36 pm	1st	Capricorn	Graft or bud plants. Trim to increase growth.
Dec. 7, 12:44 am- Dec. 8, 4:36 am	1st	Pisces	Plant grains, leafy annuals. Fertilize (chemical). Graft or bud plants. Irrigate. Trim to increase growth.
Dec. 8, 4:36 am- Dec. 9, 4:02 am	2nd	Pisces	Plant grains, leafy annuals. Fertilize (chemical). Graft or bud plants. Irrigate. Trim to increase growth.

Dates	Qtr.	Sign	Activity
Dec. 11, 8:46 am- Dec. 13, 2:59 pm	2nd	Taurus	Plant annuals for hardiness. Trim to increase growth.
Dec. 15, 11:16 am- Dec. 15, 11:01 pm	3rd	Gemini	Cultivate. Destroy weeds and pests. Harvest fruits and root crops for food. Trim to retard growth.
Dec. 15, 11:01 pm- Dec. 18, 9:18 am	3rd	Cancer	Plant biennials, perennials, bulbs and roots. Prune. Irrigate. Fertilize (organic).
Dec. 18, 9:18 am- Dec. 20, 9:39 pm	3rd	Leo	Cultivate. Destroy weeds and pests. Harvest fruits and root crops for food. Trim to retard growth.
Dec. 20, 9:39 pm- Dec. 23, 10:26 am	3rd	Virgo	Cultivate, especially medicinal plants. Destroy weeds and pests. Trim to retard growth.
Dec. 25, 9:04 pm- Dec. 28, 3:43 am	4th	Scorpio	Plant biennials, perennials, bulbs and roots. Prune. Irrigate. Fertilize (organic).
Dec. 28, 3:43 am- Dec. 30, 6:35 am	4th	Sagittarius	Cultivate. Destroy weeds and pests. Harvest fruits and root crops for food. Trim to retard growth.
Dec. 30, 6:35 am- Dec. 30, 10:12 pm	4th	Capricorn	Plant potatoes and tubers. Trim to retard growth.

2005 Dates to Destroy Weeds and Pests

Date	Time	Date	Time	Sign	Qtr.
Jan. 6	10:44 pm	Jan. 8	11:11 pm	Sagittarius	4th
Jan. 25	5:32 am	Jan. 27	6:24 am	Leo	3rd
Jan. 27	6:24 am	Jan. 29	5:13 pm	Virgo	3rd
Feb. 3	7:21 am	Feb. 5	9:32 am	Sagittarius	4th
Feb. 7	9:26 am	Feb. 8	5:28 pm	Aquarius	4th
Feb. 23	11:54 pm	Feb. 25	10:59 pm	Virgo	3rd
Mar. 2	1:29 pm	Mar. 3	12:36 pm	Sagittarius	3rd
Mar. 3	12:36 pm	Mar. 4	5:12 pm	Sagittarius	4th
Mar. 6	6:49 pm	Mar. 8	7:32 pm	Aquarius	4th
Mar. 29	6:56 pm	Mar. 31	10:48 pm	Sagittarius	3rd
Apr. 3	1:31 am	Apr. 5	3:45 am	Aquarius	4th
Apr. 7	6:28 am	Apr. 8	3:32 pm	Aries	4th
Apr. 26	1:46 am	Apr. 28	4:33 am	Sagittarius	3rd
May 30	6:54 am	May 1	1:24 am	Aquarius	3rd
May 1	1:24 am	May 2	9:43 am	Aquarius	4th
May 4	1:36 pm	May 6	7:01 pm	Aries	4th
May 23	3:18 pm	May 25	12:11 pm	Sagittarius	3rd
May 27	1:10 pm	May 29	3:09 pm	Aquarius	3rd
Jun. 31	7:07 pm	Jun. 3	1:20 am	Aries	4th
Jun. 5	9:36 am	Jun. 6	4:55 pm	Gemini	4th
Jun. 23	9:36 pm	Jun. 25	10:03 pm	Aquarius	3rd
Jun. 28	12:51 am	Jun. 28	1:23 pm	Aries	3rd
Jun. 28	1:23 pm	Jun. 30	6:45 am	Aries	4th
Jul. 2	3:26 pm	Jul. 5	2:07 am	Gemini	4th
Jul. 21	7:55 am	Jul. 23	7:12 am	Aquarius	3rd
Jul. 25	8:23 am	Jul. 27	12:54 pm	Aries	3rd

Date	Time	Date	Time	Sign	Qtr.
Aug. 29	9:02 pm	Aug. 1	7:52 am	Gemini	4th
Aug. 3	8:10 pm	Aug. 4	10:05 pm	Leo	4th
Aug. 19	12:53 pm	Aug. 19	5:52 pm	Aquarius	3rd
Aug. 21	6:01 pm	Aug. 23	8:58 pm	Aries	3rd
Aug. 26	3:43 am	Aug. 26	10:18 am	Gemini	3rd
Aug. 26	10:18 am	Aug. 28	1:57 pm	Gemini	4th
Sep. 31	2:14 am	Sep. 2	2:56 pm	Leo	4th
Sep. 2	2:56 pm	Sep. 3	1:45 pm	Virgo	4th
Sep. 18	4:43 am	Sep. 20	6:47 am	Aries	3rd
Sep. 22	12:07 pm	Sep. 24	9:10 pm	Gemini	3rd
Sep. 27	9:03 am	Sep. 29	9:44 pm	Leo	4th
Oct. 29	9:44 pm	Oct. 2	9:24 am	Virgo	4th
Oct. 17	7:14 am	Oct. 17	5:04 pm	Aries	3rd
Oct. 19	9:44 pm	Oct. 22	5:41 am	Gemini	3rd
Oct. 24	4:48 pm	Oct. 24	8:17 pm	Leo	3rd
Oct. 24	8:17 pm	Oct. 27	5:28 am	Leo	4th
Oct. 27	5:28 am	Oct. 29	5:15 pm	Virgo	4th
Nov. 16	7:10 am	Nov. 18	2:42 pm	Gemini	3rd
Nov. 21	1:10 am	Nov. 23	1:41 pm	Leo	3rd
Nov. 23	1:41 pm	Nov. 23	5:11 pm	Virgo	3rd
Nov. 23	5:11 pm	Nov. 26	1:58 am	Virgo	4th
Dec. 30	5:32 pm	Dec. 1	10:01 am	Sagittarius	4th
Dec. 15	11:16 am	Dec. 15	11:01 pm	Gemini	3rd
Dec. 18	9:18 am	Dec. 20	9:39 pm	Leo	3rd
Dec. 20	9:39 pm	Dec. 23	10:26 am	Virgo	3rd
Dec. 28	3:43 am	Dec. 30	6:35 am	Sagittarius	4th

2005 Egg-setting Dates

Dates to be Born	Sign	Qtr.	Set Eggs
Jan. 12 9:50 pm-Jan. 15 12:27 am	Pisces	1st	Dec. 22
Jan. 17 7:06 am-Jan. 19 5:24 pm	Taurus	2nd	Dec. 27
Feb. 9 8:59 am-Feb. 11 10:21 am	Pisces	1st	Jan. 20
Feb. 13 3:18 pm-Feb. 16 12:18 am	Taurus	1st	Jan. 23
Feb. 18 12:13 pm-Feb. 21 12:54 am	Cancer	2nd	Jan. 31
Mar. 13 1:05 am-Mar. 15 8:44 am	Taurus	1st	Feb. 21
Mar. 17 7:44 pm-Mar. 20 8:17 am	Cancer	2nd	Feb. 26
Apr. 9 11:50 am-Apr 11 6:55 pm	Taurus	1st	Mar. 19
Apr. 14 5:03 am-Sat. 16 5:17 pm	Cancer	1st	Mar. 24
Apr. 21 3:27 pm-Apr. 23 10:25 pm	Libra	2nd	Mar. 31
May 11 1:20 pm-May 14 1:17 am	Cancer	1st	Apr. 20
May 19 12:30 am-May 21 7:49 am	Libra	2nd	Apr. 27
Jun. 7 8:46 pm-Jun 10 8:39 am	Cancer	1st	May 17
Jun 15 8:59 am-Jun. 17 5:23 pm	Libra	2nd	May 26
Jul. 12 4:09 pm-Jul. 15 1:51 am	Libra	1st	Jun. 24
Aug. 8 10:08 pm-Aug. 11 8:35 am	Libra	1st	Jul. 20
Sep. 5 3:52 am-Sep. 7 2:10 pm	Libra	1st	Aug. 16
Sep. 16 5:24 am-Sep. 18 5:43 am	Pisces	2nd	Aug. 27
Oct. 13 2:05 pm-Oct. 15 3:39 pm	Pisces	2nd	Sep. 22
Nov. 9 7:22 pm-Nov. 11 10:22 pm	Pisces	2nd	Oct. 20
Nov. 14 2:02 am-Nov. 16 7:10 am	Taurus	2nd	Oct. 26
Dec. 7 12:44 am-Dec. 9 4:02 am	Pisces	1st	Nov. 16
Dec 11 8:46 am-Dec. 13 2:59 pm	Taurus	2nd	Nov. 22

Companion-planting Guide
Plant Helpers and Hinderers

Plant	Helped By	Hindered By
Asparagus	Tomato, parsley, basil	
Bean	Carrot, cucumber, cabbage, beet, corn	Onion, gladiola
Bush bean	Cucumber, cabbage, strawberry	Fennel, onion
Beet	Onion, cabbage, lettuce	Pale bean
Cabbage	Beet, potato, onion, celery	Strawberry, tomato
Carrot	Pea, lettuce, chive, radish, leek, onion	Dill
Celery	Leek, bush bean	
Chive	Bean	
Corn	Potato, bean, pea, melon, squash, pumpkin, cucumber	
Cucumber	Bean, cabbage, radish, sunflower, lettuce	Potato, herbs
Eggplant	Bean	
Lettuce	Strawberry, carrot	
Melon	Morning glory	
Onion, leek	Beet, chamomile, carrot, lettuce	Pea, bean
Garlic	Summer savory	
Pea	Radish, carrot, corn cucumber, bean, turnip	Onion
Potato	Bean, corn, pea, cabbage, hemp, cucumber	Sunflower

Plant	Helped By	Hindered By
Radish	Pea, lettuce, nasturtium, cucumbers	Hyssop
Spinach	Strawberry	
Squash, Pumpkin	Nasturtium, Corn	Potatoes
Tomatoes	Asparagus, parsley, chives, onions, carrot, marigold, nasturtium	Dill, cabbage, fennel
Turnip	Pea, bean	

Plant Companions and Uses

Plant	Companions and Uses
Anise	Coriander
Basil	Tomato; dislikes rue; repels flies and mosquitoes
Borage	Tomato and squash
Buttercup	Clover; hinders delphinium, peony, monkshood, columbine
Chamomile	Helps peppermint, wheat, onions, and cabbage; large amounts destructive
Catnip	Repels flea beetles
Chervil	Radish
Chives	Carrot; prone to apple scab and powdery mildew
Coriander	Hinders seed formation in fennel
Cosmos	Repels corn earworms
Dill	Cabbage; hinders carrot and tomato
Fennel	Disliked by all garden plants
Garlic	Aids vetch and roses; hinders peas and beans
Hemp	Beneficial as a neighbor to most plants
Horseradish	Repels potato bugs

Plant	Companions and Uses
Horsetail	Makes fungicide spray
Hyssop	Attracts cabbage fly away from cabbages; harmful to radishes
Lovage	Improves hardiness and flavor of neighbor plants
Marigold	Pest repellent; use against Mexican bean beetles and nematodes
Mint	Repels ants, flea beetles and cabbage worm butterflies
Morning glory	Corn; helps melon germination
Nasturtium	Cabbage, cucumbers; deters aphids, squash bugs, and pumpkin beetles
Nettle	Increase oil content in neighbors
Parsley	Tomatoes, asparagus
Purslane	Good ground cover
Rosemary	Repels cabbage moths, bean beetles, and carrot flies
Sage	Repels cabbage moths and carrot flies
Savory	Deters bean beetles
Sunflower	Hinders potatoes; improves soil
Tansy	Deters Japanese beetles, striped cucumber beetles, and squash bugs
Thyme	Repels cabbage worms
Yarrow	Increases essential oils of neighbors

2005 Weather

by Kris Brandt Riske

Astrometeorology—astrological weather forecasting—reveals seasonal and weekly weather trends based on the cardinal ingresses (Summer and Winter Solstices, and Spring and Autumn Equinoxes) and the four monthly lunar phases. The planetary alignments and the longitudes and latitudes they influence have the strongest effect, but the zodiacal signs are also involved in creating weather conditions.

The components of a thunderstorm, for example, are heat, wind, and electricity. A Mars-Jupiter configuration generates the necessary heat and Mercury adds wind and electricity. A severe thunderstorm, and those that produce tornadoes, usually involve Mercury, Mars, Uranus, or Neptune. The zodiacal signs add their energy to the planetary mix to increase or decrease the chance of weather phenomena and their severity.

In general, the fire signs (Aries, Leo, Sagittarius) indicate heat and dryness, both of which peak when Mars, the planet with a similar nature, is in these signs. Water signs (Cancer, Scorpio, Pisces) are conducive to precipitation, and air signs (Gemini,

Libra, Aquarius) to cool temperatures and wind. Earth signs (Taurus, Virgo, Capricorn) vary from wet to dry, heat to cold. The signs and their prevailing weather conditions are listed here:

Aries: Heat, dry, wind
Taurus: Moderate temperatures, precipitation
Gemini: Cool temperatures, wind, dry
Cancer: Cold, steady precipitation
Leo: Heat, dry, lightning
Virgo: Cold, dry, windy
Libra: Cool, windy, fair
Scorpio: Extreme temperatures, abundant precipitation
Sagittarius: Warm, fair, moderate wind
Capricorn: Cold, wet, damp
Aquarius: Cold, dry, high pressure, lightning
Pisces: Wet, cool, low pressure

Take note of the Moon's sign at each lunar phase. It reveals the prevailing weather conditions for the next six to seven days. The same is true of Mercury and Venus. These two influential weather planets transit the entire zodiac each year, unless retrograde patterns add their influence.

Planetary Influences

People relied on astrology to forecast weather for thousands of years. They were able to predict drought, floods, and temperature variations through interpreting planetary alignments. In recent years there has been a renewed interest in astrometeorology, the ancient branch of astrology that focuses on weather forecasting. Unlike meteorology, which at best can forecast weather trends a week in advance, astrometeorology is limitless. A weather forecast can be composed for any date—tomorrow, next week, or a thousand years in the future. Astrometeorology reveals seasonal and weekly weather trends based on the cardinal ingresses (Summer and Winter Solstices, and Spring and Fall Equinoxes) and the four monthly quarterly lunar phases in combination with the transiting planets. According to astrometeorolgy, each planet governs certain weather phenomena. When certain planets are aligned with other planets, weather—precipitation, cloudy or clear skies, tornados, hurricanes, and other conditions—are generated.

Sun and Moon

The Sun governs the constitution of the weather and, like the Moon, it serves as a trigger for other planetary configurations that results in weather events. When the Sun is prominent in a cardinal ingress or lunar phase chart, the area is often warm and sunny. The Moon can bring or withhold moisture, depending upon its sign placement.

Mercury

Mercury is also a triggering planet, but its main influence is wind direction and velocity. In its stationary periods, Mercury reflects high winds, and its influence is always prominent in major weather events, such as hurricanes and tornados, when it tends to lower the temperature.

Venus

Venus governs moisture, clouds, and humidity. It brings warming trends that produce sunny, pleasant weather if in positive aspect to other planets. In some signs—Libra, Virgo, Gemini, Sagittarius—Venus is drier. It is at its wettest when placed in Cancer, Scorpio, Pisces, or Taurus.

Mars

Mars is associated with heat, drought, and wind, and can raise the temperature to record-setting levels when in a fire sign (Aries, Leo, Sagittarius). Mars also provides the spark that generates thunderstorms and is prominent in tornado and hurricane configurations.

Jupiter

Jupiter, a fair-weather planet, tends toward higher temperatures when in Aries, Leo, or Sagittarius. It is associated with high-pressure systems and is a contributing factor at times to dryness. Storms are often amplified by Jupiter.

Saturn

Saturn is associated with low pressure systems, cloudy to overcast skies, and excessive precipitation. Temperatures drop when Saturn is involved. Major winter storms always have a strong Saturn influence, as do storms that produce a slow, steady downpour for hours or days.

Uranus

Like Jupiter, Uranus indicates high pressure systems. It reflects descending cold air and, when prominent, is responsible for a jet stream that extends far south. Uranus can bring drought in winter, and it is involved in thunderstorms, tornados, and hurricanes.

Neptune

Neptune is the wettest planet. It signals low pressure systems and is dominant when hurricanes are in the forecast. When Neptune is strongly placed, flood danger is high. It's often associated with winter thaws. Temperatures, humidity, and cloudiness increase where Neptune influences weather.

Pluto

Pluto is associated with weather extremes, as well as unseasonably warm temperatures and drought. It reflects the high winds involved in major hurricanes, storms, and tornados.

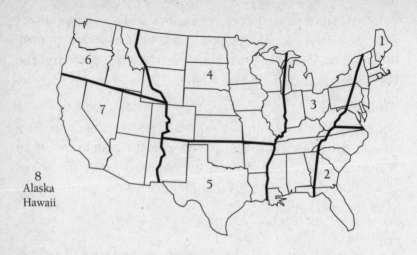

Winter

Zone 1: Northern areas are windy, cloudy, and cold with abundant precipitation.

Zone 2: Cold, windy, and cloudy weather prevails to the north. Southern areas cool after storms, but are otherwise seasonal to above with precipitation that ranges from average to below.

Zone 3: Western areas see average precipitation and warm temperatures. Weather is windy and cooler to the east with more precipitation as storms center in that area.

Zone 4: Cloudy and windy west, precipitation is abundant. Western Plains are seasonal; eastern areas drier and warmer.

Zone 5: Western areas are cloudy, wet, and windy; conditions to the east are drier. Temperatures range from seasonal to above.

Zone 6: Central areas are cloudy with major storms and temperatures ranging from seasonal to below. Fairer and drier weather prevails to the east; western areas are cold and wet.

Zone 7: Northern coastal areas are wet, windy, and seasonal, while southern coastal areas see average precipitation. Seasonal temperatures and precipitation prevail in central areas, and eastern areas are warmer, fairer and drier with more storms and precipitation to the north.

Zone 8: Alaska—Alaska is cloudy and seasonal with precipitation ranging from normal to above. Eastern areas are warmer. Hawaii—Warm and seasonal, Hawaii's precipitation levels are normal to below with rain in western areas.

Spring

Zone 1: The zone is cloudy and cool with major storms and abundant precipitation.

Zone 2: Southern areas are humid with elevated temperatures and average precipitation. Northern areas are cool with above average precipitation.

Zone 3: Precipitation is average to below as fair, windy skies and rising temperatures prevail west and central. Northeastern areas of the zone are cloudy and cool, with storms and abundant precipitation.

Zone 4: Temperatures are seasonal to above and precipitation average to below, with more rain to the east.

Zone 5: Windy and warm throughout much of the zone; precipitation centers in central and eastern areas.

Zone 6: Storms bring cold and cloudy weather to western and central areas, while fairer, warmer weather and average precipitation prevail to the east.

Zone 7: Major storms signal cold cloudy weather west that moves into central areas, where temperatures are also cool but precipitation is lower. Eastern areas are warmer and windy with average precipitation.

Zone 8: Alaska—The zone is seasonal with average precipitation. Hawaii—Windy with rising temperatures and precipitation that ranges from normal to dry.

Summer

Zone 1: Temperatures are below normal and precipitation above throughout the zone.

Zone 2: The zone is windy with severe thunderstorms and precipitation that ranges from average to above. Temperatures are cooler north.

Zone 3: Hot and dry to the west; eastern areas see more precipitation with severe thunderstorms.

Zone 4: Severe thunderstorms bring precipitation to the eastern Plains, but the rest of the zone is fair, hot, and dry.

Zone 5: Mostly hot and dry; eastern areas have some severe storms. Humidity rises central and east.

Zone 6: Fair and hot with variable clouds; the zone also has cooling storms and average precipitation. Central areas are cooler.

Zone 7: Precipitation is average to below with elevated temperatures. Eastern areas are drier.

Zone 8: Alaska—Temperatures range from seasonal to above, and precipitation from average to below with periodic major storms.

Hawaii—Temperatures rise and precipitation is average to below.

Autumn

Zone 1: The zone is windy, with average precipitation and seasonal temperatures.

Zone 2: Northern areas are seasonal and windy with average precipitation. Heat prevails to the south with average precipitation.

Zone 3: Mostly dry with temperatures that range from seasonal to above; eastern areas see more precipitation.

Zone 4: Western areas are dry and warm. Eastern areas see more precipitation and major storms; temperatures are seasonal.

Zone 5: Much of the zone is dry with seasonal temperatures. Precipitation and storms center east.

Zone 6: Major storms, wind, and cool temperatures are in the forecast for western areas. Central and eastern areas are warmer with abundant precipitation.

Zone 7: Much of the zone sees abundant precipitation; temperatures are cool west, while the desert is warm and dry.

Zone 8: Alaska—Central and eastern areas see abundant precipitation, and the west is drier. Temperatures range from seasonal to above.

Hawaii—Above normal temperatures, wind and humidity accompany average precipitation.

Weekly Forecasts

January 1–8

Zone 1: Conditions are overcast, windy, cold, and stormy throughout the zone, with the heaviest precipitation in southern and central areas.

Zone 2: Northern and coastal areas overcast, cold, and heavy precipitation. Cold dips south and become more so late in the week, when cloudy skies bring precipitation.

Zone 3: Seasonal temperatures and partly cloudy skies prevail west. Colder and fair skies in central areas follow precipitation, which moves east, bringing heavy downfall to the northeast.

Zone 4: Clouds and precipitation move into the northwest and western plains. Conditions are cold and dry central and east with variable clouds and scattered precipitation.

Zone 5: Increasing clouds west signal precipitation midweek that moves into the central areas of the zone. Temperatures vary from seasonal to colder central and east as the storm front approaches.

Zone 6: Western areas are cloudy, windy, and cool with scattered precipitation, more developing at week's end. Midzone is cold and fair to partly cloudy much of the week, with a storm moving into the area on weekend. Wind and precipitation to the east accompany a storm, followed by clear, cold weather.

Zone 7: Seasonal to cool west and central with variable clouds and precipitation that centers south. Heavy precipitation blankets the east, which is cold and stormy before clearing; warmer temperatures by week's end.

Zone 8: Alaska—Increasing clouds and precipitation signal a storm front with high winds and cold temperatures moving east from midzone in. The most eastern areas of the zone see seasonal temperatures and drier conditions with scattered precipitation.

Hawaii—Warm and dry west. Eastern areas see cooler temperatures with cloudy cover, winds, and precipitation before a warming trend sets in.

January 9–16

Zone 1: Cold temperatures and fair to partly cloudy skies prevail throughout the zone except northeast, where heavy precipitation precedes clearing skies and cold.

Zone 2: Northern areas are clear and cold. Precipitation and low temperatures prevail to the south, with warming at week's end.

Zone 3: West is cold, overcast, and stormy; warmer east with scattered precipitation. Northeastern areas are clear and cold.

Zone 4: Seasonal west prior to a storm front. Central zones see seasonal to above temps with a thaw; colder with wet east.

Zone 5: Temperatures are seasonal to above west. In central and eastern areas, conditions are stormy, overcast, cold and wet; abundant moisture east.

Zone 6: Temperatures seasonal to above and warming west, scattered precipitation and snow melt. Central areas cooler, windy, and partly cloud to cloudy; eastern areas see heavy precipitation as a front moves through prior to falling temperatures.

Zone 7: Seasonal west with scattered precipitation, and windy, cloudy, and cooler central. Abundant downfall to the east accompanies seasonal temperatures.

Zone 8: Alaska—Seasonal to cool temperatures accompany a storm with heavy precipitation west and central. Very cold temperatures prevail to the east.

Hawaii—Abundant precipitation signals flooding potential, with central areas receiving heaviest downfall; temperatures are seasonal to cool.

January 17–24

Zone 1: Windy with precipitation through midweek, with temperatures seasonal to below. Heaviest downfall occurs south, where a new weather front arrives at week's end.

Zone 2: Precipitation throughout the zone midweek, with flooding potential in coastal areas, Florida, and the Carolinas. Temperatures are seasonal to above.

Zone 3: Scattered precipitation and seasonal temperatures west, while central areas are seasonal and windy with precipitation midweek. The week begins and ends with precipitation, some heavy, east and northeast, with flooding potential east.

Zone 4: Cloudy and cool west with precipitation late in the week. Variable cloudiness and seasonal temperatures prevail central, but eastern areas are cold with scattered precipitation.

Zone 5: A storm front enters western zone at week's end; temperatures are seasonal to below east and central before a warming trend.

Zone 6: A cold front brings precipitation to much of zone, with abundant moisture east. Temperatures are seasonal to below.

Zone 7: Western areas see precipitation with the heaviest in northern coastal areas and inland as a storm tracks east with increasing clouds. Cold temperatures and abundant moisture arrive in eastern areas the end of the week.

Zone 8: Alaska—Central areas are very cold and overcast with scattered precipitation prior to stormy conditions at week's end. To the east, weather is warmer, with precipitation, thaw and flooding potential; coastal areas are foggy.

Hawaii—Temperatures are seasonal to cool and windy west and central, with precipitation. Clouds are variable east, where conditions are warmer.

January 25–31

Zone 1: Temperatures to the south are seasonal to cool under fair skies, while northern areas are cold and windy with fair to partly cloudy skies and scattered precipitation.

Zone 2: Southern areas are overcast and stormy with abundant precipitation. To the north, conditions are fair and cool.

Zone 3: Temperatures are seasonal to above west, but cooler and windy central, with precipitation, some heavy. Conditions are clear and seasonal east.

Zone 4: Winds pick up and temperatures decline northwest as a front moves through early in the week. Central areas are seasonal, and warmer, drier weather prevails to the east with clear to partly cloudy skies.

Zone 5: Weather is seasonal and partly cloudy west. Central areas see scattered precipitation with temperatures seasonal to above.

Zone 6: Overcast skies signal heavy precipitation and cold temperatures west, and midzone areas are seasonal prior to the arrival of a cold front with precipitation. Heavy downfall east precedes clear and cold weather east

Zone 7: Northern coastal areas see cold temperatures and precipitation as a front moves through the area and inland, bringing moisture throughout the zone. Stormy conditions with high winds prevail in eastern areas, bringing heavy precipitation and falling temperatures.

Zone 8: Alaska—A cold front brings precipitation to western and central areas, and areas to the east are fair, windy, and seasonal to cool.

Hawaii—Fair weather precedes windy conditions, cooler temperatures, and precipitation later in the week.

February 1–7

Zone 1: Stormy conditions prior to clearing skies and colder temperatures.

Zone 2: Temperatures are seasonal to below under cloudy skies, and northern areas see abundant precipitation.

Zone 3: Mostly fair and cold; cloudy east with wind and precipitation to the northeast and then clearing and cold.

Zone 4: A storm front to the west yields abundant precipitation and cold; fair to partly cloudy and cold with scattered precipitation on the Plains; eastern areas are very cold with precipitation.

Zone 5: Temperatures are seasonal to below throughout zone. West sees abundant precipitation; conditions windy and mostly fair central and east with scattered precipitation.

Zone 6: Most of the zone sees precipitation, followed by colder temperatures; eastern areas are fair.

Zone 7: Storm front brings precipitation, some heavy, to west and central areas with temperatures seasonal to below; warmer and windy with precipitation east.

Zone 8: Alaska—Windy with temperatures and precipitation seasonal to above in central and west areas; colder east.

Hawaii—Mostly fair with some scattered precipitation and temperatures rising with a warming trend.

February 8–14

Zone 1: Stormy conditions produce abundant precipitation; temperatures are seasonal.

Zone 2: Precipitation, some heavy, throughout zone accompanies temperatures seasonal to below.

Zone 3: Mostly fair and seasonal; northeastern areas are windy and cold with precipitation.

Zone 4: Fair to partly cloudy northwest before a front moves in; western areas fair to partly cloudy with temperatures from seasonal to above. Central areas cloudy and cooler before a warming trend; east is fair and seasonal.

Zone 5: Fair west with temperatures from seasonal to above; cooler and cloudy with precipitation east.

Zone 6: Temperatures fall under increasing clouds as a front moves through the zone bringing precipitation.

Zone 7: Northern coastal and central areas see precipitation, while eastern areas are partly cloudy with scattered precipitation; temperatures seasonal.

Zone 8: Alaska—Fair and seasonal, west and central areas see precipitation late in the week.

Hawaii—Temperatures seasonal to cool, windy and wet, bringing flooding potential as a front moves through.

February 15–22

Zone 1: Cloudy, windy, and wet throughout zone; temperatures seasonal to below.

Zone 2: Weather is seasonal north with scattered precipitation, while southern areas are cloudy with precipitation and tornado potential.

Zone 3: Cold and stormy much of the week, with potential for tornados.

Zone 4: Storm causes flooding potential west before moving into the Plains and east. Warmer west, very cold east.

Zone 5: Stormy across the zone, temperatures range from seasonal to below. Eastern areas are stormy early in the week.

Zone 6: Wind in western areas and falling temperatures signal an approaching storm that moves into the central portion of the zone. Eastern areas are seasonal and windy and see precipitation at week's end.

Zone 7: Seasonal, breezy weather west precedes an advancing storm that moves into the central mountains and eastern areas, bringing cooler temperatures.

Zone 8: Alaska—Eastern areas are cold with precipitation; west and central areas see abundant precipitation with temperatures seasonal to below.

Hawaii—Hawaii is cloudy and cool with precipitation.

February 23–28

Zone 1: Precipitation much of the week with temperatures from seasonal to much below.

Zone 2: Precipitation under variable clouds; temperatures seasonal to above in southern areas.

Zone 3: Temperatures seasonal to below with scattered precipitation west and northeast. Increasing clouds and wind east signal an approaching front.

Zone 4: Conditions windy west with precipitation; windy and cold central; partly cloudy to cloudy, wet and cold east.

Zone 5: Temperatures seasonal to below; windy east; western and central areas see scattered precipitation.

Zone 6: Windy with increasing clouds west as a front moves in and continues to the east; cold and wet in central and east.

Zone 7: Northern coastal areas are windy and seasonal with precipitation. Central and eastern areas are cold with precipitation, some heavy, with a second front approaching at week's end.

Zone 8: Alaska—Storm in west moves into central and eastern areas of the zone, bringing wet and cooler temperatures.

Hawaii—Seasonal and windy with scattered precipitation.

March 1–8

Zone 1: Windy conditions and seasonal temperatures accompany precipitation.

Zone 2: Windy with precipitation to the north; seasonal with precipitation at week's end in the south.

Zone 3: Stormy west and central, with thunderstorms and tornado potential; eastern areas see precipitation later in the week.

Zone 4: Mostly fair west, central areas see scattered precipitation and areas to the east are cloudy; cold and wet as a storm with high winds passes through.

Zone 5: Stormy and wet west, central areas see scattered precipitation. Eastern areas see thunderstorms, some severe with tornado potential.

Zone 6: Much of the zone is fair and breezy with scattered precipitation; weather is cooler inland.

Zone 7: Windy and seasonal with scattered precipitation to the west, areas to the east are drier.

Zone 8: Alaska—Seasonal and dry to the west; a front brings precipitation to central and eastern areas.

Hawaii—Windy with scattered precipitation; temperatures are seasonal to above.

March 9–16

Zone 1: A front moves into the zone, bringing precipitation with high winds and cold.

Zone 2: Cool and cloudy with precipitation to the north; southern are mostly cloudy and wet, followed by cooler temperatures.

Zone 3: Western and eastern areas see precipitation; central areas fair and cold and windy with scattered precipitation and variable cloudiness.

Zone 4: Stormy and cold to the west with precipitation; rest of zone sees scattered precipitation and variable cloudiness; temperatures seasonal to below.

Zone 5: Stormy and cold west; central and east are windy with variable cloudiness and precipitation; seasonal to the south.

Zone 6: Western areas are fair to partly cloudy with temperatures ranging from seasonal to above; central and eastern areas windy and colder with precipitation, especially to the east.

Zone 7: Seasonal and cool throughout much of the zone; eastern areas see variable clouds with a chance for precipitation and warmer temperatures.

Zone 8: Alaska—Stormy conditions lower temperatures to the east, while seasonal conditions are in the forecast for western and central areas.

Hawaii—Windy and mostly dry and fair, temperatures range from seasonal to below.

March 17–24

Zone 1: Conditions are seasonal, clear, and cold.

Zone 2: Windy with a chance for precipitation throughout the zone; temperatures are seasonal to cool.

Zone 3: Much of the zone is cloudy, cool, and windy with precipitation as a front moves through, bringing precipitation to western and central areas; northeast is windy; temperatures are cooler central.

Zone 4: Windy and wet west; central areas are also windy but fair. Clouds, wet, and cold prevail east as a front moves through.

Zone 5: Wind and precipitation, some heavy, in western areas; central portions are fair and seasonal; east is windy with scattered precipitation.

Zone 6: Cloudy, windy, and cold west; partly cloudy to cloudy and cold central and east with precipitation.

Zone 7: Northern coastal areas windy and seasonal; warmer and variable cloudiness to the south; eastern areas cloudy and windy with precipitation.

Zone 8: Alaska—Abundant precipitation east; other areas partly cloudy to cloudy with scattered precipitation; temperatures are seasonal.

Hawaii—Seasonal, warm, and partly cloudy.

March 25–31

Zone 1: Stormy and cold, with some areas receiving abundant precipitation.

Zone 2: Colder north; thunderstorms, some severe, with excessive precipitation are in the forecast zone-wide.

Zone 3: Weather is cool, cloudy, and wet west and central, while central and eastern areas see thunderstorms, some severe with abundant downfall; temperatures are warmer east.

Zone 4: Temperatures seasonal to above west and central; cooler east with a chance for precipitation.

Zone 5: Most of the zone has a chance for thunderstorms, some with abundant rain, and temperatures seasonal to below.

Zone 6: Fair to partly cloudy west, with scattered precipitation; cold, cloudy, and fair in central areas; windy to the east.

Zone 7: Cloudy and cool central and west; warmer south; eastern areas are fair and seasonal.

Zone 8: Alaska—Weather is cold east, and seasonal west and central with a chance for precipitation.

Hawaii—Temperatures range from seasonal to below under mostly fair skies; central areas have a chance for showers.

April 1–7

Zone 1: Temperatures seasonal to below; skies are fair to partly cloudy and windy with a chance for precipitation.

Zone 2: Fair, windy, and dry, with temperatures seasonal to below.

Zone 3: West and central are cloudy and cold with abundant precipitation, while eastern zone is fair, windy, and seasonal.

Zone 4: Windy, dry, and fair west; precipitation expected for central and eastern areas as a front moves through; temperatures seasonal to below.

Zone 5: Temperatures are seasonal to below; thunderstorms, some severe, bring heavy precipitation to some areas central and east.

Zone 6: Increasing clouds to the west; central and eastern areas are partly cloudy and windy, with a chance for precipitation east.

Zone 7: Northern coastal areas are cool, partly cloudy, and windy; south warmer and mostly dry, as is much of the zone, with seasonal temperatures; chance for precipitation east.

Zone 8: Alaska—Western and central areas are overcast and cold with precipitation, while eastern areas are fair and warmer; coastal areas see fog.

Hawaii—Temperatures seasonal to below under partly cloudy to cloudy skies with precipitation, some abundant, later in the week.

April 8–15

Zone 1: Temperatures are seasonal to above with scattered thunderstorms, high winds; some areas receiving abundant downfall.

Zone 2: Cloudy and windy throughout the zone, temperatures are seasonal to below under cloudy skies that yield precipitation.

Zone 3: Heat in the west sparks scattered thunderstorms in that area and central, where it's cooler and cloudy; fair with scattered thunderstorms and temperatures seasonal to above east.

Zone 4: Thunderstorms, some severe with high winds and tornado potential, are in the forecast for western and central areas of the zone; fair to partly cloudy and warmer with scattered thunderstorms in the east.

Zone 5: Western and central areas see severe thunderstorms with tornado potential, and weather to the east is fair to partly cloudy with scattered precipitation.

Zone 6: A front moves through west and central areas, bringing overcast skies, cold temperatures, and abundant downfall; eastern areas are cold and windy with a chance for precipitation.

Zone 7: Northern coastal areas are cloudy and wet prior to clearing as a front moves into central area; windy and mostly dry to the south, with a chance for rain later in the week; desert areas are dry, windy, and hot.

Zone 8: Alaska—Windy to the east, partly cloudy, and seasonal. Hawaii—Most of the zone is cloudy and cool, with the heaviest downfall in central and eastern areas.

April 16–23

Zone 1: Partly cloudy to cloudy with precipitation to the south; northern areas are very windy and cool with precipitation.

Zone 2: Seasonal with scattered precipitation north; south is cooler after thunderstorms, some with high winds and tornado potential.

Zone 3: Much of zone is partly cloudy to cloudy and cool with scattered precipitation; thunderstorms in the east, some severe, with tornado potential, and then cooling.

Zone 4: Western and central areas are warm and windy with scattered thunderstorms, while the east is cooler and cloudy with precipitation.

Zone 5: Temperatures are seasonal to above, with thunderstorms west and central, some with tornado potential; there's a chance for precipitation east.

Zone 6: West and central areas are wet and windy much of the week; fair weather prevails east, followed by precipitation and cooler temperatures later in the week.

Zone 7: An advancing front brings precipitation to most of the zone; cold north; desert areas are dry and hot.

Zone 8: Alaska—Western and central areas are windy with variable cloudiness and a chance for precipitation; eastern areas are warmer.

Hawaii—Seasonal conditions prevail under fair to partly cloudy skies, with a chance for showers.

April 24–30

Zone 1: Stormy conditions and cool temperatures prevail, with significant downfall north.

Zone 2: Temperatures in southern areas seasonal to above, sparking thunderstorms, some severe; northern areas see variable cloudiness with scattered precipitation.

Zone 3: Temperatures seasonal to above throughout the zone; central and western areas windy with scattered thunderstorms; thunderstorms in the east, some severe, as a front moves in from the west.

Zone 4: Skies are partly cloudy west and central; wind signals thunderstorms, some with abundant downfall, central and east.

Zone 5: Central and eastern areas have scattered thunderstorms, and skies are partly cloudy to cloudy with temperatures ranging from seasonal to above.

Zone 6: Cool and cloudy west and central; mountain areas are wet prior to clearing as a weather front moves east, bringing precipitation to that area.

Zone 7: Much of the zone is cool, cloudy, and windy, with precipitation; eastern areas are fair to partly cloudy with rising temperatures and scattered thunderstorms.

Zone 8: Alaska—Mostly fair and seasonal, western areas are windy and eastern portion of the zone see precipitation.

Hawaii—Hawaii is fair, breezy, and seasonal.

May 1–7

Zone 1: Stormy and cool north; areas to the south are hot with scattered thunderstorms.

Zone 2: Temperatures are seasonal to above with wind and scattered precipitation, some abundant, in southern areas.

Zone 3: Much of the zone is wet; some areas receive excessive downfall as humidity and temperatures rise; eastern areas are mostly dry.

Zone 4: Western and central areas are dry and hot; precipitation, some abundant, centers east, which is cloudy and cooler.

Zone 5: Hot and mostly dry; eastern areas have a chance for scattered thunderstorms.

Zone 6: Windy weather prevails as a front moves across much of the zone, bringing abundant downfall to central and eastern areas, which are windy and stormy.

Zone 7: Cloudy, cool, and stormy in much of the zone; desert areas are hot and dry.

Zone 8: Alaska—Temperatures are cold east and seasonal west, with precipitation and wind in central areas.

Hawaii—Mostly fair to partly cloudy; windy weather and seasonal temperatures signal showers later in the week.

May 8–15

Zone 1: Thunderstorms, some severe, are in the forecast, along with heat and humidity.

Zone 2: Temperatures and humidity rise, sparking severe thunderstorms, some with tornado potential.

Zone 3: Western areas fair; heat and humidity rise east and central, where thunderstorms with tornado potential are possible.

Zone 4: Northwest is stormy later in the week, with abundant precipitation that moves into the Plains, where it's windy with increasing cloudiness; eastern areas are mostly dry and seasonal.

Zone 5: Weather is fair west; central and eastern areas see scattered thunderstorms; temperatures throughout the zone are seasonal to above; eastern areas are windy.

Zone 6: Western areas see precipitation, while central areas are fair and dry with precipitation later in the week; stormy conditions, with high winds and tornado potential are in the forecast for eastern areas at week's end.

Zone 7: A front moves through northern coastal areas and across the zone, bringing precipitation to northern areas, while southern coastal areas have a chance for precipitation; desert areas are hot, dry, windy, and partly cloudy.

Zone 8: Alaska—Stormy central and east with high winds; western areas are fair and seasonal.

Hawaii—Windy and stormy, with abundant precipitation.

May 16–22

Zone 1: The zone is overcast, cool, and stormy.

Zone 2: Northern areas are cloudy with precipitation; southern areas humid with temperatures from seasonal to above and a chance for showers.

Zone 3: Strong thunderstorms with tornado potential develop in western and central areas, while the northeast is stormy and cool, with some areas seeing abundant precipitation.

Zone 4: The Plains area is humid, and sees scattered thunderstorms, some severe, with tornado potential; western areas are partly cloudy with scattered thunderstorms, and temperatures range from seasonal to above throughout the zone.

Zone 5: Hot and mostly dry throughout the zone; areas to the west are partly cloudy; humidity rises in the central and east areas, with scattered thunderstorms, some severe, and tornado potential.

Zone 6: Most of the zone sees precipitation and cloudy skies, as a storm with high winds moves through central areas and into the east, bringing cooler temperatures.

Zone 7: Areas to the west see precipitation, and conditions are stormy central and east as a front moves through; desert is hot and humid.

Zone 8: Alaska—Stormy central and west with abundant precipitation; conditions are fair east; temperatures are seasonal. Hawaii—Windy, mostly fair and seasonal, with scattered showers.

May 23–29

Zone 1: Cool and cloudy with scattered thunderstorms to the north; southern areas are seasonal, partly cloudy, breezy, and warmer.

Zone 2: The zone is hot and humid with scattered thunderstorms.

Zone 3: Heat and humidity spark scattered thunderstorms throughout much of the zone, while eastern areas are windy, hot, mostly dry, and fair.

Zone 4: Western areas are windy with thunderstorms; the Plains are fair to partly cloudy and dry; eastern areas are humid with scattered thunderstorms; temperatures rise throughout the zone.

Zone 5: Hot and mostly dry and fair; western and central areas see scattered thunderstorms; eastern areas are cooler.

Zone 6: Most of the zone is fair to partly cloudy with temperatures seasonal to above; eastern areas are windy with showers and thunderstorms.

Zone 7: Dry and fair to partly cloudy; hot and windy in the desert; eastern areas see scattered thunderstorms.

Zone 8: Alaska—Eastern and central areas are seasonal with scattered precipitation; western areas are warmer and drier. Hawaii—Seasonal and fair to partly cloudy with showers east and central.

May 30–31

Zone 1: Temperatures range from seasonal to above with showers; northern areas see severe thunderstorms.

Zone 2: Weather is seasonal north; hot and partly cloudy to cloudy south with scattered thunderstorms.

Zone 3: Hot weather sparks thunderstorms, some severe, east and central; western areas are windy and hot.

Zone 4: Scattered thunderstorms in central areas are the exception to the hot and dry weather that prevails throughout the zone; eastern areas are windy.

Zone 5: Hot and mostly dry throughout the zone, central areas are partly cloudy with scattered thunderstorms.

Zone 6: Temperatures rise; eastern areas have a chance for showers; thunderstorms with high winds pop up in central areas.

Zone 7: Northern coastal areas are seasonal but dry, while other areas are hot, windy, and dry, with a chance for showers to the east.

Zone 8: Alaska—Alaska is seasonal with a chance for precipitation east.

Hawaii—Temperatures range from seasonal to above, with showers in western areas.

June 1–5

Zone 1: Hot weather sparks scattered showers and thunderstorms with high winds.

Zone 2: Northern areas see scattered shows, and severe thunderstorms with tornado potential accompany hot weather to the south.

Zone 3: Hot and mostly dry west and central; hot weather is also the norm to the east, where severe thunderstorms with abundant rainfall and tornado potential is high.

Zone 4: Hot weather signals scattered showers and thunderstorms west and central; eastern areas are hot and dry.

Zone 5: Temperatures rise throughout zone sparking severe thunderstorms, tornado potential, and abundant precipitation.

Zone 6: Much of the zone sees scattered showers and thunderstorms, and temperatures range from seasonal to above.

Zone 7: Weather is mostly hot, dry, and fair.

Zone 8: Alaska—Fair and seasonal with showers in central areas.

Hawaii—Scattered showers accompany seasonal conditions and skies that are fair to partly cloudy.

June 6–13

Zone 1: Temperatures range from seasonal to above, skies are fair to partly cloudy with a chance for showers and thunderstorms.

Zone 2: Hot, humid weather sparks thunderstorms, some severe with high winds, tornado potential, and abundant rainfall.

Zone 3: Thunderstorms, some severe with heavy downfall and tornado potential, accompany hot, humid weather.

Zone 4: The zone is mostly dry and fair to partly cloudy with seasonal temperatures and scattered thunderstorms, some severe, to the east.

Zone 5: Cloudy skies, wind, and thunderstorms are in the forecast for western areas; seasonal and breezy central and east, which sees scattered thunderstorms.

Zone 6: Most of the zone is dry, windy, and partly cloudy with seasonal temperatures; western areas see precipitation.

Zone 7: Hot, fair, and dry throughout the zone; western areas have a chance for precipitation.

Zone 8: Alaska—Mostly fair to partly cloudy and windy; central areas are cooler; warmer with scattered precipitation in the east. Hawaii—Seasonal and fair to partly cloudy with thunderstorms followed by cooler temperatures.

June 14–20

Zone 1: Temperatures are seasonal to above and the zone sees scattered thunderstorms.

Zone 2: Rising temperatures under partly cloudy to cloudy skies accompanies showers and thunderstorms.

Zone 3: Much of the zone has a chance for showers, especially east where cloudiness and cooler temperatures prevail; western and central areas are fair to partly cloudy and hot.

Zone 4: Weather is seasonal west, with rising temperatures throughout the zone; western areas are partly cloudy to cloudy with a chance for thunderstorms; eastern and central areas are mostly fair and sunny with a chance for showers east.

Zone 5: Hot, humid weather prevails throughout the zone; central and eastern areas have a chance for precipitation.

Zone 6: Mostly dry, windy, and fair to partly cloudy; western areas are cooler with showers.

Zone 7: Weather is cooler with a chance for showers in northern coastal areas; other areas of the zone are windy and fair to partly cloudy with temperatures seasonal to above and mostly dry.

Zone 8: Alaska—Seasonal, mostly fair and windy with scattered showers.

Hawaii—Temperatures rise under fair, breezy skies.

June 21–27

Zone 1: The zone is fair to partly cloudy and seasonal with scattered thunderstorms.

Zone 2: Humid and seasonal, southern areas see rain and thunderstorms, some severe with tornado potential, and abundant downfall.

Zone 3: Hot weather sparks severe thunderstorms with tornado potential and abundant rain west and central, while conditions to the east are hot and humid, with a chance for showers.

Zone 4: Hot weather dominates the zone, especially west, which has scattered precipitation; humid with precipitation east, while the Plains are partly cloudy with scattered thunderstorms.

Zone 5: Hot, dry weather prevails throughout the zone, which is mostly dry and fair; central areas have a chance for showers.

Zone 6: Weather is seasonal and fair west; temperatures rise in central and eastern areas, which see scattered thunderstorms.

Zone 7: Much of the zone is fair with scattered thunderstorms and temperatures ranging from seasonal to above; desert areas are humid and partly cloudy.

Zone 8: Alaska—Fair and warmer east with precipitation, and cloudy and cooler west and central with precipitation, some heavy. Hawaii—Fair to partly cloudy with clouds gradually increasing to bring precipitation, some abundant.

June 28–30

Zone 1: Northern areas have a chance for showers; the zone is windy and seasonal with variable cloudiness.

Zone 2: Hot and humid; northern areas have a chance for precipitation.

Zone 3: The zone is hot and mostly dry, with eastern areas having more cloudiness and a chance for showers.

Zone 4: Fair to partly cloudy and dry; temperatures soar, especially to the east and in desert areas.

Zone 5: Dry, hot, and fair to partly cloudy throughout the zone; western areas have a chance for showers, and humidity rises midzone.

Zone 6: The zone is mostly dry with a chance for showers west and central; temperatures are seasonal to above under fair to partly cloudy skies.

Zone 7: Mostly dry with rising temperatures under fair to partly cloudy skies; western areas have a chance for showers.

Zone 8: Alaska—Seasonal and fair.

Hawaii—Fair with temperatures ranging from seasonal to above and a chance for showers.

July 1–5

Zone 1: The zone is seasonal with scattered thunderstorms.

Zone 2: Hot and humid; the zone is fair to partly cloudy.

Zone 3: Weather is hot and humid, but cooler east, with a chance for thunderstorms east and central.

Zone 4: Mostly dry with temperatures seasonal to above; there's a chance for scattered precipitation.

Zone 5: The zone is hot, humid, and fair to partly cloudy; eastern and central areas have a chance for scattered thunderstorms.

Zone 6: Fair to partly cloudy and hot throughout the zone, eastern and central areas have a chance for scattered thunderstorms.

Zone 7: Northern coastal areas have a chance for scattered precipitation, while areas to the east are mostly dry; hot weather prevails under fair to partly cloudy skies; desert areas are very hot.

Zone 8: Alaska—Temperatures range form seasonal to above under mostly fair skies, with a chance for showers west and central.

Hawaii—Windy with rising temperatures and scattered showers.

July 6–13

Zone 1: Seasonal and windy with a chance for precipitation.

Zone 2: Seasonal, windy, and fair to partly cloudy; the zone has a chance for precipitation.

Zone 3: Hot and humid west and central with thunderstorms; eastern areas are cooler and cloudy.

Zone 4: Western areas are fair to partly cloudy with scattered showers and temperatures seasonal to above; heat and humidity prevail to the east, sparking severe thunderstorms with tornado potential.

Zone 5: Hot, humid, and fair to partly cloudy throughout the zone, with western areas seeing scattered thunderstorms.

Zone 6: Conditions are windy with temperatures seasonal to above throughout the zone; scattered precipitation west and central.

Zone 7: Fair to partly cloudy with scattered showers, thunderstorms, and temperatures that range from seasonal to above.

Zone 8: Alaska—Fair with temperatures from seasonal to above throughout the zone; central and eastern areas have a chance for showers.

Hawaii—Windy and fair to partly cloudy with scattered showers and rising temperatures.

July 14–20

Zone 1: Hot, humid, and windy throughout the zone; northern areas see scattered thunderstorms.

Zone 2: Fair to partly cloudy along with heat and humidity, and a chance for precipitation.

Zone 3: Scattered thunderstorms, some severe with tornado potential, are in the forecast for western and central areas, which are hot and humid; northeastern areas are windy and partly cloudy.

Zone 4: Hot throughout the zone; Plains are mostly dry, while eastern areas see scattered thunderstorms, some severe; a chance for showers in the west.

Zone 5: Skies are partly cloudy west and fair central and east, where high temperatures spark scattered thunderstorms, some severe.

Zone 6: Western areas are fair, and central and eastern areas see showers, some with abundant downfall; temperatures are seasonal to above.

Zone 7: Northern coastal areas are fair, while southern and eastern areas see precipitation, some heavy; temperatures are seasonal to above.

Zone 8: Alaska—Fair to seasonal with a chance for showers. Hawaii—Fair to partly cloudy with temperatures ranging from seasonal to above.

July 21–26

Zone 1: Stormy with abundant precipitation south; and northern areas are windy with showers and scattered thunderstorms.

Zone 2: Weather is hot throughout the zone; stormy north with scattered precipitation south.

Zone 3: The zone is hot and humid with scattered showers west; severe thunderstorms with tornado potential central and east, which also sees abundant precipitation.

Zone 4: Western areas see scattered thunderstorms, while the Plains are fair, hot, and humid; eastern areas have a chance for showers and thunderstorms as temperatures rise.

Zone 5: Fair to partly cloudy skies and scattered showers prevail to the west, while other areas of the zone are hot, humid, and windy; there's a chance for precipitation east.

Zone 6: Central and western areas are seasonal to above with scattered showers and thunderstorms; conditions are dry to the east; much of the zone is windy.

Zone 7: Western areas see scattered precipitation, central areas are partly cloudy with a chance for showers; eastern areas are dry with very hot weather in the desert.

Zone 8: Alaska—Temperatures are seasonal to above under fair skies.

Hawaii—Cloudy skies yield abundant precipitation, followed by cooler temperatures.

July 27–31

Zone 1: Hot, humid weather prevails, with a chance for showers to the south.

Zone 2: Northern areas have a chance for showers, and thunderstorms are in the forecast for southern areas, possibly from a tropical storm.

Zone 3: Hot and humid throughout the zone, with central and eastern areas seeing showers and thunderstorms.

Zone 4: Weather is hot, fair, and dry west, with a chance for scattered thunderstorms; severe thunderstorms pop up in central and eastern areas of the zone as temperatures rise.

Zone 5: Thunderstorms, some severe in central areas, result from temperatures that are seasonal to above.

Zone 6: The zone is fair to partly cloudy and windy with temperatures seasonal to above; central and eastern areas have a chance for showers.

Zone 7: Scattered showers and thunderstorms are in the forecast for much of the zone, which is fair to partly cloudy; eastern areas are hot with a chance for precipitation.

Zone 8: Alaska—Conditions are seasonal and windy with scattered precipitation.

Hawaii—Breezy, seasonal, and fair to partly cloudy with scattered thunderstorms.

August 1–3

Zone 1: The zone is fair to partly cloudy with temperatures seasonal to above and a chance for showers south.

Zone 2: Fair and humid throughout the zone, hot weather prevails to the south.

Zone 3: Temperatures are above normal throughout the zone; conditions are dry west and central, with a chance for rain to the east as clouds increase.

Zone 4: The zone is fair and dry with temperatures ranging from seasonal to above.

Zone 5: Scattered showers and thunderstorms accompany hot, humid, windy weather.

Zone 6: Fair and dry; temperatures are seasonal to above.

Zone 7: Central areas have a chance for precipitation, but fair, dry, hot weather dominates throughout the zone.

Zone 8: Alaska—Mostly fair throughout the zone, eastern areas see showers.

Hawaii—Weather is fair and seasonal.

August 4–11

Zone 1: Humidity and temperatures rise under fair to partly cloudy skies with a chance for showers.

Zone 2: The zone is hot, fair, and mostly dry, with scattered showers.

Zone 3: Hot, humid conditions west and central trigger showers and thunderstorms, some with abundant precipitation and tornado potential; eastern areas are hot and fair to partly cloudy with scattered thunderstorms.

Zone 4: Hot weather throughout the zone sparks thunderstorms, the most severe with the highest downfall occurring east.

Zone 5: Severe thunderstorms, some with abundant precipitation, result from high temperatures to the west; eastern and central areas are also hot and windy with scattered thunderstorms.

Zone 6: The zone is fair and dry and temperatures ranging from seasonal to above.

Zone 7: Western and central areas are fair to partly cloudy with temperatures seasonal to above; hot weather east sparks scattered thunderstorms.

Zone 8: Alaska—Precipitation, some heavy, along with strong winds are in the forecast for eastern and central Alaska; western areas are fair and seasonal.

Hawaii—Fair with temperatures seasonal to above.

August 12–18

Zone 1: Weather is fair, hot, and humid, with a chance for showers to the north.

Zone 2: The zone is hot and humid, with thunderstorms south and scattered showers and thunderstorms north.

Zone 3: Western areas are partly cloudy with precipitation at week's end, central areas see scattered thunderstorms and eastern areas are dry; temperatures are seasonal to above.

Zone 4: Showers and thunderstorms, some severe and with abundant precipitation west and central, are in the forecast, along with high temperatures; eastern areas have a chance for rain at week's end.

Zone 5: Temperatures rise throughout the zone, sparking thunderstorms, which are severe to the east with high winds, possibly from a tropical storm.

Zone 6: Western areas are fair with increasing clouds that signal precipitation the end of the week; thunderstorms, some severe, are in the forecast for central and eastern areas; temperatures are hot throughout the zone.

Zone 7: Western areas are fair to partly cloud with rain later in the week; central areas are mostly dry and fair to partly cloudy with high temperatures; the east has a chance for rain.

Zone 8: Alaska—Weather is fair and seasonal.

Hawaii—Temperatures are seasonal to above with scattered thunderstorms.

August 19–25

Zone 1: The zone is hot, humid, and fair to partly cloudy with scattered thunderstorms.

Zone 2: Temperatures are seasonal to above with scattered showers and thunderstorms.

Zone 3: Much of the zone is hot and dry; eastern areas are partly cloudy with a chance for showers.

Zone 4: Hot and humid weather sparks severe thunderstorms with tornado potential in central areas and a chance for showers to the east.

Zone 5: The zone is hot and humid, with major thunderstorms with tornado potential and heavy precipitation in central areas; areas to the east see scattered thunderstorms.

Zone 6: Western and central areas have a chance for showers; skies are partly cloudy to cloudy and temperatures seasonal east, with a chance for showers.

Zone 7: Most of the zone sees scattered thunderstorms; the desert is mostly cloudy, hot, and humid.

Zone 8: Alaska—Cloudy and windy conditions accompany precipitation in central areas, while the east and west are fair; temperatures are seasonal to cool.

Hawaii—Scattered thunderstorms accompany windy conditions and fair to partly cloudy skies.

August 26–31

Zone 1: Abundant precipitation accompanies windy, overcast skies, possibly from a hurricane that passes north off the coast.

Zone 2: Weather is fair and seasonal south; northern areas, especially coastal regions, are cloudy and cooler with showers.

Zone 3: The end of the week brings thunderstorms and cooler temperatures to the west and central areas of the zone; eastern areas are cloudy, windy, and cooler with precipitation.

Zone 4: Temperatures cool after showers and thunderstorms west, while central areas see high temperatures and severe thunderstorms with tornado potential; conditions are seasonal east with precipitation at week's end.

Zone 5: Cloudy skies signal precipitation to the west; central and eastern areas of the zone are hot and humid, with abundant precipitation from thunderstorms with tornado potential.

Zone 6: Western areas are windy, hot, and fair to partly cloudy with precipitation, some heavy, central and eastern areas are cooler and cloudy.

Zone 7: Northern coastal areas see partly cloudy to cloudy skies and showers, while seasonal conditions prevail to the south; cloudy skies bring precipitation to central areas; major thunderstorms, heavy precipitation, high humidity, and high temperatures are in the forecast for the east.

Zone 8: Alaska—Central and eastern areas are fair and seasonal, while low pressure signals stormy conditions and abundant precipitation to the west.

Hawaii—Much of the zone is seasonal, but eastern areas are wet, possibly from a typhoon.

September 1–10

Zone 1: Conditions are windy as a front moves through the zone, bringing more precipitation north with scattered thunderstorms; temperatures are seasonal to above.

Zone 2: Skies are partly cloudy to cloudy throughout the zone, with scattered showers north; high temperatures spark severe thunderstorms, some with tornado potential, to the south.

Zone 3: High winds accompany thunderstorms in the west, while central areas see thunderstorms, some severe with tornado potential; conditions are cooler east and windy with scattered thunderstorms.

Zone 4: Weather is hot to the west with a chance of showers early in the week and thunderstorms at week's end that also pop up in the Plains; eastern areas are hot, humid, and windy under partly cloudy to cloudy skies with a chance for rain.

Zone 5: The end of the week brings showers to the Plains and severe thunderstorms to the west; hot weather east sparks thunderstorms with high winds and tornado potential.

Zone 6: Much of the zone sees cloudy skies, heat, and precipitation as a front brings significant downfall to the west and moves to the east.

Zone 7: Western areas see showers, and northern coastal areas are stormy with significant precipitation as a weather front moves into and across much of the zone; eastern areas are drier and windy with a chance for precipitation at week's end.

Zone 8: Alaska—Above average temperatures and precipitation visit central and eastern areas, while the west is windy with a warming trend.

Hawaii—Windy with significant showers and thunderstorms, possibly from a typhoon in the area.

September 11–16

Zone 1: Temperatures are seasonal under partly cloudy to cloudy skies, with wind and scattered thunderstorms.

Zone 2: Hot and humid conditions throughout the zone spark severe thunderstorms with high winds in southern areas.

Zone 3: Weather is hot and humid in much of the zone, with scattered thunderstorms, some severe, in western areas; the east sees thunderstorms later in the week, and the northeast is cloudy and humid with seasonal temperatures.

Zone 4: Fair skies and temperatures ranging from seasonal to above are in the forecast for the west and western Plains, and precipitation falls in central areas and to the east, which is cloudy, humid, and windy; high temperatures spark major thunderstorms with high winds in the Mississippi River Valley.

Zone 5: Humidity and temperatures seasonal to above signal scattered thunderstorms under partly cloudy to cloudy skies central and east as a front moves through the area; areas to the west are fair and seasonal.

Zone 6: Windy conditions prevail throughout the zone, especially central, where higher temperatures spark scattered thunderstorms; western areas have a chance for showers, and the east is fair and seasonal.

Zone 7: Northern coastal areas are windy with showers, southern coastal areas are hot with a chance for showers, and heat rises in central areas of the zone with scattered thunderstorms; conditions are dry, fair and seasonal to the east.

Zone 8: Alaska—Eastern areas are warmer than central and west, which are fair to partly cloudy and seasonal.

Hawaii—Weather is fair to partly cloudy and seasonal with a chance for showers.

September 17–23

Zone 1: Windy conditions and stormy, overcast skies signal abundant precipitation and hurricane potential.

Zone 2: Overcast skies, possibly from a hurricane, yield excessive precipitation north; partly cloudy to cloudy south, with showers.

Zone 3: Temperatures are seasonal to above with scattered thunderstorms throughout much of the zone. To the east, cooler temperatures, wind, and overcast skies trigger abundant rainfall.

Zone 4: Western areas are partly cloudy to cloudy with a chance for showers; hot weather dominates central and east with scattered thunderstorms, partly cloudy skies, and wind.

Zone 5: Skies are partly cloudy to cloudy with temperatures seasonal to above and scattered showers and thunderstorms. Eastern areas are windy.

Zone 6: The wind picks up as a storm front moves through the zone, bringing heavy precipitation to some areas. Temperatures are seasonal.

Zone 7: Much of the zone is partly cloud to cloudy with precipitation, some heavy, and temperatures seasonal to above. Eastern areas are hot with scattered thunderstorms.

Zone 8: Alaska—Western and central areas see precipitation with high winds, and temperatures throughout the zone range from seasonal to above.

Hawaii—Hot, humid, windy conditions prevail, with scattered showers.

September 24–30

Zone 1: Weather is cloudy, cool, and windy to the north, and fair and seasonal south.

Zone 2: The zone is fair and seasonal north, with scattered thunderstorms and high temperatures to the south.

Zone 3: Cloudy skies west and central, along with warm, humid air, signal a chance for showers; areas east are hot and dry with scattered showers; seasonal conditions prevail northeast.

Zone 4: Temperatures are seasonal to above throughout the zone, with scattered showers in central areas, and wind and showers east.

Zone 5: Skies are partly cloudy and temperatures seasonal to above in western areas; central and eastern areas are cooler with wind and a chance for precipitation.

Zone 6: Seasonal conditions and partly cloudy to cloudy skies signal a chance for showers; weather is warmer to the east.

Zone 7: Western and central areas are seasonal with a chance for showers under partly cloudy to cloudy skies, while eastern areas are windy with scattered thunderstorms and higher temperatures.

Zone 8: Alaska—Weather is overcast, cool, and windy with precipitation east and central, and seasonal and windy west.

Hawaii—The zone is partly cloudy to cloudy and windy with showers.

October 1–9

Zone 1: Mostly fair; the zone is cool and windy with scattered thunderstorms.

Zone 2: Areas to the north are fair and seasonal, while scattered thunderstorms, cloudy skies, and humidity prevail to the south.

Zone 3: Wind and cloudy skies accompany thunderstorms are followed by lower temperatures.

Zone 4: Western areas see variable cloudiness with thunderstorms, some severe; other areas are fair to partly cloudy with temperatures that range from seasonal to above.

Zone 5: Central and western areas are windy with thunderstorms popping up later in the week to the east; east is warm and humid.

Zone 6: Central areas of the zone see thunderstorms and abundant precipitation as a front advances to the east, bringing precipitation later in the week; western areas are fair to partly cloudy and warm.

Zone 7: Northern coastal areas are windy, fair to partly cloudy and warm with showers, while southern coastal and central areas have abundant downfall and high winds; the east is fair and seasonal with showers at week's end.

Zone 8: Alaska—Weather is fair and windy east, with precipitation central and west, and temperatures seasonal to above. Hawaii—The zone is breezy and fair to partly cloudy with showers, and temperatures are seasonal to above.

October 10–16

Zone 1: The zone is windy, fair, and cool.

Zone 2: Northern areas are windy and fair; areas south are cloudy and warm with scattered precipitation.

Zone 3: Overcast, cold, and stormy west and central; eastern areas are fair to partly cloudy and seasonal, with wind and scattered precipitation northeast.

Zone 4: Stormy conditions replace fair weather as a front moves through western and central areas of the zone; eastern areas are windy, stormy, and cold.

Zone 5: Scattered thunderstorms bring cooler weather west and central; eastern areas are windy and mostly fair and seasonal.

Zone 6: Western areas are breezy, cloudy, and warm with showers; central areas of the zone are cloudy with scattered thunderstorms; fair to partly cloudy skies and seasonal temperatures prevail east.

Zone 7: Cloudy and stormy west, central areas are very windy with scattered thunderstorms and then much cooler; eastern areas are fair to partly cloudy, dry, and seasonal.

Zone 8: Alaska—Fair and cool west and central, eastern areas see abundant precipitation from a storm front.

Hawaii—Wind, thunderstorms, and rising temperatures prevail.

October 17–23

Zone 1: Abundant precipitation and cold temperatures accompany a windy front that moves through the zone.

Zone 2: Northern areas are windy, cloudy, and cool with precipitation; southern areas are seasonal to cool with a chance for precipitation.

Zone 3: Temperatures seasonal to above and fair to partly cloudy skies yield scattered precipitation west; eastern areas are cooler and cloudy with precipitation.

Zone 4: Precipitation accompanies cool, cloudy, and windy weather west, while conditions are seasonal to cool and fair to partly cloudy central and east with frost.

Zone 5: Western areas are windy with scattered thunderstorms; cooler weather prevails east, and central and eastern areas see scattered thunderstorms.

Zone 6: Precipitation accompanies cloudy, cool weather west, while central and eastern areas are mostly fair, windy, and seasonal to cool with scattered precipitation.

Zone 7: The zone is windy with fair to partly cloudy skies and scattered precipitation; eastern areas are cooler.

Zone 8: Alaska—Cloudy skies and showers are in the forecast for eastern areas; wind and precipitation prevail west, while central portions of the zone are fair and seasonal.

Hawaii—Mostly fair and seasonal; a windy front later in the week brings thunderstorms to western areas.

October 24–31

Zone 1: The zone is cool and fair to partly cloudy with precipitation north.

Zone 2: Fair and seasonal south; northern areas are cooler and fair.

Zone 3: Seasonal temperatures, wind, and scattered precipitation are in the forecast for western and central areas; fair weather prevails east, and frost accompanies cooler temperatures.

Zone 4: The zone is partly cloudy to cloudy, with cooler temperatures and precipitation west, while central and eastern areas are windy and warmer.

Zone 5: Seasonal temperatures and partly cloudy to cloudy skies signal precipitation throughout the zone, with abundant downfall east, where conditions are warm and humid.

Zone 6: Temperatures are seasonal to above under fair skies, but cooler at higher elevations and partly cloudy west.

Zone 7: Central and eastern areas are windy, and skies are fair throughout the zone, with temperatures seasonal to above.

Zone 8: Alaska—Fair skies prevail west, with precipitation central and east.

Hawaii—Showers and thunderstorms accompany warm, humid, cloudy weather.

November 1–7

Zone 1: Fair skies yield to increasing clouds and wind as precipitation arrives in southern areas; fair and seasonal north.

Zone 2: Northern areas see wind and precipitation, and precipitation, while wind and cool temperatures dominate to the south.

Zone 3: Weather is windy, fair, and seasonal west; cold with variable cloudiness and precipitation east.

Zone 4: A storm brings excessive precipitation to western areas, while the central portion of the zone is seasonal; windy and fair to partly cloudy east, with a chance for precipitation.

Zone 5: Western areas see abundant precipitation and temperatures that range from seasonal to above; fair to partly cloudy skies for central and eastern areas.

Zone 6: Western and central areas are mostly fair with a chance for precipitation; stormy conditions east brings abundant precipitation and cool temperatures.

Zone 7: Fair and warm west and central, while eastern areas are cloudy and cooler with precipitation.

Zone 8: Alaska—Most of the zone is cloudy and seasonal, with fog in coastal areas; central and eastern portions of the zone see precipitation.

Hawaii—Cloudy skies, wind and high humidity yield precipitation, some abundant, and cool temperatures.

November 8–14

Zone 1: Cloudy, windy, stormy weather dominates as a front moves through the zone.

Zone 2: Northern areas are cloudy with precipitation and then clear, while wet, cool, windy weather prevails to the south.

Zone 3: Western areas of the zone are seasonal with scattered precipitation and variable cloudiness; central and eastern areas see cooler weather with precipitation.

Zone 4: Weather is fair and seasonal west; cooler in the central areas, with scattered precipitation, wind, and variable cloudiness; stormy east.

Zone 5: Western skies are fair to partly cloudy, while central and eastern areas are cold, cloudy, and wet with high winds.

Zone 6: A storm front moves through the zone bringing precipitation, some abundant, to all areas.

Zone 7: Western and central areas see precipitation, some heavy, as a storm moves through much of the zone; eastern areas are mostly fair and seasonal.

Zone 8: Alaska—Windy weather and cloudy skies bring precipitation and stormy conditions; temperatures are seasonal.

Hawaii—Seasonal with scattered showers; eastern areas are windy.

November 15–22

Zone 1: Weather is cloudy, cool, and windy with precipitation, some abundant.

Zone 2: Cloudy skies and precipitation prevail to the north, while southern areas are seasonal and fair to partly cloudy.

Zone 3: Much of the zone is windy, cloudy, and wet with temperatures that range from seasonal to below.

Zone 4: Western areas are fair; central areas seasonal with precipitation; cold, windy weather with precipitation prevails to the east.

Zone 5: Precipitation moves across much of the zone, and temperatures are cold to the east.

Zone 6: Fair and seasonal west; cold and stormy central and east with high winds.

Zone 7: Western and central areas see fair skies and a warming trend as a storm front moves east; much of the zone is windy.

Zone 8: Alaska—Fair and cold.

Hawaii—The zone is fair to partly cloudy and seasonal.

November 23–30

Zone 1: Fair to partly cloudy skies and seasonal conditions prevail throughout the zone.

Zone 2: The zone is cloudy, windy, and cool with precipitation, and then clearing and warmer.

Zone 3: Fair, cool, windy weather with precipitation dominates throughout the zone.

Zone 4: Cold and wet west moves into the western Plains, bringing cooler temperatures; central and eastern areas are seasonal.

Zone 5: Much of the zone is cool, with warmer temperatures to the east. Western and central areas see precipitation.

Zone 6: Central and eastern areas are cold, with fair to partly cloudy skies throughout the zone.

Zone 7: Fair to partly cloudy and seasonal west and east, temperatures are cooler central with precipitation.

Zone 8: Alaska—Central and eastern areas are windy and wet with seasonal temperatures, and fair skies prevail west.

Hawaii—Weather is fair before skies turn cloudy, bringing showers and cooler temperatures.

December 1–7

Zone 1: The zone is overcast with precipitation and seasonal temperatures.

Zone 2: Northern areas are overcast and stormy, while the south sees thunderstorms with high winds and tornado potential.

Zone 3: Windy, fair, and seasonal west; central and eastern areas are stormy with overcast skies, cold temperatures, and high winds.

Zone 4: Stormy conditions prevail northwest and in the foothills; central areas are seasonal, and the east is cloudy with precipitation.

Zone 5: Cloudy and windy west with precipitation, central areas are fair to partly cloudy and seasonal; the east is cold with precipitation.

Zone 6: High winds, overcast skies and stormy conditions prevail west and central; eastern areas are seasonal and partly cloudy.

Zone 7: Western and central areas are stormy as a front moves through the region, while the east sees fair to partly cloudy skies with a chance for precipitation.

Zone 8: Alaska—fair central and east, western areas are cloudy with precipitation.

Hawaii—Temperatures are seasonal under fair to partly cloudy skies.

December 8–14

Zone 1: The zone is fair, windy, and cold with a chance for precipitation.

Zone 2: Northern areas are windy and cold with a chance for precipitation; conditions to the south are fair to partly cloudy and seasonal to cool.

Zone 3: Western and central areas see severe thunderstorms with tornado potential under cloudy skies, while the east is windy and partly cloudy to cloudy, with a chance for precipitation.

Zone 4: Windy, wet weather prevails across much of the zone, and the east is colder.

Zone 5: Skies are fair to partly cloudy east, while western and central areas are cloudy with precipitation.

Zone 6: The zone is fair to partly cloudy with temperatures that range from seasonal to below, with a chance for precipitation west.

Zone 7: Conditions are fair to partly cloudy across much of the zone with wind in central areas; temperatures are seasonal; southern coastal and inland areas see thunderstorms.

Zone 8: Alaska—The east is seasonal, while western and central areas are cold and stormy as a front advances.

Hawaii—Mostly cloudy; temperatures are seasonal to cool with thunderstorms.

December 15–22

Zone 1: Mostly fair to partly cloud; the zone is windy and seasonal with a chance for precipitation.

Zone 2: Cloudy throughout the zone, temperatures are seasonal north and cold south, with precipitation and tornado potential in some areas.

Zone 3: Western areas are windy with a chance for precipitation; the east is cloudy, windy, and cold with precipitation.

Zone 4: The northwest sees precipitation, and cloudy skies prevail wes; central areas are fair and cool, and the east is windy with a chance for precipitation.

Zone 5: Much of the zone is fair and seasonal; western areas are cloudy with a chance for precipitation.

Zone 6: Weather is fair and seasonal west, while central areas see precipitation, some heavy; conditions are stormy and cold with high winds to the east.

Zone 7: Southern coastal and inland areas see precipitation, some heavy, as does the central portion of the zone; eastern areas are stormy with high winds and thunderstorms to the south.

Zone 8: Alaska—Precipitation spans the zone with variable cloudiness and seasonal temperatures.

Hawaii—Temperatures are seasonal to below with showers and windy under partly cloudy to cloudy skies.

December 23–31

Zone 1: The zone is stormy, overcast, and cold with high winds.

Zone 2: Northern areas see overcast skies and precipitation; to the south, cold temperatures accompany abundant precipitation, from rain to sleet to snow.

Zone 3: Temperatures are seasonal to below, and western areas are windy and dry; to the east, skies are overcast and stormy.

Zone 4: Cold temperatures and precipitation are in the forecast for western areas, and temperatures throughout the zone are seasonal to below; other areas are mostly dry with a chance for precipitation.

Zone 5: Windy and mostly dry throughout the zone, temperatures are seasonal to below.

Zone 6: Much of the zone is cloudy with precipitation, and temperatures are seasonal to below; eastern areas are fair and cold.

Zone 7: Western and central areas are cloudy and windy with precipitation; cool temperatures prevail east with precipitation north.

Zone 8: Alaska—The zone is windy, fair, and seasonal.

Hawaii—Mostly fair with a chance for showers, temperatures are seasonal to cool with a warming trend later in the week.

A Planetary Perspective of Our Times

What are the planets saying about our world? Find out in Llewellyn's new *Starview Almanac*. Renowned astrologers provide reliable insight into politics, entertainment, health, and fashion. Forecasts and trends relating to current events and issues, such as homeland security and America's obesity problem, are discussed without astrological terminology. Also included are financial and weather forecasts for 2005, profiles of famous people, facts about living with Mercury-retrograde periods, and a weekly calendar with fun forecasts by Sally Cragin.

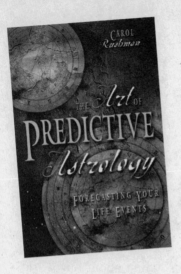

You Can Become an Expert at Seeing the Future in Anyone's Chart!

Insight into the future is a large part of the intrigue and mystery of astrology. *The Art of Predictive Astrology* by Carol Rushman clearly lays out a step-by-step system that astrologers can use to forecast significant events including love and financial success. When finished with the book, readers will be able to predict cycles and trends for the next several years, and give their clients fifteen important dates for the coming year. An emphasis is on progressions, eclipses, and lunations as important predictive tools.

The Art of Predictive Astrology:
Forecasting Your Life Events
Carole Rushman
0-7387-0164-5, 288 pp., 6 x 9
U.S. $14.95   CAN. $23.95
To order call 1-877-NEW-WRLD

Be Your Own Astrologer

Mapping Your Birthchart removes the mystery from astrology so you can look at any chart and get a basic understanding of the person behind it. Learn the importance of the planets, the different signs of the zodiac, and how they relate to your everyday life. Stephanie Jean Clement introduces the basics of the astrology chart, devotes a chapter to each planet—with information about signs, houses, and aspects—provides simple explanations of astrological and psychological factors, and includes examples from the charts of well-known people including Tiger Woods, Celine Dion, and George W. Bush. The free CD-ROM included with this book allows you to calculate and interpret your birthchart, and print out astrological reports and charts for yourself, your family, and friends.

Mapping Your Birthchart:
Understanding Your Needs and Potential

Stephanie Jean Clement, Ph.D.

0-7387-0202-1, 240 pp., 7½ x 9⅛
Includes CD-ROM
U.S $19.95 CAN. $30.95
To order call 1-877-NEW-WRLD

The Most Popular Astrological Calendar in the World

A must for everyone who wants to plan 2005 wisely, with an amazing amount of astrological data laid out on forty pages. Colorful, contemporary art by Ciro Marchetti kicks off each month, and monthly horoscopes by Carole Schwalm include the most rewarding and challenging dates for each sign. You'll find major daily aspects, planetary sign changes, and the Moon's sign, phase, and void-of-course times. The calendar also includes a table of retrograde periods and ephemerides for each month.

Llewellyn's *Astrological Calendar 2005*
40 pp., 13 x 9½
12 full-color paintings
0-7387-0135-1
U.S. $12.95   CAN. $17.50
To order call 1-877-NEW-WRLD

Take a Tour of the Zodiac

This book provides a revealing new look at the astrological signs, from Aries to Pisces. Gain a deeper understanding of how each sign motivates you to grow and evolve in consciousness. How does Aries work with Pisces? What does Gemini share in common with Scorpio? *All Around the Zodiac* is the only book on the market to explore these sign combinations to such a degree.

Not your typical Sun sign guide, this book is broken into three parts. Part 1 defines the signs, part 2 analyzes the expression of sixty-six pairs of signs, and part 3 designates the expression of the planets and houses in the signs.

All Around the Zodiac:
Exploring Astrology's Twelve Signs
Bil Tierney

480 pp., 6 x 9, 0-7387-0111-4
U.S. $19.95   CAN. $29.95
To order call 1-877-NEW-WRLD

A Pocketful of Stars

*C*onsult the stars anytime, anywhere, with this compact cosmic database that slides easily into your purse or briefcase. A National Calendar Award Winner, Llewellyn's *Astrological Pocket Planner* does what no other datebook does: It lets you trace the movements of the planets last year, this year, and next year. You'll find a regular datebook section for jotting your 2005 appointments, complete with major planetary aspects; a three-year ephemeris and aspectarian for 2004–2006; a listing of the planetary aspects; a time-zone chart; and a retrograde table.

Llewellyn's *2005 Astrological Pocket Planner*
192 pp. • 4¼ x 6
0-7387-0144-0
U.S. $7.95   CAN. $10.50
To order call 1-877-NEW-WRLD

Walk With the Gods

Enter a new dimension of spiritual self-discovery when you probe the mythic archetypes represented in your astrological birth chart. Myth has always been closely linked with astrology. Experience these myths and gain a deeper perspective on your eternal self.

Learn how the characteristics of the gods developed into the meanings associated with particular planets and signs. Look deeply into your own personal myths, and enjoy a living connection to the world of the deities within you. When you finally stand in the presence of an important archetype (through the techniques of dreamwork, symbolic amplification, or active imagination described in the book), you will have the opportunity to receive a message from the god or goddess.

Mythic Astrology
Ariel Guttman & Kenneth Johnson

400 pp. • 7 x 10
0-87542-248-9 •
U.S. $24.95   CAN. $38.50
To order call 1-877-NEW-WRLD

Read Your Future in the Cards

Tarot enthusiasts rejoice! Look for an array of news, advice, and in-depth discussions on everything tarot in Llewellyn's new *Tarot Reader*.

Renowned authors and tarot specialists deliver deck reviews and articles concerning card interpretation, spreads, magic, tarot history, and professional tarot reading. Each year's almanac will also feature a calendar with pertinent astrological information, such as Moon signs and times. This year's *Tarot Reader* includes articles by Ruth Ann and Wald Amberstone, Joan Cole, Mary K. Greer, and James Wells.

Notes:

Notes:

Notes:

Notes: